# The ancient borough of Bridgewater in the county of Somerset

Arthur Herbert Powell

THE PRESENT TOWN BRIDGE, BRIDGWATER

THE

# ANCIENT BOROUGH

OF

# BRIDGWATER

IN THE COUNTY OF SOMERSET

BY THE

## REV. ARTHUR HERBERT POWELL, M.A., LL.D.

VICAR AND RURAL DEAN OF BRIDGWATER

Author of "Our Eternal Life Here"; "God Speaking in Nature";
"The Influence of Jeremy Bentham upon Modern
Thought and Legislation"; "Sources of
Eighteenth Century Deism," etc.

WITH MAP AND ILLUSTRATIONS

BRIDGWATER: PAGE AND SON

1907

# PREFACE

THIS book is an attempt to set forth some of the incidents of the past history of a town whose antiquity is great, and whose story has been singularly varied. From the early part of the thirteenth century up to the close of the seventeenth the place throbbed with energy; they were five centuries whose characteristic, here, was *action*. It is with this period, in the main, that the following pages are concerned. From the dawn of the eighteenth century, and onwards, a quieter mood crept over Bridgwater. To chronicle this later period would require a separate volume, and entirely different treatment. It is, therefore excluded from the scope of the book. Perhaps another hand may some day take up the task.

The difficulty has lain chiefly in selecting from the abundance of documentary and other evidence which has been available. A vast number of notes, carefully prepared, have had to be omitted by reason of the need of keeping the book within the due limit of size. A possible objection might be taken to the title, for although the town is always spoken of as the Ancient Borough, it was created a county by Henry VIII when he raised Henry Daubeney to the earldom of Bridgwater. This creation, so far as I know, has never been annulled, and presumably it exists still. But the town

# PREFACE

authorities, who at that time were in possession of ample privileges, allowed the higher title and privilege to lapse by non-use. Queen Elizabeth's Charter refers to "Our Town or Burrough of Bridgwater in our County of Somersett," hence my adoption of the usual designation.

It is mainly to the inhabitants of the town and neighbourhood that the book is addressed, rather than to the antiquary or the historian. It has afforded me the keenest pleasure to observe the interest which Bridgwater·people take in the history of their town, and I am grateful to them for the kindly welcome which they have given to this book.

A word should be said as to the exceeding value and interest of the original documents which are now in the possession of the municipal rulers of this place. These parchments are replete with information, and I earnestly hope that they may some day be published. In many an English borough the choicest historical documents are similarly stored away. All these, it is hoped, may some day be given to the public, and their hidden knowledge revealed to the student·and to those who have every right to possess it.

Chapters I, II, IV, XIII, and XIV are contributed by my friend the Rev. W. H. P. Greswell. They will be found to be of deep interest, since they are the work of a very competent hand. I have many thanks to express to many friends for help given to me in various ways. First, to Mr. Greswell, not only for his literary contribution, but also for advice given and for help rendered in every direction. I am indebted

# PREFACE

to the Mayor and Corporation of Bridgwater for permission to see the municipal and other documents of
which they have the custody, and notably to the Town
Clerk for his extreme courtesy in giving me access
to them. To Mr. Broadmead of Enmore Castle I am
grateful for constant reference to his excellent Somerset
library, and to some valuable Bridgwater documents,
which he possesses. Mr. G. W. Jarman has been
most kind in helping me to explore the battlefield of
Sedgemoor; Mr. Godfrey Page and Mr. Cottam, F R A.S.,
have with great kindness provided me with some excellent drawings and a map; Mr. Kitch has been most
diligent in photographing, and in other helpful ways.
I am indebted to Mr. Charles Major for a photograph
of Idstock ruined chapel, and also for much information about the old town. To Mr. Maurice Page I wish
also to offer my hearty thanks for his great care and
diligence in all the work which he has so kindly and
well done in matters connected with the preparation of
the book.

ARTHUR H. POWELL.

# CONTENTS

# LIST OF ILLUSTRATIONS

# THE ANCIENT BOROUGH

## OF

# BRIDGWATER

## CHAPTER I

### EARLY DAYS

THE name of the town of Bridgwater was originally Brugge, Bruge, Brigge, Brigga, or at Domesday Brugie, and simply meant a bridge. In 1086, therefore, the date of the great Norman Survey, there was already an important place here, settled by Saxons, and called by them Bruge, attracting traffic to itself and probably dependent upon it to some extent. Unlike its neighbour Axbridge, under the Mendips, it did not introduce the name of the River Parret upon which it stood. According to the Domesday Survey, the Saxon owner of Bridgwater was Merlesuain, or Merleswain, and he was supplanted at the Conquest by a follower of King William the Conqueror, called Walter de Douai, a Fleming, who was a constant companion of the King, and held a large number of manors along the valley of the Parret (to which it may be necessary to refer presently), with the head of his barony at Castle Cary, at the very source of the Cary River. Walter de Douai, or perhaps his son Walter (for this point is a little uncertain), built

B

or took charge of the bridge at Bridgwater, and so the place was always called Brugge Walter or Brigge-walter, or, to show its origin more clearly, Pons Walteri. Just as Stoke at the mouth of the Parret, meaning simply a settlement in Saxon times, became amplified into Stoke Courcy when the Norman family of de Courcy settled there, so Brugge became Brugge-walter, after Walscinus or Walter of Douai. Now and then the town is certainly spelt "Burge," as if it might have been so called from a burgh or borough; but there were no borough privileges or castle previous to the reign of King John (1199–1216), and the real name of Brugge was stereotyped long before this. The Somerset folk to this day speak of Bridgwater as if it were "Burgwaater," but this dialectal variation must be explained by the fact that not only in Bridgwater, but in many other words, there is a change or meta-thesis of the letter "r." For instance, great is often pro-nounced as if it were "gert," and Richard as "Hur-chard," red as "hurd," and even bridge itself as "burge," and so on.

The first history of Bridgwater, therefore, is the history of a bridge in Saxon and possibly in British times. Far back in the centuries there may have been a "hard" or a ford, across which men could wade or ride or drive stock, and such towns as Wallingford on the Thames and Oxford on the Isis bear testimony to the fact that a settlement may first spring up round a ford. At Bridgwater it may have been possible to cross somewhere along the line of the present bridge. Curiously enough, we must look eight miles lower down the River Parret for a notable and historic ford, viz. at Combwich Passage. If Combwich (anciently spelt Comwith or Cumwych in Bridgwater documents) is really the Kinwith of the Saxon Chronicle and the

Cymwich of Roger de Hoveden, and Cannington the
" Kinwith Castle" where Saxons and Danes fought in
A.D. 878, there would appear to be little doubt that the
really important passage across the Parret was here at
the terminus of the Rodway, or old roadway, that led
from the Quantocks to Combwich and the little Pill
'there. This roadway is still visible, and can be easily
traced back to Fiddington and Over Stowey, and
finally to Triscombe Stone, or thereabouts, on the
Quantock Hills. Along its course it forms more than
one parish boundary, thus proving that it was older
than the parishes themselves. Across the Parret, and
on the east side, the objective of the roadway was the
strong hill or entrenchment of Brent Knoll, and to
travellers coming from the west to North Somerset
or Bristol it furnishes a more direct route than any
road leading to and through Bridgwater. Indeed,
within the memory of old men Combwich Passage by
the White House used to be always the place where
the Parret was forded, or passengers were ferried
across on their way to and from Bristol. Warner, in
his *Walks , Through Some of the Western Counties*,
written in 1800, mentions "the passage house on the
banks of the Parret, about 2½ miles from the Shoulder
of Mutton Inn," and says, "I ferried over the River
Parret at that time quite at ebb, and not more than a
quarter of a mile across."

Although Mr. Warner somewhat exaggerates the
distance, it is clear that a bridge at Combwich Passage
would always have been a formidable undertaking, more
formidable than the bridge at the mouth of the Teign
above Teignmouth, and, in very early days, even the
stern requirements of the " trinoda necessitas" (*arx,
pons, expeditio*) might scarcely have served to bring it
into being. A ford, or "drift," as they call it in South

Africa, it always might be and nothing more, across which the lumbering wains might travel at low water. But it was reserved for Bridgwater when the Parret had narrowed its course and the banks were closer to have a permanent bridge. The well-known "bore" was an ever-present problem, but it could be spanned best just here.

We may well wonder what kind of bridge existed in Saxon and pre-Domesday times. Probably it was of wood, for the Saxons were better workers of wood than of stone, and the bridge of those days might have been of a primitive kind, sufficing for foot passengers only, the vehicular traffic finding its way across "the hard," as at Combwich. The Flemish Walter de Douai may have given some new feature to the "Pons Walteri," for he must have seen and known of many bridges in Flanders and at the continental "Bruges" itself, where there were of old fifty-four bridges, so geographers tell us. Or, as the distant lord of Castle Cary, with the oversight of the Parret River Valley, he may have been satisfied with a military pontoon, with defences either side. No one seems, however, to be absolutely positive as to the actual position of the "Pons Walteri."

If it is a matter of conjecture, we may suppose, naturally enough, that the bridge was not far off the Castle, if not in direct communication with it. In his *History of Bridgwater* Mr. Jarman alludes (p. 22) to a rock in the centre of the river which used to be pointed out as one of the foundations of the old Brewer Bridge. It spanned the river from the Castle to the place known as Castle Field. This bridge must have lasted more than two hundred years, and was probably existing in 1365, for, in a deed of 37 Ed. III, mention is made of a piece of ground in Cook's Row and a

4

tenement opposite the Castle "as you go from the Great Bridge to the Market Place" (p. 167).

That there were some rocks, probably flat ledges of the blue lias, in the bed of the River Parret at this particular spot appears from the wording of King Edward IV's Charter, recited in the Charter of Henry VII.

In this document it was stipulated that the Mayor, Bayliffs and Burgesses of Bridgwater should for ever have and receive for every "plough" or cart drawn and passing with merchandise or grosswood over the bridge of the town one penny, and the money thereby arising was to be applied for and about the mending and fortifying the bridge there from time to time: And that it should be lawful for them, the said Mayor, Bayliffs and Burgesses and their Successors, to cleanse, secure and amend the banks and walls of the water within the Town and Borough aforesaid and the Liberties and precincts thereof:

And the rocks and stones lying and being in the bottom of the same water it should be lawful for them to draw from thence, as often as it should be necessary, for the safe bringing and lying of ships and other vessels there: And to have and retain the same stones for the mending and repairing of the bridge aforesaid, and for paving the said Town or Borough without any let, hindrance or impediment of us, our Heirs, or Successors, or of any other our ministers whatsoever.

This grant certainly gives us a little glimpse into the probable physical aspect of the Parret bed here-abouts. The channel must have been more confined than at present, the rocks may have been high enough to facilitate the setting the foundations of a bridge, and, indeed, have naturally indicated the best spot to span

5

the flood. The "bore," rushing up this confined place, would have been a far more notable phenomenon than it is at present. The ships themselves, to begin with, would have found shallower water and less room to anchor in than, perhaps, at the "Head of Comwithe"; but, in process of time, the quarrying of the stones at low water would clear and deepen the waterway. The blocks of blue lias would make, as always, good paving stones for the streets of the borough, and a double purpose be effected by their removal.

There are more historical details about what may be called "Trivet's Bridge," a triple-arched, strongly-built stone structure with houses on both sides of the roadway. Frequent references are made in the Commonalty Accounts to repairs made in these houses. The position of this bridge is probably that of the present structure, and it may have replaced the old Brewer Bridge. Amongst the town MSS. an early document sets forth the liability of Bridgwater men with regard to the *new* bridge, and stipulating that if it was not completed by a certain time, Thomas Lyons and John Fytleton (the latter a member for the town of Bridgwater in the year 1379) were to pay £200. This looks like a very heavy fine for those days, but the important point about this extract is that we get a date. This surely is the bridge of seventy "steppys" which William of Worcester mentions, and it is the bridge which Leland, the travelling antiquary of Henry VIII's time, saw, which he says was begun by William Brewer, the first lord of the town, and finished by Trivet. This statement is a little misleading, as the distance of time between the first William Brewer and Trivet was 150 years, Lord Brewer dying in 1227, and Sir John Trivet living in Richard II's reign (1377–99). In an ancient record amongst the Bridgwater accounts there is a very interesting reference to this bridge. "It appeareth that Sir John Trivett, knight, gave in Richard the Second's tyme (1377–99), 300 marcs towardes buildinge of the new bridge, and the Stewardes and Comunaltie bound themselves to performe the rest of the charge in building of the said bridge, as by several readings in French dated at the tyme aforesaid, hit doth appear."

The Trivet family were well known in West Somerset and owned, at one time, the manors of Combwich, Otterhampton, and left their name to Chilton Trivet. Their badge is still to be seen on the porch of Dodington Church and in Dodington Hall. A John Trivet represented Bridgwater in Parliament in 1348, and he may have been the benefactor of Bridgwater and the contributor to the bridge.

Sir John Trivet's badge of three trivets was affixed to the coping of the bridge, and the old structure was called Trivet's Bridge. It was in existence in Commonwealth days, and right up to 1795, and must not be confused with the gateway and drawbridge at Eastover which figures in the famous siege of Bridgwater. In 1795 Trivet's Bridge, a sketch of which still exists, was replaced by a new structure which, however, had a comparatively short life, giving place, in 1883, to the modern bridge with its span of seventy-five feet.

In the old charters of Bridgwater defining the boundaries of the borough, by river as well as by land, there is constant reference to Lymebridge on the south side, the point where the boundaries began. Some piles found in the river just above the present site of Bridgwater Infirmary (Jarman's *History of Bridgwater*, p. 22), together with a reference made by Oldmixon to a communication across the river between Hamp House and Sydenham House, may lend colour to the supposition that there was an old wooden bridge here. This would always have been distinct from the Great Bridge.

The River Parret, anciently called Pedret (600), or Peret or Pedrida in the A.-S. Chronicle (658), deserves more than a passing notice. Taking its rise in the high ground about Crewkerne and Pendomer, it flows north-wards towards the Bristol Channel, or "Severn Sea," its usual name in former days. In its course it is joined by many tributaries, such as the River Ile or Ivel at a point near Thorney, which gives a name to Ivelchester or Ilchester, Ile Abbots, Ile Brewer, Ilminster, and Ilton. It is also joined by the River Yeo (which gives its name to Yeovil), about half a mile above Langport Bridge. This part of the river from its sources to Langport may be called the "Upper Parret," and a very good view of the moors and low-lying meadows, especially in time of flooding, may be obtained from the churchyard at Langport, or any high point above Aller and along Ham Hill. On more than one occasion the writer has viewed this country when periodically inundated from 1866–1906, and has skated over miles of the moors.

The nomenclature of the River Parret has occasionally varied. Not far from Montacute its upper waters have been known as the waters of the River Credy. Camden, the Elizabethan antiquary, calls the Parret the Ivel and the Parret mouth the Ivel mouth; but this is in direct conflict with the old Saxon chroniclers, who speak of the Pedridamuda, i.e. the mouth of the Parret (845), and all ancient chroniclers. Even in Henry VIII's reign Leland falls into the error, surely, of calling the Parret the Ivel. But the antiquity of the name and of the river which far back in history gave its name to North and South Petherton, often spelt Pederton or Pedreton, is evident.

8

It also gave a name to Puriton (Domesday Peritone) at the end of the Polden Hills and, at its very source, to North and South Perrot, called anciently "Peret." The river bisects the county of Somerset from south to north.

The total watershed of the Parret and its three tributaries, the Ile, the Yeo and the Tone, is calculated to be 362,860 acres, of which the Upper Parret with the Ile and Yeo comprises about 186,880 acres, and the Lower Parret with the Tone about 175,980 acres. In certain seasons the flooded area of the Upper district is nearly 25,000 acres, and that of the Lower 15,000 acres. The watershed of the Cary is calculated at 44,930 acres, the area liable to floods at 13,958 acres. The Brue can hardly be termed a tributary of the Parret, as it joins it so low down and near its mouth, but it may be worth noting that this river, with which really the Parret is in communication as a waterway, has a watershed of 136,850 acres and an area of 13,520 acres liable to floods.[1] The Brue is historically interesting as the river valley of ancient Glastonbury. As it flows from Langport to Bridgwater the Parret is joined by the River Tone, which rises far to the west on the Brendon Hills and in its turn gives a name to Taunton. In old documents the River Tone is written Tân, and Taunton dean is written Tân dean. The most conspicuous feature of the moors and levels at the junction of the Parret and Tone is the Borough, or tumulus, near Athelney, whence an excellent view may be obtained of what may be termed the Lower Valley of the Parret. Not far from Borough Bridge the Parret received the waters, in former times, of the River Cary, the sources of which lie close under the historic site of Castle Cary. In order

[1] Grantham's "Report on the Floods of Somerset." Presented to the House of Commons, 1873.

to facilitate certain drainage schemes the River Cary
was diverted from its original course and canalized
along the main King Sedgemoor drain, so that it is
now made to flow out into the Lower Parret at Dunball
Clyce. Further to the east lies the valley of the Axe
with a watershed of 62,720 acres and an area of 2266
acres liable to floods. From these official figures it will
be possible to realize the nature of the Parret valley
as well as that of the adjoining valleys of the Brue
and the Axe. Taken together they present the
view of a series of low-lying moors stretching across
the centre of the county of Somerset.

These moors are in general on a level with the sea
water in ordinary tides, but considerably below it
during high spring or equinoctial tides. The levels
are secured from floods at these critical times by strong
banks called sea-walls, extending both along the shores
of the Severn Sea and also the sides of the rivers.
The mouths of some of the rivers and outfalls are
secured against the inrush of the sea by sluice-gates.
For centuries it has been the work of Commissioners
of Sewers and Dyke Reeves to regulate the flow of the
waters by widening the natural outfalls and keeping
the "rhines" or drains clean. But occasionally the
forces of Nature are too strong for the devices of man.
Sometimes the sudden melting of snow or an exceptional downpour of rain, happening in March or
September, during the period of the highest tides,
results in a flood and in widespread havoc, simply from
the reason that the fresh water is pent and backed up
in certain areas by the incoming "bore," and cannot
find its natural outlet quickly enough. Langport is
still subject to periodical visitations, although it is
twenty-five miles from the mouth of the Parret.

Bridgwater itself is in a better position with regard

to floods, but exceptional high tides have been known
to flood Castle Street with three feet of salt water.
Tidal observations taken at Bridgwater, which is
fourteen miles by the windings of the river from Burnham at its mouth and eleven miles from Langport, are
very interesting. At the bridge the spring tides will
rise sometimes to a maximum height of twenty feet,
measuring from a gravelly place in the bed of the
river. The " bore " takes about four hours to traverse
the fourteen miles from Burnham, going quickly in
narrow places but slower up broad reaches. Now and
then there is a second " bore " following after the first,
but this is exceptional. Curiously enough, the tidal
wave having gathered its first impulse from the sea
will continue to run up the River Parret beyond Bridgwater towards Langport, but in the lower reaches the
back movement will have begun, so that the unusual
phenomenon is presented of a river flowing upwards
and downwards at the same time. Some neap tides do
not reach much further than Borough Bridge, five
miles beyond Bridgwater. The tides vary with the
winds outside, the east or north-east winds keeping
down the level of the spring tides, the south or south-
west, the prevalent winds, raising it. The effect of a
south-west gale from the Atlantic piling up the water
in Bridgwater Bay is very marked. On September 10th,
1903, a great south-west gale, which reached a velocity
of sixty miles an hour, raised the water to a level of
more than six feet above the calculated height of the
tide at Burnham. Given the force of wind outside,
a skilled observer could foretell the height of water.
In 1703 it is related how during the exceptional storm
a vessel in the Parret was driven ashore and left
upon the land several hundred yards above the ordinary high-water mark, and also how the country folk

set up marks on their houses and trees to show how high the waters flowed.

There is more than one "level" along the banks of the Parret. The Bridgwater Level has been described in Billingsley's *Survey of Somerset* as comprising the flat country lying between the range of the Polden Hills and the River Parret, bounded on the north-west by Bridgwater Bay and on the south-east by Ham Hill. The higher districts include the large tracts of alluvial land known as Pawlet Hams and Horsey Slimes. But this definition is not very satisfactory, and to arrive at the proper conclusions it is safer to consult the latest ordnance surveys as in Bartholomew's reduced maps. "Burnham Level," "Huntspill Level," "Puriton Level," "Petherton Level," are local definitions, but they do not exactly tally with land conformations. On the ordnance survey there are many places where the land is only 15 feet and even less above the ordnance datum. The zero of the gauge at Bridgwater Bridge is 5·62 feet above ordnance datum, so that a 20-foot tide at the bridge would be 25·62 feet above ordnance datum and consequently 15·62 feet above those portions of land only 10 feet above ordnance datum. In the case of fresh-water floods happening coincidently with high spring tides the danger is obvious.

The following is a quaint description of the disastrous effects of the breaking of the bank or sea-wall at Burnham in the year 1607.

" Suddenly, without notice, the country for 20 miles by 5 was flooded to the depth of 11 or 12 feet, the deepest part being at Kingston Seymour. At Huntspill 28 were drowned. . . . Brean was swallowed up. Of 9 houses there, 7 were destroyed and with them 26 persons lost their lives. . . . Ken was almost out of kenning. In this parish stood a fair large building belonging to the Lady Straunge, into which all were invited to shelter. The horses stood in the hall above their middle in water. . . . In Berrow a maid coming from milking was round about beset and climbing up a bank remained there 24 hours, the rats, mice and wants (moles) being in swarms about her to save their lives. All this blew profit to some, as seafaring men came in boats and went away richly laden. Others, sheep-byters, killed the sheep for their tallow only, leaving the carcasses. Conies sought refuge on the backs of the sheep but were at last drowned with them. As soon as possible, 500 men at 12d. a day were put to work at Burnham, the Justices helping not with their eyes only but also with their hands."

This terrible catastrophe was of a very unusual kind and is not likely to be repeated, although Mr. Grantham, in his Report of 1873, observes that not only in 1607 but also in 1703 and in 1811 the sea has rushed in and flowed up as far as Glastonbury. The weakness of the Burnham defences lay in the divided responsibilities of many riparian owners working their "doles" at that time according to no fixed plan.

Bridgwater in its very early beginnings bore a considerable resemblance to Axbridge or to Over-Weare on the Axe as the terminus of a tidal river. On the score of time the thirty-two burgesses of Axbridge had the advantage, for they got their charters from the Saxon kings and as favoured king's "vills." The privileges of Bridgwater were acquired in Norman times and some centuries afterwards.

In modern times it is curious how history has repeated itself. In the colony of Nova Scotia there is a Bridgwater situated on a tidal river at a distance of fourteen miles from its mouth. In five places in our

Empire Bridgwater is reproduced: in Newfoundland on the east coast near Freshwater; in Nova Scotia, already noticed; in Victoria, where, in the south-west of the colony, a cape, bay, and town carry the name; in Tasmania; and in New South Wales.

There is just another town which challenges a comparison with Bridgwater, and this is its neighbour and rival Taunton. As in the case of Bridgwater so with Taunton, the annals of the town are extremely interesting and provide a study in themselves, as they go far back into Saxon times like Axbridge, Somerton, and Langport. But in a certain sense these become stereotyped when in A.D. 790 Frithogitha gave the manor of Taunton to the bishopric of Winchester, and King Ethelwulf, the father of Alfred, enlarged it of his gracious bounty. In Taunton we breathe a different—perhaps a more ecclesiastical—atmosphere altogether, with laws surviving through the centuries right up to modern times. The *Customs of Taunton Dean,* or Tândean, reflect the spirit of Saxon legislation since the days of Ina and Alfred.

Taunton's agricultural prosperity was won from the "dean" or rich valley around it just as the wealth of Bridgwater arose from the marshes and knee-deep pasture lands of the Lower Parret, but the men of Bridgwater had another string to their bow in their trading, commercial and shipping position. They held the coign of vantage here, seized by a rapacious baron in the first place with his anchorage, pontage and port dues, but presently to be passed on to the burgesses and the modern mayor and corporation. At Taunton the Bishop of Winchester may have been a good overlord enough but he was too far distant, and when the diocese of Bath and Wells was split off from Winchester the growing inconvenience and anomaly must have been felt for centuries. For instance, it was no great advantage for the Taunton men and the dwellers of Taunton Dean to pay rich rent to such a bishop as Henry Beaufort, the famous Cardinal, who certainly did not spend his money in Taunton Dean.

Bridgwater, therefore, reaped much in the past not only from her natural river surroundings but also from other more intangible and fortuitous events. She scored her first victory over Langport under William Briwere; she had a kind of river and navigation precedency over Taunton; her burgesses gained the reversion of the baronial privileges falling in like a lease in due time. The only possible rival was Combwich, but the river was too wide there, and the position was dangerous and exposed to piratical raids. The chances of Downend gradually became obliterated by the working of natural causes; and so, betwixt and between, the town grew from a primitive bridge, first to a mediæval castle, eclipsing the old " Caput Baroniae " of Walter de Douai at Castle Cary; then to a favourite hunting centre, finally blossoming into a self-governing borough.

A single modern industry of Bridgwater seems to illustrate the peculiar position of the town as the exact topographical point of converging interests that have helped to localise it and to place it where it is. In making Bath bricks (for these useful household articles are really products of Bridgwater and not Bath) a certain proportion of sand and Parret alluvial deposit is required, tempered and mixed to exact proportions. The chief agency is the ebb and flow of the Parret bore, keeping it in suspense here and accumulating it there, until by the inscrutable working of the great water sieve the detritus is fit for human manipulation. Earth, air and water all combine to churn the mixture, and no human hand can rival Nature's workshop. The gift is adventitious, and the curious fact is that only within a mile or so of the bridge at Bridgwater can the suitable compound be found. So, indeed, the prosperity of the ancient borough is due far back in history to the inscrutable churnings of unseen forces. Natural agencies have been at work, and human hands have seemed now to interfere, now to forward, and now to depreciate the task. But by ordinances beyond man's control and by influences converging with a kind of magnetic force the old bridge arose as the Rialto of the foaming Parret, whence sailors adventured far and near to the markets of the world.

# CHAPTER II

## THE NORMAN SETTLEMENT

BOTH before and after the fateful battle of Senlac there must have been much hurry and alarm along the valley of the Parret. Whether across the ford of Combwich, the bridge of Bridgwater, Borough Bridge, at the confluence of the Tone and Parret, South Petherton Bridge, or Langport Bridge, eager messengers, bowmen, and steel-clad knights, rushing to the assistance of the great Saxon cause, must have passed and repassed. Never perhaps was there such tumult, never such a momentous national crisis since the days when the Roman legionaries encamped at Vespasian's camp in Selwood and met the British chiefs. Or when, four hundred years and more afterwards, the British forces under Geraint and King Arthur, rallying round tall Camelot and the Tower of War, exchanged those mighty blows with the Saxons at Llongporth, or Langport itself. Or when, after a space of another 400 years, the summons went forth from King Alfred, hiding in the forest of North Petherton and along the ridges of Quantocks, to all the faithful men of Somerset and to the royal herdsmen and swineherds of this region to meet at "Egbright's Stone." East, west, south, and north the troopers had hurried to that noted rendezvous in the depth of leafy Selwood, creeping round, it may have been, on the south by Othery or by South

C

Petherton, on the north by Brugie or Bridgwater itself, singly or in small parties, all determined with strong hearts and resolute wills to deal death and destruction upon the heathen Danes who had wrought such havoc everywhere. Almost within sight and sound of Brugie was that battle fought at Edington— so we may well place it—upon the Polden Hills.

Now it was the turn of the Saxons themselves, for under the sway of the mild and saintly Edward the Confessor their national unity and national aspirations seemed to suffer an eclipse. Duke William, nurtured in war from the very cradle, stern and ruthless in demeanour, crafty in politics, and great as an organizer, had secured the reversion of the English crown to himself, so far as putting himself technically in the right was concerned. There might have been—and probably there were—advocates of the Norman claim in Somerset and in the valley of the Parret, but the majority of the thanes and earls were whole-hearted Saxons. Had not Edward the Confessor been crowned himself at a Witenagemot at Gillingham, close to Sherborne, and on the borders of Somerset and Dorset? Were they likely to forget their choice and the oath of allegiance?

The Saxon chronicler, Ethelwerd, in describing King Alfred's extremities in 878, just before the battle of Edington, remarks that he fought "daily battles against the barbarians, having with him the province of Somerset only: no others assisted him, except the servants who made use of the king's pastures." Loyalty to Alfred's line and to the Wessex princes of the House of Cerdic must have been a tradition not lightly to be forgotten, especially when it was remembered how such loyalty had been sealed by the great glory of a successful campaign, and how, as a

climax to all, Guthrum, the Danish king, at Aller
itself, close to North Petherton, had received Christian
baptism and a new name.

The King's pastures and—it must be added—the
King's forests were goodly and wide in Somerset.
There were the five forests of Selwood, Mendip,
Neroche, North Petherton, and Exmoor, all hunting
centres of the Saxon kings. Mendip and Axbridge
were notable centres, and in the days of S. Dunstan
King Edmund had urged his horse along the cliffs of
Cheddar in that classic hunt; Edward the Elder had
sojourned at the old Taunton Priory on a hunting and
hawking tour westwards (901); and Somerton, with its
ancient warren, bounded on one side by the Roman
foss and on the other by the Cary River, had sporting
annals second to none in the kingdom. Eastward of
Somerset and right into Hampshire, to Gillingham
Forest, to Cranbourne Chase, and to regions covered
afterwards by the huge "New Forest," the Saxon
preserves ran.

These forests and king's pastures held many brave
and good archers and men-at-arms. The hundreds of
Carhampton, Williton, Cannington, Andersfeld were
royal hundreds, and the musters there must have
furnished a goodly spectacle of West-country men. We
would gladly have welcomed a roll of these men,
just as we welcome those Elizabethan musters when
the summons went forth to rally round the Tudor
Queen against the usurping Spaniard. But history is
silent, and we can only guess at the number and names
of these Saxon thanes who went first, it might have
been, with Comes Haroldus to Stamford Bridge, and
then southwards to Senlac.

We can only guess, too, at the way the news was
carried westwards to the valley of the Parret, to say

how Harold fell. Perhaps the ominous rumour of the bowing of the Cross at Waltham—that cross which tradition said had been taken from the hill of Montacute itself to begin with—was passed from one to another of these Somerset men, who, awestruck at the reputed portent, read into it some stroke of an over-ruling power. Had Harold really perjured himself over those relics? Had that cross, before which he prostrated himself in prayer, really intimated to him that fate which awaited him next morning at Senlac? Was King William's founding of Battle Abbey in honour of S. Martin of Marmoutier really a proof not only of personal piety but also of Divine grace?

Then there was that other great portent, the comet of 1066, such as never had been seen before. The historian Palgrave assigns a great importance to this, and dwells upon the fact how "night after night the appalled multitude gazed at the messenger of evil, the long-haired star, darting its awful splendour from horizon to zenith. Crowds, young and old, watched the token far beyond the midnight hour, and when they retired to their broken rest, its bright image, floating before their eyes, disturbed their slumbers. Even if this were but an idle opinion, yet it was an opinion which became a reality, as the moral world was then constituted. The conviction that the phenomena of nature and the destiny of mankind were bound up in a mystic unity gave more boldness to the fortunate, and increased the cares of the despondent. And the English, throughout all the Anglo-Norman period, acknowledged their subjection to be a kind of national punishment."

Such thoughts may have confused the loyalty of Saxon thanes and made them waver. The passes of Selwood had been entrusted to a family of the name of Stourton—so called from the Stour—and it is the tradition of the lords Stourton that their ancestor, who must indeed have occupied the important fastnesses round Pen Pits and Vespasian's Camp, came to terms with the Conqueror. All this and much more must have flashed through the country and formed a topic of conversation along all the highways of the country and the bridges of the Parret, not the least being the bridge at Bridgwater. For it was from this bridge, more almost than any other, that the Saxon must have looked seaward and have wondered whether by some disastrous turn they might have to take refuge in Ireland, as Harold's son did, or perhaps in South Wales and Monmouth, where Harold's triumphs were still a bright spot in the Saxon annals.

When, after Senlac, the strong castle of Dover, one of the very few existing in England, had been taken; when Canterbury, where Archbishop Stigand ruled and Agelnoth, apparently one of the Godwin family, commanded the military forces, had made a formal submission; when Winchester had proffered obedience; nay, when London itself had surrendered, her citizens bearing with them the keys of the city and delivering to William the person of the infant Atheling as he sat in the palace where the Confessor had been accustomed to wear his crown, then indeed the cause of the Saxons seemed to be hopelessly lost. Stigand, the Archbishop, had proffered his formal submission, Edwin and Morcar had given their adhesion to the Norman, and it was a well-known fact that Eadnoth, the standard-bearer or marshal of the Saxon hosts—an hereditary and honourable post—had acknowledged William's claims.

The siege and fall of Exeter form a very distinct phase in the conquest of the west, for Exeter would by no means accept the Norman domination except upon certain conditions, even if the city would go as far as this. Indeed, the men of Exeter and others with them desired to form a general league amongst the English burghs against the common enemy. But Exeter fell, and one of the most pathetic results briefly narrated in the Anglo-Saxon Chronicle runs thus :—

"This year (1067) Harold's mother, Githa, and the wives of many good men with her, went to the Flat Holm (Bradanreolic) and there abode some time ; and afterwards went from thence over sea to S. Omers."

The Saxons of Brugie and the Saxon followers of Haroldus Comes in the valley of the Parret must have known of this supreme climax in the fortunes of the House, and their hearts must have gone out in sympathy to the forlorn Royal Lady seeking such precarious asylum in the lonely island of the Severn Sea. How did the fugitive reach the spot from Exeter? Was it by an escape which followed the rough tracks of Dartmoor Forest to Hartland, where indeed there existed a monastery founded and endowed by the Queen-mother herself in honour of S. Nectan ; or, more likely, was it by following the valley of the River Exe by Tiverton, by Bampton, by Dulverton, and so to Porlock, a favoured Saxon centre? Thence by boat to the Flat Holm was a short and easy transit.

Still all was not lost, and from Ireland might come a rescuing hand, and so the Chronicle briefly says: "During these things one of Harold's sons came with a fleet from Ireland unexpectedly into the mouth of the River Avon and soon plundered all that neighbourhood. They went to Bristol and would have stormed the town, but the inhabitants opposed them bravely. Seeing they could get nothing from the town, they went to their ships with the booty they had got by plundering and went to Somersetshire, when they went up the country. Eadnoth, Master of the Horse, fought with them, but he was slain there and many good men on both sides; and those who were left departed thence."

This is a curious turn in the history of the Norman Conquest of the county of Somerset. Eadnoth adhered to King William's cause and fought against the sons of Harold. He lost his life in the task, but evidently he showed which way his sympathies went. Perhaps, also, the sons of Harold were not as popular as Harold himself, and their descent upon Somerset was in the guise rather of pirates and freebooters than of consistent Royalists and Legitimists. Everything seemed to tell in favour of the adventurous William the Bastard; so much so that he seemed in reality to have the blessing of Providence. Locally, it is an interesting speculation to wonder what particular part of Somerset the son of Harold ravaged, and deductions have been made from the state of those manors which seem to have lost value between the days of Edward the Confessor and 1086, the date of the Great Survey. Amongst them are many showing signs of great impoverishment in the valley of the Parret and the Quantock country, such as Pignes—part of Bridgwater itself—Cossington, Combwich, Gothelney in Charlinch, Radlet and Planesfield in Overstowey, Durborough, close to Stoke Courcy, Stowey itself, where Haroldus Comes had been a landowner, Stoke Courcy, Stringston, under the Quantocks, and Knowle in Baudrip parish and Edington on the Poldens. Lower down, the manors of Quantockshead, Carhampton, and many in the vicinity of Porlock itself show signs of depreciation. No doubt the invasion was on a large scale, for there were fifty-two ships, and these were manned partly by Danes from Ireland and partly by English exiles (Freeman, *Norman Conquest*, Vol. IV, p. 225, and *Som. Arch. Proceedings*, Vol. XXV, p. 22).

Yet another striking event which must have resounded through the valley of the Parret and aroused the deep passions and sympathies of its inhabitants, and this was the famous siege of the castle of Montacute, where King William had installed his half-brother, Robert Count of Mortain, with great powers to rule the country. This trust the Count seems to have abused, and although it may be presumed that many of the Saxon thanes were ready to acknowledge King William, it was not in their disposition to submit tamely to King William's officers, who through underlings and subordinates treated them badly. So there was a great rising in Somerset and Dorset, but unfortunately for the Saxon cause there was no head and no one great plan, and it was remorselessly crushed by the warlike Bishop of Coutances at the head of an army composed of Saxons of London, Winchester and Salisbury.

Montacute, that lonely hill now crowned by a deep growth of trees, was once the site of a strong castle, the ruins of which have now entirely disappeared. But to this castle, next in importance to Bristol in the west as a Norman administrative centre, was paid the hated Romfeoh or tax to Rome. In an old Wells document there is a mandate from William the Conqueror to William de Corcelle, father of the great Quantock Baron, Roger de Courcelle. "We command you to see that the Rome denarii (or Peter's pence) be paid at the coming Feast of S. Michael and make this known at Montacute and Bristol." Apart from its local interest this mandate sheds a light upon the changed circumstances of the land. Rome had a footing which she never possessed before in England, and it is not surprising to read how in April, 1070, at Winchester, William the Conqueror received his crown from the Pope through the hands of Hermenfried, Bishop of Sion, and Peter the Bibliothecarius or Keeper of the Records of the Holy See, called Peter of S. Maria in Trastevere. This ambiguous act, "wholly passed over by the English historians as distasteful to them," so Palgrave remarks, is, however, simply an amplification of that official act by which Pope Alexander sanctioned Duke William's expedition to England to punish Harold. That consecrated banner, the gonfanon of S. Peter, when it floated victoriously over the stricken field of Senlac, meant a kind of spiritual and ecclesiastical change for England. Could it be welcome to the Saxons? Especially when introduced under such circumstances of humiliation? The old question was destined to arise again in King John's day, and of King John Somerset and Bridgwater knew a good deal.

The change was one of those which made itself felt even in the remotest parishes. The Normans were, as we know, great benefactors of the monks and of the monastic orders, giving in the first place much property which belonged to them simply by the rude processes of indiscriminate plunder. Churches and their advowsons were handed over to priories and abbeys in Normandy, as in the case of Stoke Courcy and of Bridgwater Parish Church itself, which was given to the monks of S. Martin of Marmoutier, the privileged holders of Battle Abbey, an abbey made independent, by the way, of the English Church and the great see of Canterbury. But how were these parish churches served by absentee Norman monks? Instead of the old resident parson, vicars were appointed on a slender pittance, and so a form of appropriation of Church property

25

was introduced unknown to Saxon times. By the aid
and awe of a foreign power and the see of Rome a bad
custom was imperiously put upon the poor English
clergy. As an old writer remarks, "between such
monastic and papal ambition and avarice the practice
of appropriation, which crept in with William the Conqueror, became the custom of the land within the space
of a few reigns, and the infection spread till above
a third part of the benefices, and these the richest,
became attached to monasteries. It was a craft with
the monks to get their rules relaxed, and either to
personally serve these cures or else to do it by vicars in
the cheapest way."

In the history, however, of Bridgwater it is of more
particular interest to know what changes of ownership
there were both in the vill itself and also in North
Petherton hundred. In Bridgwater and Wembdon
we have seen that the Saxon owner in the time of
King Edward the Confessor was Merlesuain. Who
was this Merlesuain? Could he have been that Saxon
thane Merlesweyne who fled with Edgar Atheling and
his mother Agatha and his sisters, Margaret and
Christina, to Scotland to seek the protection of King
Malcolm? He is found also in 1069 at the siege of
York helping in the last struggles of the great cause
alongside of Gos Patrick and Edwin and Morcar.
Besides Bridgwater and Wembdon, it may be noticed
that Merleswain is said to have held Stockland,
Quantockshead, Bagborough, Hewish and Newhall—
in fact, the whole Domesday property of Ralph
Paganel, the ancestor of the Paganels who succeeded
to Walter de Douai at Bridgwater.

At any rate, the Merelesuain of Brugie and Wembdon disappears, and his place is filled by Walscinus
de Duaco, or better known as Walter de Douai, a

Fleming. It must always be remembered that in that great and composite host of King William's followers who landed at Kent there were a large number of Flandrenses, stout men of Flanders, fellow-countrymen of Matilda, King William's wife and consort, and subjects of Baldwin Count of Flanders. In a well-known Charter of Banwell there are the signatures, not only of King William and of Matilda and of Richard the son of whom we hear so little, but also of Walter the "Flemminc." This was, we take it, Walter of Douai, and he was a most influential follower of the King.

The Flemings lived of old in the country that spread from the borders of Normandy almost to the Rhine. The name of Calais was Vlaemskeland, and the cities of Flanders were centres of mediæval art and industry. The looms of Arras wove the tapestries which constitute the splendour of the Vatican, and Queen Matilda has by her Flemish handicraft handed down to posterity one of the most enduring monuments of her husband's successes in the famous Bayeux tapestry. These Flemings were great wanderers also, and going to Scotland as sailors and adventurers, laid the beginnings of influential Scotch families. There were Flemings of Aberdeen, Flemings of Lanark and Flemings of Dumbarton, and from Flemish stock sprang the Douglases, the Leslies, and the Bruces.

Under William the Conqueror the Flemish bands were mercenary troops, but they became too powerful to be disbanded, and so formed an important element in the Norman settlement. The difficulties of such a country as the valley of the Parret were familiar to these stout warriors, who came from somewhat similar regions in the Low Countries. Over and over again England and the Low Countries have been associated together in war and trade, and perhaps the most agreeable invasion, as far as England was concerned, took place in Tudor days, when Flemish weavers were settled at Glastonbury and elsewhere in Somerset, helping forward the trade and industry of the county.

A short description of Walter de Douai's barony is locally very instructive. Next to Roger de Corcelle, with his eighty-seven Somerset manors, and William de Mohun, at Dunster, with fifty-four manors, Walter de Douai was the most powerful layman in the neighbourhood, excepting, of course, the Earl of Mortain, the Conqueror's half-brother, at Montacute Castle. The manors given to Walter de Douai seem, however, to have been given with a distinct idea of military strategy, and this idea was to guard the rivers Parret and the Axe from source to outfall into the Severn Sea, a task this Fleming was, no doubt, well able to fulfil. At the same time he commanded and intercepted the main lines of inland communication, whether it was by the old Roman road that led from Bath and Bristol over the Mendips, or further south by the roads that converged upon Ilchester, or, on the side of the Severn Sea, by such lines of communication that crossed the Parret at Brugie itself or Combwich Passage, the early importance of which latter place has been already noted.

The " caput Baroniae " was at Castle Cary, a place perhaps so called from the old caer or castrum that might have existed either on the site of the old castle itself or on the adjoining ridges of " Lodge Hill " and " Park Hill." The outlook from these eminences is over a wide and extensive tract of land. On the east is Selwood, the passes of which we must suppose were entrusted to Rodolphus de Stourton to keep in virtue of his homage to King William; to the north-west, Glastonbury Tor; and, due west, spreading out like a map, the valley of the River Parret, reaching right up to North Petherton hundred and the distant boundary of the eastern ridge of Quantock.

Indeed, Castle Cary, standing a little north of South Cadbury, occupied in Norman times the same important and strategical position that King Arthur's Tower of War at Camelot occupied in British days, both of them standing a little east of the Fosse Way and the old Roman road to Bath. Together with Castle Cary, Walter de Douai received Harptree, on the east side of Mendip, commanding the Roman road that followed the line of Mendip, and ultimately had its terminus at the mouth of the Axe and Brean Down. Both Richmont Castle at East Harptree, and Castle Cary were celebrated places in the time of King Stephen, and were held by the Perceval or Lovel family for the Empress Matilda, a proof of their early importance. There under the walls of Castle Cary issued the fountains of the River Cary, the eastern feeder of the Parret, now canalized, as already mentioned, and having its outfall, for drainage purposes, at Highbridge, but at the time of the Norman Conquest flowing along its natural channel adjoining the River Parret, not far from Borough Bridge.

Together with Castle Cary Walter de Douai held Wincanton, Milton-Clevedon, Ansford, close to Castle Cary, Brocton or Bratton (Seymour) to the south, North Barrow, Sparkford, a manor in the immediate vicinity of the noted Cadbury Castle and lying on the road from Castle Cary to Ilchester. There was a feudal connection between Castle Cary and the old Roman town of Ilchester, as we are told that a burgess of the place paid rent to Walter de Douai. It may be re-

29

marked that of the manors held in the neighbourhood of Castle Cary and Harptree the greater part, like Spark-ford, soon passed on to the Lovel barons.

Next to Castle Cary the most important place was Bridgwater and the adjoining manors along the valley of the Parret, e.g. Creech S. Michael, high up the river, and, nearer Bridgwater, Wembdon, Bradney, Horsey, Donham or Dunball, Baudrip, East Bower, Walpole in Paulet parish, Huntspill and Alston-maris in Huntspill, Paulet, Stretcholt, Burnham at the mouth of the Parret itself, and Huish, a manor in Burnham. Many of these manors fell under the territorial division of North Petherton hundred, but it is worth noting that Walter de Douai held the fords and bridges. He held the bridge at Bridgwater; he held Stretcholt and Paulet dominating Combwich Passage; and he held Burnham at the very mouth of the Parret. Together with William de Falaise at Stoke Courcy Castle, Walter de Douai may be said to have been the master of the Parret, although his strongest fort and castle was at the source of the Parret waters, whilst William de la Falaise's was on Bridgwater Bay.

In a similar way Walter de Douai had the oversight of the Axe River and held Compton on the Axe, Weare or Werre on the Axe, Bagewerre or Badgworth, Alston (Sutton) in Weare, Turnock or Tarnick near Biddesham, and Allerton, known better as Chapel Allerton. These manors formed a goodly section and block by them-selves, rich beyond measure, not only as places where the reclaimed marsh ground would be valuable for grazing, but also as places where profit might be made from the traders and vessels bringing merchandise up the Axe, as at Weare (or Overweare) two miles below Axbridge. For Weare at one time was a borough in itself. If Walter de Douai held nothing at Axbridge, this must be explained by the fact that Axbridge had been from time immemorial a royal burgh associated closely with the Royal Forest of Mendip.

At the mouth of the Axe Walter de Douai was placed in charge of Worle, the old camp lying above the modern Weston-super-Mare and Brean or Brean Down. As if to show his sense of the importance of these two headlands lying east and west of the mouth of the Axe, Walter de Douai held them both in his own hands, just as he did Huntspill and Burnham at the mouth of the Parret. From Domesday it also looks as if he held Donham or Dunball in his own hands, and Donham is described as a virgate of land and part of some gift which the king made, lying "inter duas aquas." What these two "waters" were does not appear, but the land may have been an island or peninsula formed by the loop of the Parret close to Dunball.

To sum up—the new Norman Lord of Bridgwater was an extremely powerful baron, and from the heights above his strong Norman keep at Castle Cary he could look westward and northwards and survey his broad domains reaching down to the sparkling waters of the Severn Sea. We do not know what became of the Saxon thanes. There was Alnod, who held Bradney close to Bridgwater in the time of Edward the Confessor and probably gave his name to Alnodestone or Alston-maris in Huntspill. There was the Saxon Elsi at Castle Cary, Wincanton, Brocton, West Barrow, and there was a certain Aluuacre who held Overweare, Milton-Clevedon, Sparkford, Huntspill, Compton, Harptree, and so on, and as for Merleswain we have already speculated whether he could have been the powerful thane who fled to Scotland. But darkness covers the Saxon landowners after the Conquest. With bitter hearts they must have witnessed the absolute extinction of their family histories. Even to pronounce the names of the old manors with the Norman tag must have been gall and wormwood. The sacred hill of Leodgaresburgh was changed to Montacute from the name of a Montacute in Normandy. Shepton became Shepton-Montacute, another Shepton became Shepton-Malet. Stowey was called Stowey Columbers, Stoke became Stoke-Courcy, Cutcombe became Cutcombe Mohun, Harptree became Harptree Gournay, part of Stockland was called Stockland Lovel, one manor of Huntspill became Huntspill-Mareis, and another moiety Huntspill Cogan, and plain Brugie became, as we have seen, Brugge Walter.

William the Conqueror began by acting leniently to the English who acknowledged his rights, but as time went on and one revolt after another, crushed with an iron heel, embittered all relations, he waxed sterner. It was said that sixty thousand knights received their fees from the Conqueror, but, granting some exaggeration, there was a great host of Normans, Flemings, Angevins, Bretons, and others who by his gift stepped into the heritage of Anglo-Danish and English nobility and gentry. As the historian Palgrave remarks (*Hist. of Normandy*, Vol. III, p. 480), the great majority of the adventurers who fought under William's flag had been rude and poor and despicable in their own land ; the rascallions of Northern Gaul. These, suddenly enriched, lost all compass and bearing of mind, and no one circumstance vexed the spirit of the English more than to see the fair and noble English maidens and widows forced to accept these despised adventurers as husbands.

The list of the thanes of the King as described in Domesday is a short one. There is a Brictric who held under the King a place called Buckland, and Tuckswell in Over Stowey, and he may have been the Brictric who held Clive or Kilve in the time of Edward the Confessor. With him was associated a certain thane called Ulward, who may have given his name to Ulwardeston, or Woollston, a farm in Stoke Courcy parish and close to Stockland. Then there was an Anglo-Dane amongst the thanes called Harding, the son of Alnod, already mentioned. A Saxon Dodo held Dodington as part, then, of Nether Stowey, and Hosmer held a virgate of land in Otterhampton, which it is said "his father held before him" in the time of King Edward. But the change was generally typified in the transfer of such a manor as Perleston or Parleston in Kilve, where it is recorded in the Great Survey " Perlo held it in the time of King Edward the Confessor, and paid Danegeld for half a hide," etc., Normanus tenet—without even specifying who the Norman adventurer was.

Or, perhaps, the original Saxon owner sinks down to a position of a tenant such as Eldred, who held part of Selve or Monksilver in the time of Edward the Confessor, and then holds under the great fief of Roger de Corcelle, so powerful on the Quantocks and in the neighbourhood of Bridgwater and Stoke Courcy. Just indeed as the Saxon Alric, who held Halsway and Colford in Stogumber parish as owner in King Edward's time, and then as tenant under Roger de Courcelle.

Feeling themselves aliens in England, the more notable Saxon thanes and earls fled to Ireland (as many of them doubtless did from North Somerset); to Denmark, to the Elbe, but most of all to the south, and even to Byzantium, where the English guard were deemed the most trusty defenders of the Eastern emperor.

D                    33

# THE ANCIENT BOROUGH OF BRIDGWATER

It is a curious fact that so many of King William's personal attendants and servants were found settled in the valley of the Parret.[1] For instance, Robert de Odburville or Ambreville, who was a kind of Forest Baron and ruled at Melcome in North Petherton and at Bower in Bridgwater itself, held under Humphrey the Chamberlain, who was installed himself at Curry. Johannes Hostiarius, i.e. John the doorkeeper, held Pegens or Pignes in Bridgwater itself, and also Huntstile, with Pury or Perry in Wembdon, under the Chief Chamberlain. Ansger the hearth-keeper held Chilton and also Michaelchurch and Sheerston, the hamlet in North Petherton, with Durleigh; and another Ansger, described as the Coquus or the royal cook, held Lilstock. The wife of another cook called Manasses held a place called Haia, probably some park or enclosure. A Parcarius or park-keeper, called Anchitil, held North Newton in Petherton parish itself, and also a place called Honibere, close to Stoke Courcy. The presence of these servants and attendants of the King in the neighbourhood has given rise to a conjecture that King William himself may have held a hunting court here, but at present there is no corroborative evidence to show for certain that such was the case; nor is it possible to prove that the Conqueror was ever at Bridgwater itself.

[1] *Forests and Deer Parks of Somerset,* by Rev W. Greswell.

# CHAPTER III

## THE LOST CHURCH OF ST. BRIDGET

THE glory of Bridgwater, in mediæval days, was
divided between its feudal castle and its splendid
parish church. William Briwere founded the former ;
the latter was in existence before the time of the
Norman Conquest. Before, however, these two institutions come to be dealt with in turn, it may be well to
glance at the dim traces we possess of another church
which once existed in the town. Amongst the many
valuable and choice documents now in the possession
of the Corporation of Bridgwater is one dating from
the latter part of the thirteenth century, probably from
the reign of Edward I. It conveys certain properties
to old St. Bridget's Church. The seal of the deed is
lost ; the wording is as follows.

"Know present and to come that I William de
Wemedone, son of Daniel de Edmestone, have given,
granted, and by this my present charter confirmed to
Peter de Bruges, Rector of the church of St. Bridget,
all my meadow in Crow Pulle which I had of the gift
of Daniel de Edmestone, my father, pertaining to my
tenement of La Wytescote. Which said meadow lies
between the meadow which was Walter de Cheselade's
towards the east and Hugh de la Churcheye's meadow
towards the west, and extends in length towards the
south side and the north. To have and to hold the
aforesaid meadow with all its appurtenances to the aforesaid Peter and his heirs of the chief lords of the same

35

fee freely, quietly, well, and in peace by hereditary right for ever, with free ingress and egress. Doing therefor to the same chief lords the services due and accustomed, as much as pertain to so much free meadow in the same fee. The aforesaid Peter and his heirs also rendering to me and my heirs or assigns one rose at the Feast of the Nativity of St. John the Baptist for all service and secular demand. And I the said William and my heirs or assigns will warrant, acquit and defend the aforesaid meadow with all its appurtenances to the aforesaid Peter and his heirs against all mortals for ever. And for this gift, grant and confirmation of the present charter the said Peter gave me three marks of silver in hand. In witness whereof I have set my seal to this present charter. These being witnesses: Hugh de Popham; Robert de Burty; Walter de Sydenham; Hugh Godwyne; William le Large; Robert of the Bakehouse (de Pistrino); William the Clerk; and others."

The document is endorsed by the grantor, William of Wembdon.

Several of these witnesses appear also in other current documents, and some are well-known men. But of the church of St. Bridget in Bridgwater no further trace as yet has been discovered. It has disappeared, as have so many ancient buildings, entirely from history and from sight. Crowpulle, now known as Crowpill, was and is a little stream flowing on the north side of the town eastwards into the River Parret, close by where the docks now are situate. Its vicinity is fairly well indicated by the Crowpill Inn, on the Chilton Road.

Saint Brigid, Bridget, Brigida, or Brighid was a most notable person who flourished, it is stated, in the fifth century. Her name was afterwards curtailed into

St. Bride. The centre of her influence was at Kildare, in Ireland, and it spread to England and Scotland. Many churches were dedicated to her, and so greatly was she revered that the Gaelic poets looked upon her as equal in greatness to St. Mary the Virgin.

> Except Mary none was similar
> As we esteem unto Brighid.
> May the blessing of Brighid and of God
> Be upon those join in reciting this.
> By whom may I be guarded—
> Mary and Saint Brighid.

It is advanced, with much probability, that the name of St. Bridget is an offspring of Druidic worship.[1] "Brighid was not a personal name but an official title, nor is it a title of one person and age only, but of all ages and persons within the limits of that dispensation. Brighid, the favourite Gaelic name, was recognized as the Vesta of fire wherever the Gaelic traditions were kept up." When the Druids took their departure from Anglesea they made their home in Kildare, set up their sanctuary, where burnt the miraculous fire, where was the cauldron which typified renovation, with the priestess or goddess Brighid at the head of the worship. "With the cauldron and the perpetual fire was connected the choir or sisterhood of the sacred virgins or Druidesses, the vestal keepers of the fire and the cauldron." There is no doubt that Kildare became famous for the miracles said to be performed there by the glorious Brighid, and that Pagan customs were known to survive in that place even as late as the beginning of the thirteenth century. Henry of London, Archbishop of Dublin, in 1220 put an end to many irregularities connected with Brighid's rites, though the cult lingered here and there, in remote places, up to the time of the Reformation.

[1] See Mr. Christopher Irvine's *St. Brighid and Her Times.*

"There was at Kildare," writes Mr. Irvine, "while Ireland was yet the Holy Island (of Druidism), a central authority of Druidism, a circular *pyrèum*, with all its mystic rites and sacred vestas, under the sway of Brighid. It seems easy enough to perceive that Druidism in its ideal representation, Christianized, is the true explanation of St. Brighid the divine virgin, no matter at what date her sanctuary at Kildare first called itself Christian."[1]

However all this may be, and whatever may have been the origin of St. Bridget and her story, it is undoubted that in mediæval times she was looked upon in Britain as a Christian saint, and was reverenced as such. Two other churches in Somerset are dedicated to her memory, at Brean and at Chelvey. It was said that she came to Glastonbury in 488 A.D., and that after her return thence to Ireland a chapel on the Island of Beckery (near Glastonbury, hard by the River Brue), formerly dedicated to St. Mary Magdalene, was known henceforth as St. Bridget's Chapel. The surrounding fields, known as "Brides," suggest the truth of the tradition. Only the foundations of the chapel—or rather of two chapels, one within the other —remain. It was once believed that St. Bridget's burial place was at Glastonbury, but this honour was also claimed by Kildare, and by Abernethy in Scotland. Somerset has always had frequent communication with Ireland, from the very earliest days. It was therefore natural enough that Beckery and Bridgwater, Brean and Chelvey—all situated within easy communication with the Severn Sea—should have churches of St. Bridget. At Cannington there is St. Bride's Field, still marked on the map. It may once have formed part of the endowment of our lost Bridgwater church.

[1] *St. Brighid and Her Times.*

There is an interesting will of Edmund de Saint Maur, Knight, dated 1421, which shows the testator's love for St. Bridget.

"On the day of St. Laurence, A.D. 1421, I, Edmund de Saint Maur, Knight, Lord of St. Bridget, in Lower Gwent [a province in South Wales] and of Chelvey in the county of Somerset, make my will in this manner:

"I bequeath my body to be buried in the Church of St. Bridget of Chelvey, if I chance to die in England; and if I chance to die in Wales, I will that my body shall be buried in the Church of St. Bridget in Lower Gwent." Then Sir Edmund proceeds with his other bequests. "I bequeath to the Augustinian Friars of Bristol 10s., to be distributed amongst them one by one, to celebrate for my soul in honour of the four evangelists. To the Friars Preachers of Bristol 6s. 8d., to be distributed among them one by one, to celebrate for my soul in honour of the Father and the Son and the Holy Ghost. To the Friars Minor there, 10s. as above, to celebrate in honour of all the apostles and saints of God. To the Friars Carmelites of Bristol 20s. as above, to wit, one-half in honour of all the martyrs, and the other half in honour of all the confessors of God. To the Friars Minor there, 10s. as above, to celebrate for my soul in honour of the blessed Michael and Gabriel, Archangels. To the Friars Carmelites, 5s. as above, to celebrate in honour of St. Mary Magdalene, and all the virgins and all the angels of God." Lastly, with divers sums bequeathed to Sir Robert FitzJames, Rector of Backwell, and to others, he continues, "I bequeath to the fabric of the Chapel of the Blessed Mary of St. Bridget in Lower Gwent 100s." This was a very large sum of money. St. Bridget had in Sir Edmund Saint Maur a faithful servant indeed.

Now at this very period, i.e. the end of the thirteenth century, there was no lack of churches in Bridgwater, which was then what we should now call quite a small town. St. Mary's Church was, and had long been, in the full vigour of active work. The Hospital of St. John in Eastover had its chapel. So also had the House of the Friars Minor in Friarn Street. There was a chapel within the walls of Bridgwater Castle. Wembdon Church lay close by, and most of the great manor houses in the neighbourhood possessed oratories or chapels of their own. It may be asked, where was the use, or need, of yet another church, Saint Bridget's, in Bridgwater? In order to answer the question we must entirely divest ourselves of modern ideas. Churches to-day are built in some sort of ratio to the number of the population of a town. In mediæval times such a notion never entered any one's head. There could not be, it was held, too many churches. It gave the keenest joy to any knight or landowner or merchant to build, to endow, or partly endow, a church or a chantry. It was not only one of the very few outlets for the expenditure of a man's wealth, it was also reckoned to be a most pious act, which would be of much efficacy in gaining for the donor the favour of God and of the saints. Moreover, the churches were always open; their altars were accessible to rich and poor alike, and the beautiful buildings were very largely used by the people. Not only were religious services conducted in them; wills were proved there, bargains were ratified, courts were held, and many secular transactions gained additional security and validity by taking place within the church's walls. Thus, in a document dated July 3rd, 1480, Robert Catesby, clerk; Nicholas Catesby, gentleman; and Thomas Barker execute a bond to John Kendall and John Hugyns, esquires

(Bridgwater merchants), in £25, to ensure the payment of a sum of £10 to the two latter on the twentieth day after Michaelmas next ensuing. The money was to be paid in the church of St. Bridget (St. Bride) in Fleet Street, London, between the hours of seven and ten in the morning. The sacred place wherein the debt was to be paid no doubt added to the fear of failure to redeem what was due, and also strengthened the probability to the creditors that the promise would be faithfully kept. Business hours in Fleet Street have changed since 1480. Few churches now are open daily for worship, or for any other purpose, before seven o'clock in the morning, and very few heads of mercantile firms, or even their responsible representatives, are ready to settle accounts at that early hour. *Tempora mutantur, nos et mutamur in illis.*

So far as is known, even the memory of there having once been a St. Bridget's Church in Bridgwater has almost vanished. One or two old inhabitants, on being questioned, have confessed to a faint recollection of having heard its former existence mentioned long ago. It is now one of the forgotten incidents of ancient times. It was probably a small chapelry, situated on the north side of the town, in the neighbourhood of Blacklands or The Mount. Its influence can hardly have been great, or its duration long, for no mention is made of any of its chaplains or rectors after the time of Peter de Bruges. Very probably its slender endowments passed into the possession of the Augustinians of St. John's Hospital in Eastover, or became merged in those of one of the endowed chantries of St. Mary's Parish Church. Such alienations were not unusual, and sometimes a small foundation became the basis of a large and later church scheme. Schemes for church and chantry building then were indeed very numerous. It is rather the custom nowadays to

41

attribute the zeal, so characteristic of the thirteenth and fourteenth centuries, to mediæval superstition. It was not so; it was the outcome, for the most part, of religious aspirations which were intensely strong, and which found their obvious satisfaction in endowing a chantry or in building a church to the honour of God. It was an Age of Faith.

> O had I lived in that great day,
>   How had its glory new
> Fill'd earth and heaven, and caught away
>   My ravished spirit too !
>
> No thoughts that to the world belong
>   Had stood against the wave
> Of love which set so deep and strong
>   From Christ's then open grave.
>
> And centuries came and ran their course,
>   And unspent all that time
> Still, still went forth that Child's dear force,
>   And still was at its prime.

Thus writes Matthew Arnold in *Obermann Once More*.

And a very different writer, of far earlier date, expresses in quaint and beautiful language the deep and absorbing devotion of an age which had never learned to doubt, and which was satisfied, heart and soul, with the simple belief in a Saviour of men.

> Let fal downe thy ne, and lift up thy hart,
>   Behold thy Maker on yon cros al to torn.
> Remember His wondis that for the did smart,
>   Gotyn without syn, and on a Virgin born.
> Al His head percid with a crown of thorns,
>   Alas ! Man, thy hart oght to brest in too.
> Bewar of the devyl when he blawis his horn,
>   And pray thy good aungel convey the.

# CHAPTER IV

## BRIDGWATER CASTLE

NORMAN castles were built in feudal days to over-awe the country and to keep the people in subjection. Almost immediately after the Conquest the stern Norman "keeps" arose, placed very often on inaccessible places and surrounded by a moat of water. The remains of such an early castle of occupation surrounded by a water-moat may surely be traced at Stoke Courcy, where the first owner was William de Falaise, a relative of King William, and coming from his birthplace in Normandy. There was a strong Norman keep with its dry moat at Nether Stowey also, which formed the head of the old Nether Stowey Barony. Both Stoke Courcy and Nether Stowey were "boroughs," but their importance was of a comparatively fleeting character. The barons in each place were men of note, but the warlike energies of the de Courcy family took them to Ulster; those of the de Candos or Columbers family at Nether Stowey to South Wales. It was a grander thing to be called "Lord of ancient Caerleon" and a Lord Marcher of Wales than Lord of Nether Stowey; and it was more imposing for John de Courcy to be Lord of Ulster than Lord of Stoke Courcy in Somerset.

The Castle of Bridgwater had a very different beginning from that of Stowey or Stoke Courcy castle. In the first place its construction, i.e. 1202, was later in time, and in the second place its first owner,

William Briwere or Brewer, was not amongst the roll of Norman families. It is said by Gerard that the first William Briwere was a foundling or perhaps a mere military adventurer picked up from the "bruera" or heath by Henry II when hunting in the New Forest. Thirdly, it is plain that Bridgwater Castle was not in the first instance ever meant to be an original "caput Baroniae." The manor of Brugie, as already pointed out, lay amongst the Domesday properties of Walter de Douai, and the head of this original barony was at Castle Cary.

Still, as far as we can see, Bridgwater Castle was constructed very much on the lines and according to the plan of the early Norman castles which, by the policy of the Conqueror (as Freeman and Palgrave remind us), sprang up all over the land. The proximity of a tidal river afforded the opportunities of having a very deep and exceptionally wide moat; the river itself with its tidal currents and slippery banks afforded a strong defence on the east. The very entrance was probably guarded, not only by a detached "barbican" or strong tower, but also by two smaller towers on this side and on that, up which a staircase would lead to the parapets, whence the defenders would hurl down what missiles they had. Through slits and apertures in the walls men with cross-bows could take their deadly aim. The walls of the great keep itself would be strong and massive, measuring ten feet or fifteen feet thick. Whoever desired to assault the walls of a Norman castle would have, in many cases, to cross a moat of water. This could be done only by filling up the moat or a portion of it with huge quantities of fascines or brushwood. But this was only part of the task. To carry the parapets of the castle by assault a huge wooden structure was often made, built up storey after storey facing the castle walls, reminding us of Virgil's Trojan horse. When completed, it was moved forward on wheels with immense toil across the portion of the moat already filled up and affording an access. Relays of assaulters would then clamber up and, letting down a gangway on the top, come to a desperate hand-to-hand struggle with the defenders. This wooden structure might be fired and all the labour lost, but to avoid this catastrophe, it was often covered with raw hides. Below, the sappers and miners with pickaxe and battering-ram might get to work at the foundations of the castle walls, protected by a kind of wooden contrivance called a "chat" or "cat," fulfilling the same purpose as a Roman *testudo*. A "chat chasteil" was the collective name for the engine of assault (*Norman Architecture*, by Viollet le Duc). Not unfrequently the sappers and miners might begin to work at some distance from the castle wall, and so try to surprise their foes from beneath their own foundations, and perhaps this may account for the many rumours of subterranean passages under old castle sites. Before the days of artillery Norman castles, however, must have been extremely difficult to carry by assault. In Bridgwater the worthy burghers might have looked to the castle as a defence, but what if the building was used against their own liberties? Within the walls was, we know, a gloomy prison, and the Lord of Bridgwater Manor had his gallows, his pillory, and ducking-stool.

When leave was given by King John to William Briwere to build (*firmare*) Bridgwater Castle he was allowed to erect one at the same time at Eslege or Stoke, in Hampshire, or on his lands in Devon, where he was Lord of Dunkeswell, on the Blackdown Hills not far from Honiton, and also of Bahantune or Bampton. William Briwere was a heart and soul supporter of King John, and is said to have ranged himself on his side against the barons and to have opposed the granting of Magna Charta. However this may be, it is certain that he entertained King John in Bridgwater Castle shortly after its erection on several occasions, from 1204–10. Apparently there was no part of England more favoured by this monarch than the county of Somerset.

Bristol Castle, with its forest and chase of Kingswood adjoining, was visited by him, and there, in 1209, it is said that the King "interdicted the capture of all birds throughout England," an early and strong presentation of the game laws. It has been suggested that this particular kind of Interdict of birds was really an answer to the terrible Interdict which had just been launched upon him by Pope Innocent, and that it was a warning to all monks, friars, and churchmen fond of hawking that for the future they would have to hold their hands.

The Castle of Bridgwater never knew more imposing days than those of King John. The Castle must frequently have been used as a kind of hunting-box, whence the heights of the neighbouring Quantock Hills, the moors, and fastnesses of North Petherton and North Curry would be traversed by the eager steps of huntsman and fowler. From the Pipe Rolls of the Bishop of Winchester (1207–8) we learn that certain payments were made for salting and drying venison from Bruges.[1] At one time, so old Gerard informs us, King John had taken over in his own hands the royal park at Petherton from William Dacus, the forester,

[1] See *Forests and Deer Parks of Somerset*, by Rev. W. Greswell.

who in 1199 had the custody of it,[1] giving him "a parcell of Ilchester" in exchange for it. However, this does not seem to have been a permanent arrangement, for in 1216 (Close Rolls) King John gave to his favourite, William Briwere, in addition to what he already possessed, the manor of Newton Forester (North Newton in North Petherton) and all appertaining to it, viz. the oversight of the Somerset Forest, also of Exmoor, Hawkridge, Exton, Withypoole. He also gave him the charge of the manor of Stoke Courcy and, presumably, the Castle also, together with Wootton Courtenay, a manor associated with Stoke Courcy in the early annals. The above were probably temporary arrangements only, made in troublous and turbulent times, for there seems to have been no permanence about them. At this date William Briwere was at the zenith of his power. In 1222 the Castle itself was either enlarged or repaired in a very substantial way, as a grant of fifty oaks was made "ad castrum nostrum de Bruges reparandum," unless indeed the repairs were made necessary by an assault of which we have no notice. William Briwere was enlarging his barns also, and had a grant of oaks from North Petherton for this purpose.

It is not too much to assume that about this time there was much military and naval activity at Bridgwater. There was the threatened invasion of Louis, King of France, spurred on by the Pope to invade England, and to meet these dangers there are several orders extant in the Close Rolls issued to William Wrotham, Archdeacon of Taunton, "for the preservation of our ships and galleys" on the south coast and elsewhere. The following entry concerns William Briwere:—

[1] Rotuli de oblatis.

"The King to William, Archdeacon of Taunton, etc. : know ye that we have given to our beloved R. de Mariscis, Archdeacon of Northumberland, and W. Briwer [Brewer] two of the ships, with all their apparel, which our sailors captured. And, therefore, we command you to retain to our use the best of those ships, and give the second best to Richard de Mariscis and the third best to W. Briwer with all their apparel. 2 June, 14 John."

There is extant also a letter dated 10 John, September 19th, at Bridgwater, written by the King, Willielmo de S. Liego, vicecomiti Pembrochiae, i.e. William Marescall, Sheriff of Pembroke, bidding him to come to him at Bridgwater. The object of this errand is not stated, but it may. have been on some business connected with the Welsh rebellion, which at this time was setting South Wales on fire. This Earl of Pembroke was one of the most powerful and able servants of King John, and, together with the Archbishop of Canterbury and others, met the rebellious barons at Brackly, near Oxford, in 1215, shortly before the signing of the Magna Charta.

After the death of King John the Earl of Pembroke became the protector of the young King, Henry III, who succeeded to the throne at the early age of ten years, as his uncle. At the beginning of his reign King Henry III, we are told, had "to remain about Gloucester, Worcester and Bristol, till his vigilant and politic ministry could find out ways to break the united forces of his enemies." Indeed, it was at Gloucester that Henry was acclaimed King by the barons on his side, who uttered that notable cry, "Fiat Rex! Fiat Rex!" and for want of a regal diadem Henry was crowned with a plain circle or chaplet of gold (Kennet's History).

48

THE WATER GATE, BRIDGWATER CASTLE

*Facing page* 48

In 16 Henry III (1230) the male line of the Briweres came to an end, their inheritance being divided amongst the daughters, Græcia, Margaret, Isabel, Alice and Joan. The Castle of Bridgwater, together with the manor and borough, and the manors of Haygrove and Odcombe, fell to the lot of the eldest sister, Græcia, who was married to William de Braose, lord of the manors of Brecknock, Radnor and Abergavenny. Græcia Braose would naturally be living at the castles of her powerful husband, and so does not appear to have occupied the Castle of Bridgwater. About 1233 there are entries in the Rolls referring to an inventory of the "armatura," or a military accoutrement; the "balistae" and catapults, and the "quarelli" or weapons of the castle belonging to the last William Briwere. They were being valued at a certain price.

About 1233–4 Alienora, the second of the daughters of King John, the wife of William Earl of Pembroke, the younger, became a resident at Bridgwater Castle. In 1233 there was an order issued to Peter de Russell to give Alienora Countess of Pembroke the grass and hay which he had of the manor of Bridgwater, and also as much firewood as she needed as long as she stayed at the Castle. This lady was known not only as the wife of William Earl of Pembroke, the younger, whom she survived, but as the wife of Simon de Montfort, whom she married in spite of a vow of perpetual chastity after widowhood (1238). In 1234 Richard de Wrotham, the chief forester of the forests of Somerset, was ordered to give her nine stags out of Mendip Forest. She is described as the "consanguinea regis," really his sister. At the same time Gilbert Marescall, Earl of Pembroke, is to have ten stags out of the park of Newton Forester, i.e. North Petherton. Gilbert was the third son of the great

William, and apparently was a resident at Bridgwater Castle, together with his sister-in-law. About the same time also there was a mandate to Richard de Wrotham to give Richard "Earl of Cornwall and Pictavia" five bucks and twenty-five does from the park of Bridgwater, i.e. Petherton Park, for replenishing his own parks. This Richard Earl of Cornwall, crowned "King of the Romans," was the younger son of King John. The earldom of Cornwall originally was associated with the earldom of Mortaigne, and included much of what is now known as "the Duchy of Cornwall." The titular honours, whatever they were, which belonged to the "King of the Romans," and of the "Holy Roman Empire," dating from A.D. 800, when the King of the Franks was crowned Emperor of the Romans by Pope Leo III, were conferred upon Richard at Aachen. Richard undertook a pilgrimage to the Holy Land in company with the Earl of Salisbury, and is certainly one of the strangest and most romantic figures of the day.

In the reign of Henry III there was another change in the succession of Bridgwater Castle and property. William Braose, the son of William Braose who had married Græcia Briwere, was massacred by Llewellyn Prince of Wales. He left four daughters, the eldest of whom was Maud, the wife of Roger de Mortimer (1247), and so the Mortimer regime began at Bridgwater, lasting for 150 years, till the Mortimer property became merged in Crown property.

The Mortimers were of Norman origin, and Roger, called the *filius episcopi*, i.e. of Hugh Bishop of Coutances, first took the name of Mortimer from the castle and village of Morte-mer-en-Brai in the Pays de Caux. Ralph Mortimer was probably at Hastings, and the House of Mortimer was connected with the

ducal Norman house. Maud de Braose was a great
heiress in her own right, and brought as her share
one-third of the great marcher-lordship of Brecon
and the still greater inheritance of the earls Marshall,
in addition to Bridgwater Castle and the Briwere inheritance. Roger Mortimer, the son of Maud and
Roger (1256–1326), is said by historians to have ruled
all Wales like a king from 1307–21. Perhaps the
family were known best as the lords of Wigmore
Castle.

During the Mortimer regime Bridgwater Castle was
governed by a constable acting for the great Mortimer
overlord. For instance, in 1323, a writ was sent to the
Constable of Bridgwater Castle directing him to keep
the prisoners in his castle in safe and sure custody that
he might be able to answer for them at the King's
command (Close Rolls).

In 1359 the Somerset property of the Mortimers was
still further enlarged by the sale and transfer of the
forestership of Somerset from Roger de Beauchamp
to Roger de Mortimer, and the extract from the Feet of
Fines runs thus :—

"At Westminster in the Octave of St. John the
Baptist between Roger de Mortimer, Earl of March,
querent, and Roger de Beauchamp and Sibilla his
wife, deforciants : For a messuage, a carucate of land
and ten marcs rent in Newton-Plecy and Parkhous, and
for the Bailiwick of the Forests of Mendip, Nerechich
and Pederton, and the custody of the Warren of
Somerton, and for the third part of the Advowson of
Hawkridge, and for the Free-chapel of Newton-Plecy,
and for the Bailiwick of the Forest of Exmore in the
County of Devon. . . . Roger and Sibilla acknowledged the right of the Earl and quit-claimed to him
for them. The Earl gave them 200 marcs of silver."

## THE ANCIENT BOROUGH OF BRIDGWATER

The fortunes of Bridgwater Castle and of Petherton Forest and Park adjoining, had been knit together closely ever since the days of King John, and this purchase ratified and strengthened the connection.

The Forestership-in-Fee of Somerset has, of course, a distinct history, and was not necessarily an appendage to the Castle of Bridgwater, although it may be remembered how, in 1216, King John had given William Briwere this important office for a time. When the Mortimer family purchased it they appointed almost in every case substitutionary foresters and did not carry out the duties of the office personally.

For many centuries Bridgwater was, in addition to its character as a borough, a forest town with the very ancient and royal park of North Petherton just outside its south gate. The influence, therefore, of the forest laws must have been strongly felt, and the contrast between municipal freedom and trading privileges on the one hand, and the irksome regulations of the King's Itinerant Forest Justices on the other must have been acutely felt. Immediately a burgess got outside the limits of his borough, who could tell whether an officious forester would not exact *chiminagium* or toll from him? or, if a packman was fulfilling an engagement at Bridgwater fair or market, a burly verderer might stop him on small pretext for cutting a holly-stick or making waste, as it was called? The man who had a mastiff or watch-dog to guard his house and had forgotten to have it "expeditated" or clawed, might be summoned before the King's Forest Justices at Ilchester at great trouble and expense. Poaching was not to be thought of, unless a man wished to face the dread alternative of being proclaimed an outlaw and sent out of the country, *minus* all his goods and chattels. Fuel was scarce in those days, before the days of Welsh coals, and it was very difficult to get a sufficient quantity of this, unless a man was on good terms with the forest officials. The proximity of the forest as a refuge for outcasts, whether feeble-witted or criminal, must have interfered with law and order, just as Kingswood Forest on the outskirts of Bristol was constantly a menace to the law-abiding citizens there. Placed thus, a forest with its practical exposition of forest laws for centuries must have exercised some kind of moral effect upon Bridgwater. Sometimes the citizens, feeling their way tentatively towards civic freedom and encouraged by wider trade privileges, would feel rebellious against a system of administration that made personal liberty a mere mockery. There were no forest laws in Devon except on Dartmoor, and the Devon sailors were out of their influence. The Parret sailors were exposed to them at every turn if they got outside the ports at Bridgwater or Axwater. Perhaps, when the Revolution did come, the memory of some or of all the inequalities of justice made the folk of Bridgwater and of Somerset more dour, more stern, and more determined than others. Certainly Cromwell had no more thorough and whole-hearted fighters than the men, for instance, of Popham's Regiment; no more intrepid leaders than Robert Blake, the very incarnation of the Bridgwater maritime spirit; no more eloquent advocate of right than Pym of Cannington.

Another dynastic change came in 1424, when the Mortimer property came into the hands of Richard Earl of Cambridge, and the grandfather of Edward IV, who married Anne Mortimer, the last heiress of the great House of Mortimer. This was the third time since the Briwere regime that Bridgwater Castle was passed on through the female line. Presently the whole property became merged with the Crown possessions.

According to an Inquisition p.m. in 1425, the Somerset property of Edmund Mortimer consisted of the forestership of Nerachich (Neroche), Exemore, Mendip, and Pederton, Bridgwater Castle, one-third of the borough, Heygrove, Odcombe, Milverton, etc.

A few typical extracts will show how the Castle of Bridgwater was held.  It became a Yorkist appointment, and as far as our evidence carries us the place was not subjected to a siege like Stoke Courcy Castle, which was destroyed by Lord Bonville in the Wars of the Roses.  Together with other places Bridgwater Castle became part of the dower or jointure of the King's mother, Cicely Duchess of York, who, as far as we know, did not live here, but received the profits that arose from the Castle and manor.  Indeed, for many years the Castle continued to be the especial property of the English queens.

In 1461 Stephen Preston, by letters patent of Richard Duke of York, father of Edward IV, was appointed keeper of Bridgwater Castle, receiving the accustomed fees and issues of that lordship, and also lieutenant and keeper of the forest and park of Petherton, "with the accustomed fees and full powers as the Rangers and Foresters have always had."  Stephen Preston did not hold the office long, for in 1465 there was a grant for life to Humphrey Stafford, Knight, Lord Stafford of Southwyke, of the office of Constable and Keeper of the Castle of Bridgwater on the death of the King's mother, Cicely Duchess of York, and also of the keepership of the King's park or forest of Pederton by Briggewater, with such fees and profits as the King's father, Richard, late Duke of York, had, with full powers to appoint and remove a lieutenant ranger and all foresters on foot.

# BRIDGWATER CASTLE

Lord Stafford did not enjoy his Yorkist honours long, for having forsaken William Herbert, the Earl of Pembroke, at Danesmore in 1469 with his archers, he was accused of lukewarmness or treachery. Letters were issued against him by King Edward IV, and instructions given for his arrest to the sheriffs of Devon and Somerset. For as a successor to the properties of the unfortunate Courtenays, fighting for the Lancastrians, he was a great Devon landowner. He was found, however, secreted in a place near Brent, not far from the River Axe, taken to Bridgwater, and executed August 17th, 1469. His body was buried, according to his will, beneath the central tower of the Abbey Church of Glastonbury.

Giles Lord Daubeny, of the great De Albiniaco family of South Petherton, had a grant of the forest, park or hay of Petherton by Briggewater with all fees, together with the Castle constableship and the forestership of Somerset, if we may so infer from a document in 1495, when "our lady Queen is said to have as dower the Forests of Racche (Neroche) and Myndeppe, the Manor of Odcombe, Manor and Burgh of Milverton, Castell of Brugewater and Manor of Heygrove—saving the rights of Lord Daubeny." These rights would be surely those of Constable of Bridgwater Castle and Forester of Somerset.

Giles Lord Daubeny was best known in Somerset for the part he took in suppressing the Perkin Warbeck rebellion, with which there was so much sympathy shown amongst the West Somerset gentry.[1] He was well known at the Court of Henry VII, being one of the heroes of Bosworth, Lord Chamberlain, Baron of the Realm, and Governor of Calais. Locally he was connected with the Luttrell, Trevelyan, and Audley

[1] Greswell's *Land of Quantock.*

families, and owned large estates in Somerset, amongst these the famous Barrington Court, part of South Petherton manor.

King Henry VII made a progress through Wells, Glastonbury, Bridgwater and Taunton in October, 1497, and probably paid a visit to Bridgwater Castle.

In 3 Henry VIII there is an enfeoffment *inter alia* to the King of the Castle and borough of Bridgwater, the manors of Heygrove, Odcombe, Milverton, Newton-Plecy, Eston (Exton?), Nerechich, Mendip, North Petherton and Exmoor.[1] When Leland came to Bridgwater he described the Castle thus (1540–2) :—

"The Castelle sumtyme a right fair and strong piece of work, but now al going to mere ruine standeth harde byneth the bridge of the west side of the haven."

The glories, therefore, of the old Castle of Bridgwater were, from one cause and another, beginning to pale in the days of Queen Elizabeth. According to an extract from a Special Commission, 1565, it is reported :—

"Item, ther ys nere adjoynyng unto the key [quay] off the said porte off Brydgewater an olde decayed Castell off the quenes majesties. Within the walles thereof ther is a Greene conteynyng an acre of ground or thereabout, the profyt whereof is taken by the Constable of the seyd Castell whiche ys a fitt place ffor the buildyng off a Custome house and will be builded for XL^li so that ther may be convenyent Stone off the seyd decayed Castell and timber out off quene majesties Wood called quenes Wood belongyng thereunto." The Queen's Wood is probably the one near Durleigh House.

King Charles the First, by Letters Patent dated July 11th, 1627, granted to Sir William Whitmore, Knt.,

[1] Catalogue of Ancient Deeds.

56

and George Whitmore, Esq., and their heirs and assigns, the manor and Castle of Bridgwater, with its appurtenances, the manor of Heygrove, and divers messuages, lands, tenements and hereditaments in Bridgwater, Heygrove, Durleigh, Chilton and North Petherton, together with all toll, courts-leet, view of frank-pledge, law-days, and assize of bread, wine and beer and all other victuals, goods and chattels of felons and fugitives, felons of themselves attainted, convicted and condemned and put in exigent [exacted and outlawed], fines, amerciaments, waifs, estrays, deodands, free warren, etc., in as large and ample a manner as heretofore used and accustomed within the same castle, manor, etc., and in as large and ample a manner and form as Jane [Seymour] Queen of England, Katherine Countess of Devon, Roger Mortimer, Earl of March, or Richard Duke of York, ever heretofore had by reason or means of any charter or grant whatever. And among other things the said King grants all that rent of four iron horse-shoes, and thirty-eight iron nails, a free rent of John Buckland for his house called "The Swan," with the appurtenances in Bridgwater . . . to hold of the King, as of the manor of East Greenwich in the county of Kent in free and common socage, and not in capite, or by knight's service.

In this deed, which smacks of the old time and customs, one wonders how much reality there was about the feudal rights and perquisites so solemnly mentioned in the Charter. Did the Whitmores dare act upon the privileges of their deeds, or, after all, was it only the sonorous echo of the old days that floated down?

The above did not exhaust the whole of the Stuart property in Bridgwater, for in a Parliamentary Survey, September, 1653, of royal property, Charles Stuart, late King of England, is said to have been the owner of "a capital messuage or mansion house," commonly called the capital messuage, in Bridgwater on the south-east part of the said town, together with mills, barn and gardens, bounded by the mill stream and St. Mary's Street. The mills were described as a water grist mill and malt mill, both under one roof and near unto the capital messuage.

After the purchase by the Whitmores, the old Castle appears to have been destroyed in great measure, if the following extract from the *Calendar of State Papers*, dated 1634, can be trusted: "Tobias Atkins confesses that at the time when Mr. Helliard had Somersetshire, by his leave the petitioner made some saltpetre out of the walls of the old Castle, lately pulled down by the owner at Bridgwater."

It was getting near the time, however, of the great siege in the Parliamentary War, and the Castle must have been fortified and placed in a state of defence before Fairfax and Cromwell came to batter it down. At this length of time it is hard to say how much of the old work ever survived the inroads of centuries, especially as the order was given by the Parliament to "slight" or dismantle the fortifications.

Coming to more modern times researches have shown that most of the site has been built over by the houses of Castle Street, King's Square, a part of Fore Street, Queen Street, and a portion of York Buildings, and that the garden in King's Square is the only portion not yet covered. As late as 1810 Mr. Jarman says that some of the walls of the Castle were standing, and for years afterwards several pits, guessed to be the remains of the keep or vaults, could be seen.

"A few years since a portion of the roadway on the higher side of King's Square suddenly gave way and disclosed what was thought to be part of the foundations. An old spoon was the only relic which came to light. The stones taken from the ruins served to build portions of the walls of new premises, and in more than one instance the ruins themselves were built into new structures. The wide moat was filled in at intervals, as it interfered with traffic or building operations; the north portion went by the name of Baily Ditch, a name not yet forgotten. Some of the houses in Fore Street were built over the moat, and as late as 1884, when rebuilding operations were going on behind Messrs. Hook's Golden Key Grocery Warehouse, the workmen made the interesting discovery of a portion of the moat, filled with black mud and refuse.

"The last wall which stood was on the spot now occupied by the large house on the north-east corner of the Square, and it had to be removed as being dangerous. Of the few well-authenticated traces which now remain of the structure may be mentioned a stone archway on the Western Quay, next Mr. Sully's office, which doubtless was a water-gate entrance. There is also an archway in the cellar of a house at the corner of Castle Street which has been regarded as part of a subterraneous passage leading across the river. This is, however, mere conjecture. For many years one portion of the Ballium was used as a timber-yard, whilst the old gate-house in earlier times was converted into a dwelling-house by a member of the Harvey family."

*Sic transit gloria mundi!* and the old Castle, which seven hundred years ago resounded doubtless with the sounds of minstrels, and was the rendezvous of many a royal hunting party with its picturesque groups of foresters, verderers, bedels, lymerers, and falconers awaiting the behest of a noble "Master of Game,"

## THE ANCIENT BOROUGH OF BRIDGWATER

has perished so completely that we can only guess its shape and size from its scattered fragments. Tradition, however, dies hard, and on this classic spot even within recent memory the youth of the town of Bridgwater, hearing the tales of the past, have resorted to the deserted outer Baily to play games of mimic warfare. Perhaps the memory that lived longest was that of the celebrated siege in the Civil War, when, after its fall, the hopes of the Loyalists which clung to this spot as an impregnable fort and rallying spot were dashed utterly to the ground.

# CHAPTER V

## BRIDGWATER WILLS IN MEDIÆVAL TIMES

THERE are few documents which illustrate more clearly the attitude of people's minds than a man's last will and testament. They not only reveal some of the motives which rule human life; they afford also a clue as to the testator's belief in a life to come, and what he believes he ought to do in order to attain that life. To begin with, he will desire to clear up his estate so as to make some provision for those who come after him; his debts must be paid; all moneys due to him must be gathered in. Apportionments are made to his wife and children, possibly also to a friend. He may wish to found an almshouse, to benefit a church, an abbey, a hospital, a chantry, a chapelry, or any of the services conducted and maintained within such religious institutions. He may desire to make a benefaction to his parish priest, or to some ecclesiastic with whom he has been connected during life. It may be his wish to benefit a religious body, e.g. the Franciscan Friars, or the Augustinian Canons, both of which had considerable influence in Bridgwater. And it would probably be his hope—certainly it was so in mediæval days—so to divide his worldly goods as best to commend himself to the religious ideals of his time. This is especially evident in the fourteenth, fifteenth, and sixteenth centuries, from which period the wills here quoted are taken. Many wills, undoubtedly, were made on the death-bed, although the more elaborate and lengthy ones were prepared with much care beforehand. In nearly every will it will be seen that something is given to the Church, or to the Church's ministers. No sentence is more usual than the euphemistic clause, *For tithes forgotyn*, so much. It suggests a squaring up of financial dues owing to the parson of the parish. The testator must leave this world at peace with all men, and specially with his spiritual counsellor.

The numerous gifts made in ancient wills to Church objects and to Church officials are very easily accounted for. In those days every charity, every scheme for the betterment of man's earthly lot, was connected with the Church. There were no polytechnics to endow, and no free libraries to assist. The care of the sick, the poor, the ignorant, the wayfarer, the pilgrim fell to the Church's lot. For these there were the hospital, the almshouses, the monastic school; the abbey with its dormitory, refectory, and food for the passing pilgrim; the friars' houses, and the great religious foundations dotted over the whole kingdom. Hence it was natural, indeed, it was inevitable, that property should be bequeathed in the manner indicated by the wills quoted in this chapter. Yet there is another element which is evident in the majority of the wills. It is the strong desire for the prayers of the Church for the departing and departed soul. Behind this desire lay the belief which is the keynote to much that was vital in the pre-Reformation beliefs of our forefathers. This was the doctrine of purgatory. Without defining with exactness the numerous intricacies, variations, and developments of the doctrine, which belong to theology rather than to history, it may be stated simply thus. The doctrine of purgatory was, that in the intermediate state between death and resurrection there are three conditions, in one of which the soul is. The saints go direct to heaven, the lost go direct to the place of punishment, but those who leave this life not accounted to be good enough for saints, neither condemned as being utterly reprobate and lost, go to an intermediate place called purgatory. There, for a longer or shorter time, they remain, suffering a greater or less degree of punishment, according as their deeds shall have been, and with regard to the sincerity of their repentance and belief. Thus Otto Frisingensis, in A.D. 1146, wrote: "Some affirm that there is in the unseen state a place of purgatory, in which those who are to be saved are either troubled with darkness only, or are refined by the fire of expiation." Later on the Council of Florence, in A.D. 1438, spoke more directly still. "If any true penitents shall depart this life in the love of God before they have made satisfaction by worthy fruits of penance for faults of commission and omission, their souls are purified after death by the pains of purgatory." A later Council confirmed this pronouncement, significantly adding to it the clause that "the souls there detained are aided by the suffrages of the faithful." Here, then, we have the belief which influenced the mediæval churchman to desire, beyond all other things, the prayers of his church—of the priests, the laity, the poor; all who could be got to pray for him—that his sojourn in those dark realms might be shortened, and his merited punishment, by the mercy of God, might be in some measure stayed. In order that these benefits might accrue, there were the chantries, at whose altars the chantry priests said masses for the dead; the parish priest, too, at the altar where the departed had no doubt often knelt while in life, could make his supplication as well. The funeral was a most solemn event, executed with the greatest care, and assisted at by as many people as could possibly be got together. Here the Mediæval Church surpassed herself in the wealth of her devotions.

In the Sarum Manual [writes Professor Swete] the rites which follow death begin with a *Commendatio animarum* . . . consisting of Psalms intermingled with prayers for the departed. The body is then washed and spread upon a bier; vespers for the day are said, followed by the vigils of the dead, the special vespers and special mattins commonly known from their respective antiphons as the *Placebo* and the *Dirige* or dirge. It is then carried in procession to the church, accompanied by a cross-bearer and acolytes with lighted tapers, a man with a bell going before the corpse to invite the prayers of the passers-by; after him come the priest and his ministers, in albs, singing Psalms, the body being followed by friends of the deceased bearing torches, with the mourners in black cloaks. In the church the dead is laid with his feet towards the high altar. Mass is then said, or if it be too late for Mass, the body remains in the church until the first Mass of the following day. After Mass the priest puts off his chasuble, and the special office for the burial of the dead (*Inhumatio defuncti*) begins. The service falls into three divisions; the first to be said in church at the head of the body, the second on the way to the grave, the third at the grave itself. The first consists of antiphons, kyries, and prayers, the precentor and choir assisting, while the priest censes the body and sprinkles it with holy water. On the way to the grave, the Psalms *In exitu Israel* and *Ad te, Domine, levavi* are sung, and the old suffrages said, " Eternal rest grant them, Lord, and let perpetual light shine upon them." The grave, of which the priest had previously cut the first sod in the form of a cross, is now opened with the Psalm *Confitemini, Domino, quia bonus*, and the antiphon "Open to me the gates of Righteousness." Then, the grave having been blessed and aspersed, prayers for the departed follow, and the priest pronounces

THE PARISH CHURCH, BRIDGWATER

*Facing page* 64

a final absolution. Earth is thrown crosswise on the body, and the interment is completed during the singing of a psalm; after which the priest says, "I commend thy soul to God the Father Almighty; earth to earth, ashes to ashes, dust to dust: in the Name of the Father, and of the Son, and of the Holy Ghost." On returning to the church the clerks sing the penitential Psalms or the *De profundis*, and the priest dismisses them with the prayer, "May the soul of this person and the souls of all the faithful departed rest in peace."[1]

This service, without doubt, has many and many a time been conducted in the church and churchyard of St. Mary's, Bridgwater.

There were points of beauty in the service, no doubt. But there was also an element of deep gloom in it all. Moreover, there was more to follow. The vigils of the dead and masses for his soul were said from time to time throughout the following month, specially on the third, seventh, and thirtieth day.

The following wills will perhaps best illustrate, without further comment, the mind and habit of men in pre-Reformation days. They are mostly taken from the Somerset Record Society's publications, Vols. XVI and XXI, and from the Rev. F. W. Weaver's *Wells Wills*, published in 1890.

The will of John Davy, Briggewater, a tanner. It is dated June 14th, 1461.

"First, I bequeath my body to be buried in the south porch of the parish church of the Blessed Virgin Mary in Brigge-water aforesaid. I bequeath to the Master of the Hospital of St. John the Baptist there, for my tithes forgotten, 6s. 8d.

To the Vicar of the parish church there, to pray for my soul, 2s. 6d.

To the four fraternities in the parish church aforesaid, to each of them 12d.

To each priest celebrating in the said parish church, 6d.

[1] *Church Services and Service Books before the Reformation*, p. 166.

To the Friars Minor of Briggewater, to pray for my soul, 5s.

To the fabric of the parish church there, 2s. 8d.

Item, I bequeath to Roger Pym my blue gown furred with fyches. Item, to Thomas Eyre one gown of medley, furred. Item, to Richard Grobham one gown of mine embroidered and furred.

Item, I bequeath to Joan, my daughter, all that my tenement wherein I now dwell in the town aforesaid, to her and the heirs of her body lawfully begotten and to be begotten, to hold of the chief lords of that fee. Nevertheless, my will is that Matilda, my wife, shall occupy the said tenement until the day of marriage of my said daughter Joan, by the rents and services thereof due and accustomed.

Item, I bequeath to the same Joan, my daughter, my three tenements with one "Cabyne" in which John Benet now dwells, in the street of the Blessed Mary in the town of Briggewater, going towards the south gate of the said town, on the east side, between the tenement in which John Walsh now dwells on the south, and my tenement in which Robert Wever now dwells on the north, to hold as above."

After other bequests to another of his daughters, and to his wife, he leaves "the residue of my goods not bequeathed to my said wife, whom I make my executrix. Proved 19th July, 1461."

Sir Leonard Hakeluyt's will, as follows, is interesting as well exhibiting the desire of churchmen of good position, of that period, to gain all that they could from the sacred offices of their church.

The third of August, A.D. 1413. I, Leonard Hakeluyt, Knight. In primis, I bequeath my body to be buried in the church of the Friars Minor of Brudgewater.

Item, I bequeath 40 *li.* to fulfil the testament of Henry de Cornwayl, deceased. If the testament of the said Henry requires more, I will that the things contained therein be fully performed for the soul of the said Henry and for the souls for which he is bound in celebrating divine services, in distribution to the poor, and in other works of charity.

Item, 40 *li.* of silver to be distributed in celebration and distribution and the works aforesaid for the soul of Thos. Hakeluyt, clerk, my uncle, and for my soul and the souls of my parents and all the faithful deceased.

To the fabric of the church of the Friars Minors of Brugewater 20 *li.* of silver to pray for my soul and Margaret, my consort's.

To the parish church of Southbrent one full suit of my vestments newly bought, and 6 marks of silver for a missal to be bought *de novo*, to pray as above. To the parish church of Berrow 5 marks for one pair of vestments, as above. To the parish church of Estbrent 5 marks for one pair of vestments for the high altar, to be bought by my executors, to pray as above. To the parish church of Schepton Malet 20 marks, to pray as above.

To Isabella Burley, my servant, 40 *li.* of silver, a silver cup with a cover, and six silver spoons. To Leonard Stapelton 100s. To Richard Herte, my servant, 10 marks. John Parant, 2 marks. John Mareyn, 10s. Robt. Arundell, 6s. 8d. John Horner, 6s. 8d. To making the way called Conynglane in the parish of Estbrent 100s., and if anything remain I will that it be expended on the way opposite the manor of Grove.

To each indigent poor person coming to the place on the day of my burial 1d.

To twelve poor, carrying twelve torches around my bier on the day of my burial, to each of them a gown with a hood of white cloth. To Richard Pecok, rector of Shepton Malet, 10 marks. To Thomas Jauncy 100s., and William Hastyng 100s.

The residue of my goods I give to Margaret, my consort, and Sir Richard Pecok, rector of Shepton Mallet, to dispose for my soul, etc. I appoint Margaret, my consort, Sir Richard Pecok, Isabella Burley, William Hastyng, and Thos. Jauncy to execute this will. Dated at Grove in Brentmarsch, Co. Somerset. Exhibited 17 August, A.D. 1413.

Following directly upon the preceding testament is the will of Margaret Hakeluyt, wife of the above.

# THE ANCIENT BOROUGH OF BRIDGWATER

I, lady Margaret Hakeluyt, 29th July, A.D. 1414, bequeath my body to be buried in the church of the Friars Minor of Bridgewater next the body of Sir Leonard Hakeluyt, knight, formerly my husband.

To Leonard Stepilton 10 *li.*, a cloth of double texture, with a towel and one pair of sheets. To Margaret Stepilton 10 marks. To John Farawey 10 marks. To Joan Reynon, my sister, a silver cup with a cover. To Isabella Burney 20 marks, a gilt cup with a cover, a cloth of a double texture, with a towel.

Item, I bequeath to my poor tenants and to indigent priests 20 *li.* To the church of Penryn a pair of vestments of green colour of velvet. To the chapel where the bodies of my father and mother are buried one pair of vestments and 40s. To Ric. Hort and Agnes his wife 13s. 4d. To Edith Gonny 13s. 4d. and a red bed with hangings. To John Parent 20s. To the high bridge in the marsh 20s. To brother Geoffrey Pollard of the Order of Friars Minor 100s. To William Hugyn of the same order 100s. and one maser. I will that the said Walter Tylly be my executor.

11th August in the year above, a commission to Master Ralph Canon, canon of Wells, and John Burney, vicar of Puryton, Sir Richard Pecok, rector of Schepton Malet, and John Corps, perpetual vicar of the church of Bridgewater, to receive the proof.

This same Lady Margaret Hakeluyt affords an instance of widows taking the vows of the religious. The Wells registers record the fact of her taking, in 1413, after her husband's death, the vow of perpetual chastity. Thus, consecrated widowhood was looked upon as an order of the religious life, and might not be abandoned without penalty.

Adam Hamelyn's will, 1493, is a very typical one.

The eve of saint Margarete the virgyne and in the yere of our lord God 1493, I, Adam Hamelyn of Brigewater, make this my present testament and last will as foloweth:
I bequeith my body to be buried in the churche of the

towne aforeseid. Also I bequeith to the high alter a cuppe of silver. Also to every alter in the same church, 12d. Also I bequeith to the seid high alter 2s.

Also I bequeith to Isabell my wife all the occupieng and keepyng of my plate and jewelles for terme of her liffe. . . .

Also I bequeith to John Hamlyn my brother a pipe of .wyne and a pipe of wode. To William Burges a cuppe of silver.

Also I give and bequeith to the seid Isabell my wif all my landes and tenementes that I have in Brigewater and in the hundred of Northpederton for terme of her lyf. And after the decesse of the seid Isabell I will that all seid landes in Northpederton aforeseid called Shobell remayne to John Wymer and Margarete and to the heires of the same Margarete ; and for defaute of issue of the seid Margarete I will that all the seid landes remayne to John Hamlyn my brother and his heires, and for defaute of issue of the seid John to remayne to my heires' that shalbe next of my blode. And for the tenement that I now dwell yn I wull that the Maier, Ballives and Burges of the town aforeseid, by the way and right of their corporacion, immediatly after the death of the seid Isabell my wif, do enter and sease in the seid tenement, and hit to hold and keep to thayme and their successors undre this condicion to this my will so that of thissues and profittes of the same tenement yerly to be had by the Chantry preste of the perpetuall Chantry in the churche aforeseid be kept a solemyne obite there for my soule and my wife's soule, our faders and moders soules and all our frendes for ever. And the residue of the revenues cummyng of the seid tenement to goo to the augmentacion and contentacion of masses to the seid chapel for ever more. . . .

All other goodes and dettes to me due I give thaym to Isabell my wif, that she doo pay my dettes, and doo for her soule and myne and all cristen soules ; the which Isabell I make my hole executrice.

Witnes herof : late being Maier of the seid towne and notary public ; John Hamlyn ; Robert Kokes ; William Burges and meny others. Proved 28th August, 1493.

John Hille, of Bridgwater, was evidently a successful merchant and a typical town citizen of the fifteenth century, and he declares at the beginning of his will that he is "sound of mind." He dates the document May 18th, 1481.

In primis I bequeath my soul to God Almighty and the Blessed Virgin Mary, and my body to be buried in the parish church of Briggevatir if it shall happen that I die within seven "*miliaria*" from the church aforesaid.

Item, I bequeath to the Hospital of St. John of Bruggewatir, impropriator of the church aforesaid, for my tithes forgotten, 20s. Item, to the vicar of the said church, 3s. 4d. Item, I give and bequeath to every stipendiary priest to celebrate divine services in the said church, 2s. Item, to every altar in the said church, 2s. Item, to the Warden of the House of the Friars Minor in the said town and the brethren of the same house serving God, 20s. Item, I bequeath to Stephen, my brother, for his service bestowed on me, one pipe of wode and one ton of iron.

His remaining bequests are not of special interest, saving a clause wherein he gives the residue of his property to his wife Thomasina, to dispose for the health of his soul and the souls of all the faithful; and also a gift to four of his friends, "for their labours," of two pipes of woad.

His wife's will, dated four years later, is of some interest as showing the mind of a prosperous and well-to-do Bridgwater lady four hundred years ago.

Thomasine Hille. My body to be buried in the parish church of the Blessed Virgin Mary, of the said town, by my husband.

I bequeath to the great altar of the church aforesaid my gown of violet in grayne furred. To Master Richard Croke, the Vicar there, one gown of violet, to pray for our souls. To each altar of the said church, 2s. To each priest serving in the said church, 2s. To the Friars Minor of the same

town to pray for our souls, 20s. I bequeath to build anew
a sufficient house built for poor men to dwell in for ever in
the town aforesaid, 40 *li*. of lawful money of England, the
bequest of my husband in his life, that the said poor men
may pray for the souls of John Hill, Thomesina his wife, of
our parents, and of all the faithful deceased.

To Thomas Philip two pipes of woad; to Nicholas Jobe
and John Stallinch each one pipe of woad. To Joan,
daughter of the said Nicholas, my best girdle ornamented
with silver and gilt. To Margaret Stallinch my gown of blue
colour, and my next best girdle of blue ornamented. To
John Stallinch one " Fethirbede " the next best. To his
wife Joan, my gown of russet furred with black skin and my
red girdle ornamented with silver, and one small red one not
ornamented. . . .

To Agnes Russell, late my servant, one pair of beads of
" corall."

To Sir John Roche, my chaplain, 20s., to pray for our
souls.

She bequeaths the residue of her property, after payment of all claims, to be distributed to the poor to pray
" for our souls and the souls of all our benefactors and
of all faithful Christians deceased." " Master Richard
Croke," the vicar of Bridgwater at that time, is one of
four witnesses to the deed.

The will of John Wheler, who was one of the chaplains in the parish church at the latter part of the
fifteenth century, is modelled on much the same lines
as those adopted by the laity of those days. He
directs that he shall be buried in the chapel of the
Blessed Virgin Mary in the parish church of Bridgwater.

I bequeath to the perpetual vicar of the church 3s. 4d. To
each priest of the said church 8d. To the three clerks of
the said church 12d. To the two wardens being in the said
church 8d. To the altar of St. Katherine of the said church
3 lbs. of wax and 20d. To the altar of the Holy Trinity

71

3 lbs. of wax and 20d. To the altar of St. Erasmus 3 lbs. of wax and 20d.

Item, I will and grant that Alice Lye, of Brygewater, shall have and hold half a burgage in "le Weststrete" . . . and the quarter of one burgage there which Walter Martyn, Bedeman, now holds, and half a burgage in "le Freryn-strete" there, for the term of her life. After her decease I will and grant that the premises shall remain to John Kendale, Robert Philipp, rector of Chilton, and others. . . . The residue of my goods I give and bequeath to John Drewe, to dispose for my soul and the souls of my benefactors as to him shall seem best. And I ordain Sir Robert Philipp, rector of Chilton, and John Bartlett, overseers of this my will. I will that the said Sir Thomas [this is an obvious error for Sir Robert] shall have for his labour one silver cup now in his hands.

A very interesting will of a wealthy layman of strong religious views and of charitable tendencies is found in the testament of James Hadley, of "Withecombe besides Dunster, esquyer." It is dated July 2nd, 1532. "I will that £37 be paid in the king's estcheker at Westminster for my father Richard Hadley whous soule God pardon." Then follows an immense list of bequests to religious purposes, places and people.

I will that £5 be paid of my owne dette to the King's treasour of his chamber, 20 marks be paid to the maister of St. John's in Brigewater by my promys to hym made the day of my marriage; to the high aulter of the temple, Withecombe, Wemedon, St. Decombe, Wiliton, St. John's at Brigwater, and Hethefeld [each] 5s., and to every other aulter in every of the said churches 12d. Cathedral church of Wells, 5s.; to the maister of the temple for tithes forgotten 20d., and to the . . . of Withecombe 12d., and to the vicare of Wemedon 5s., and to every high aulter within the hundreds of Taunton, Carhampton, Williton fremanors and North Petherton 12d., and to every curat of the same as moche. To every secular priest within the diocese of Bath and Wells not beneficed 12d.   I will that my wiff cause 3 tapers to be made, one to be set before the Rode, the other before our lady, and the third before the hed seynt of the church where I shall happen to be buried, there to borne [burn] in time of Goddıs service.   To the priory of Dunster 20s.   To the priory of Barlinche 20s.   To the Abbey of Clef 20s.   To every other house of religion within the said diocese 20s., the abbey of Glaston except, to whom I give 40s.   To the churches of Withecombe, Wiliton, St. Decombe, Hethefeld and Wembedon [each] 6s. 8d., to have my name upon the masboks [Mass-books].

To my poure tenants of Withecumbe 20s. and this quarter's rent; the same to my tenants of Wiliton, Hethefeld. To my tenants in Brıgewater and N. Petherton 10s. [each]. To my tenants of Sydeham, Bower, Slap, Donwere, Baudrip and Chilton 10s. [each place].   Forty pence to my tenants of Batelborow, and 13s. 4d. to the maintenance of Horsey Chapell.   To reparacion of the Reliks being in Withecombe church 40s., and to every man-servant taking wages his whole yere wages and to every woman taking wages as moche.   Bequests to my mother, my brother Sir Henry, my brother George, my brother Sır John, at Bruıton my brother Sir William, at Barlinche, and to every of my godchıldren.   To have a priest to sing for 5 yeres, I wıll he have out of my lands as before 8 marks by the yere and to sing where my body shall happen to be buryed.

An honest preste shall from the daie of my buryıng singe in Withecombe aforesaid for 15 yeres praying for the soules of my father Richard, my mother Phelep, my sowle, James, Friswide, Ellen and Elizabeth my wiffes and all our children, kynsfolkes and all Chrıstian sowles, and after the same 15 yere to the end of the world, as my wife and children executors will answer before God at the dredfull daie of jugement.

I give to every howseholder in Dunster, Wachett, Tanton, Brigewater, Lamport, Bruton, Yevelchester and Wells 4d., and to every hospitall of lozare and poure people within the shire of Somerset 12d.   Prisoners of Yevelchester, 13s. 4d.; to the quiete prisoners of Wells 5s.; prisoners in Bristowe, 5s.   And for as moche as I have beyne neglıgent to visit holy places and in going of pilgremage, therefore I give and bequeath to Our Blessed Lady of Cleve 5s., St. Savior of Porlock 5d., St. Culbone 3d., St. Saviore of Tanton, Bradford and Brigewater, each 5d.; to St. Jophe 3d., blessed King Henry of Windsor 3d., Maister John Shorne 3d., Holy blode of Hayles 5d., Our Lady of Walsingham 3d, St. Thomas of Canterbury 5d.

Elizabeth, my wife, sole executor; my eldest and youngest sons to be brought up to the law, and they to have in Stroud every of them 10 marks, or in the ins of court every of them £10. The lands purchased at Sydenham by me of John Pike be to whom my said wife shall limit so that they shall keep an obit for me in St. John's, Brigewater. Forty shillings to Brigewater bridge, £5 for the making of a chapell in the honour of the visitation of B.V.M. and St. Christopher. My monethes mynde to be kept at Wemedone, St. John's, Brigewater, at the parish churches of Brigewater, Withecombe, Wiliton St. Decombe's and Hethefeld, and also my twelve months mynd.

Proved March 26th, 1537.

Poor James Hadley! Not only have masses for his soul not been sung "to the end of the world," as he directed; they were not even sung for the special term of fifteen years upon which he had set his heart. In 1547, ten years after the proving of his will, the chantries were suppressed, their endowments passed into the hands of Henry VIII's nobles and favourites, and masses for the dead came to an end. In 1549 the first Prayer Book came into existence, and a new order of things was ushered into being. Wills not only tell us what things men can do; they reveal what they cannot do. Testators in 1537 little dreamed of what was coming within the period of ten brief years. James Hadley's legacies helped, probably, to fill the pockets of those who were eager enough to batten upon the spoils of the monasteries and chantry lands. Change of some sort there was bound to be; the nation expected it. But few suspected how drastic the changes would prove to be.

A further inspection of Bridgwater wills makes it clear that money and gifts, very much akin to what have been detailed in the previous wills of this chapter, continued to be left to the chantries and monasteries and kindred objects right up to the time of their dissolution. In 1530 George Matthew of Bridgwater left money to every altar in St. Mary's Church. Richard Edney, in 1529, left to Wells Cathedral 4d. ; to the high altar in Bridgwater parish church 4d. ; to every altar in the same church 2d. Richard Grygg, in the year 1530, desired to be buried in the church of St. John's Hospital

"for the which I bequethe to the sadye house a pere of sylver [ . . . ] and a salt with a cover of sylver and 5 coshyns of carpett worke ; unto the convent of the said howse to feche me [this would imply a procession with cross, lights and banner] to the church and to pray for me, a table cloth of dyaper. To Sir Will. Alyn, my gostly father, my best gowne." William Chute begs to be buried in Bridgwater churchyard, and leaves a cow for each of the altars of St. Katherine, St. Mary and the Holy Trinity. Harry Bodman, in 1533, bequeaths " to the hye auter of the parish church of Bridgwater 8d., to Trinity auter 4d., Our Lady's auter 4d., St. George's auter 4d., Rode auter 4d., St. Katheryn's auter 4d. Sir John Strete, perpetuall vicar of Bridgwater, for my tithes forgotyn a bussell of whete."

William Chrystopher of Brygwater in 1533 left to "Johane my daughter on condicion she and her assigns to kyepe yerely anniversary for the space of thirty yers for my sowle, my wiff and children's sowles, with all my frynds sowles in the parish church of Brygwater with all the prists and clarks belongyn to the forsaid church, gyving them suffycyently for their labores." Numerous similar instances might be given.

The Bridgwater Friars Minor, or Franciscan Friars, were, to judge from the many bequests made to them in all parts of the county of Somerset, exceedingly popular. In Bridgwater itself, naturally, they were highly esteemed. Between 1528 and 1536 they received bequests, *inter alia,* from the following : John Anger, of Charlinch; Will Davye, rector of Chilton Trinity; John Pyme, of Chilton Trinity; Thos. Preston, of Dowlish Wake; Joan Wedmore, widow, of Dunster; Robt. Jankyn, of Dunster; George Stonys and Thos. Skynner, of the same town; Geo. Elsworthy, rector of Exford; John Vicar, of Exton; Edmund Taylor, of Lyng; Johane Nycholl, of Munksylver; Joh. Markes, of Westmonkton; John Nekke, of North Petherton; Robt. Andersay and John Burgys, of the same place; John Everard, of Stokelond Gaunts; Margaret Bere, of Stowcurgy; and many others. The list, indeed, might be greatly lengthened.

Up to the very close of the pre-Reformation period (and indeed, though more silently, long after it) the intense desire remained in the minds of men that they should be remembered after their death. It was not only the wish to escape the pains of purgatory, it was the fear of being forgotten and out of mind. Hence came the request in the will for " my buriall, my monythes mind, twelve monyth mynd, done and kept for my sowl." At the end of the month, and of the year, Mass was to be said for the deceased ; his relatives and friends would gather around the altar to hear his name read out, to think of him, and to pray for him. " I am wylling to have a preste syng for my sowle and all crystyn sowles the space of a hole yere," James Kyng, of Weston-in-Gordano, directs in his will of 1531. He wished that his name should be read out aloud from the Bede Roll, i.e. the list recited in church at the four Ember Seasons of the faithful dead. Similarly, Joan Roke, widow, of Taunton, declares in her will that "my son's daughter shall have the house that I dwell in the space of sixty years after my decease, not to meddle with it during my life, so that she or her assigns will keep an obit every year once in the Church of St. Mary Magdalene during the term of the said three score years, for the souls of John Roke and Joan his wife, etc., 'with seven preestes and Mr. Vicarye and two clerks.'" Albert Rowley, of Taunton, directs in his will, dated August 16th, 1530, that on the day of his burial "a trentall of thirty Masses be songe for my sowle." A trental was a service of thirty Masses, sung either simultaneously or *de die in diem*. No priest could celebrate Mass more than once a day, so that the services of thirty priests would be needed in one day in order to carry out the precise directions of Albert Rowley's last wish.

Such were the beliefs of our Bridgwater folk, and of all English people, three and a half centuries ago, in reference to the religious services which they held to be fit and comely when a man passed from out the portals of this world into the greater Life beyond. We have left these ideas behind, and a nobler view— as it seems to us—has replaced them. But our forefathers clung to their convictions with great tenacity, and they believed in them, heart and soul. And since conviction is at the root of all action and healthy life, we are bound to admit that their strenuous faith sufficed them well for the battle of their daily lives.

# CHAPTER VI

## THE GREY FRIARS OF FRIARN STREET

FOLLOWING in his father's bent of mind as a benefactor to Bridgwater, and as one anxious to promote the religious ideals of his day, William Briwere the second, his son, extended a hearty welcome to the new religious brotherhood, then but lately founded, known as the Franciscan Friars. It was in 1182 that Francis of Assisi was born, and he was one of the religious enthusiasts who have moved the world. The Friars lived and worked in Bridgwater for three hundred years, and there was never, so far as is known, any grievance or evil laid against them. From the time of the erection of their house in 1230 to its dissolution under Henry VIII they lived a quiet and industrious life, fulfilling the duties of their order, and molesting no man. The ideal of Francis their founder was a noble one indeed. His famous rule was drawn up in 1209, and was approved by the General Lateran Council of 1215. As the Friars formed an important part of the religious life of the old borough for these three centuries, it may be permitted to say something about their ways and their methods of work.

At the root of everything there lay the conception of a Brotherhood of Poor Men. They were Fratres (*Frères*), Brethren. *Frère* became anglicized into Friar, and the street where they lived is correctly spelt

Friarn Street, or, in fourteenth-century usage, *Freren-Strete*. They were to keep the Holy Gospel of our Lord Jesus Christ, living in obedience and in chastity, without any possessions they could call their own. On no account were they to receive gifts of money, either by themselves or by a third person. Nothing was to be their own, neither house, nor place, nor any other thing. For the reward or hire of their labour they might accept necessaries for the body for themselves and their brethren, but this was to be received in humble manner, as becomes the servants of God and the followers of holy poverty. It was their duty to pray, and to work devoutly. One was to be chosen among them to whom they must give obedience, yet this chief brother must bear no higher title than that of minister. They were especially to take heed of all pride, vainglory, envy, covetousness, worldly care and solicitude, detraction and muttering; those who had no learning were not to run to get literature. Moreover, they were to keep no suspicious company or familiarity with women; they were not to go into the monasteries of nuns, excepting those who had special licence granted them from the See Apostolic. It was their lot to tend the sick, the outcast, and the distressed; to minister to those to whom none else ministered; to try to alleviate some of the miseries of mediæval town life. To this end their founder, Francis of Assisi, laid it down that his followers were to be meek, peaceable, modest, mild and humble. They must walk when they went forth upon their errands; they were not to ride unless some manifest necessity or infirmity obliged them. Into whatever house they entered, they were to say, " Peace be to this house." Whatever food was set before them, that they must eat.

There were in England four orders of Friars: the Dominicans, or Black Friars; the Carmelites, or White Friars; the Franciscans, or Grey Friars; and the Austin Friars. The Franciscans came to England in 1224, their first house being at Canterbury, their second in London. They spread rapidly, for this new enthusiasm captured the imaginations of men; and the towns, wherein their mission chiefly lay, eagerly welcomed them. William Briwere did quite the popular thing in settling them in Bridgwater, although, poor man, he only lived long enough to see two years of their work. For a habit the Franciscans wore a loose garment of grey reaching down to the ankles, with a cowl of the same, and a cloak over it when they went abroad. They were girded with a cord, and went barefooted. Of course they were staunch servants of Rome, and their ministers, or provincials, were to examine carefully all who wished to enter the brotherhood as to their faith and their understanding of the sacraments. Those who joined must take no wives, or if they had any, the wives must also go into monasteries, save when leave to the contrary had been granted, under vows of continency, by the bishop of the diocese. The world, and the things of the world, must be put away. When satisfied, the provincial would give them their habit of probation or trial, viz. two tunicles, without an hood, and a cloak to the waist, "unless upon any occasion it may seem good in God to do otherwise." Those who had fully promised obedience were to have one tunic with an hood, and another without an hood, if they will have them. Such as were compelled by necessity might be shod, but it was held more fitting to walk barefoot. All the brothers must be clad in mean habits, and might blessedly mend them with sacks and other pieces.

# THE GREY FRIARS

Such of the Friars as were priests (it was mainly a lay brotherhood) performed the divine office according to the usual Church use of that period. The lay brothers must say twenty-four Paternosters for their matins; five for lauds; for prime, tierce, the sixth hour, and none, seven for each; they must also pray for the dead. They must fast from the Feast of All Saints till the Nativity of Our Lord. As for the fast of forty days, which begins at the Epiphany and holds for the forty days following, they might fast for it voluntarily, but were not obliged thereto. But the other fast, i.e. till the Resurrection of Our Lord, they must keep. At other times they need not fast save on Fridays.

Yet it was none of these things which moved men when the Friars came. They were essentially preachers. Unlike the monks, who remained within their monastery walls, they went everywhere about the whole district, preaching and teaching with a fervour which had not hitherto been seen. Although they were directed not to preach within the diocese of any bishop who might forbid them, they seem to have acted as if this obligation sat lightly upon them. For they did preach, in season and out of season, and in their journeys they travelled far and wide. Their chief appeal—at least in the case of the Franciscans—was to the masses. So little had the Friars in common with the ecclesiastics of that day, whose work lay along different lines, that to the dregs of the populace St. Francis's Brethren seemed as angels of ministration. The parochial system was rigid, and many fish slipped through the meshes of the parish priest's net. There was but little preaching in the churches of that early date. There was terrible poverty, sickness, and grinding misery abroad; the houses of the poor were frequently ghastly hovels of filth and of disease; there was far more than a submerged tenth in the thirteenth century in England. In many towns the Friars Minor—as the Franciscans humbly called themselves—at first encamped in squalor and want outside the borough walls, until presently they were admitted within, and were allowed and helped to build a house to dwell in. Probably this was what happened at Bridgwater. It seems more than likely that they settled first of all in the field on the south side of the town, adjacent to the house still known as the Friars, till at last William Briwere came to their rescue, and they were welcomed to a more decent home. From that day they rose rapidly in power and in public favour, and made their influence felt far and wide in the county. Their homely and forcible sermons, which dealt, certainly at first, with moral rather than with theological questions, appealed to the laity, and especially to the ignorant and poor, with irresistible force. The movement was a moral one; when first it began it lacked almost all intellectual stimulus. It was an appeal *ad hominem;* the simple yet direct sermon, the attractive miracle-play, the portable pulpit set up in the market-place, the homely visit, the meal shared with the humblest of folk; these things told. The alms of even the poorest flowed in to the Franciscans. A new religious power had come into Bridgwater and into English life.

The Friars' house in Friarn Street[1] grew slowly, but many benefactors, small and great, at different times helped it on. William Briwere's start was a splendid thing for them, seeing that he was lord of the town. Leland relates that "one of the Lords Botreaux and his wife were especial benefactors" to it. "There-

[1] Longitudo ecclesiae Fratrum Minorum de Bryggewater 120 steppys, et ejus latitudo 30 steppys, et latitudo navis ecclesiae 14 steppys. (Leland.)

upon his heart, and his wife's body, were buried
there."[1] William de Cantelupe, too, was a beneficent
patron. Powerful influences in favour of the brotherhood grew, for on May 28th, 1282, an order was sent
to John, the son of Hugh, keeper of the King's forest
at Shirlet, "to cause the Friars Minor of Bruges to
have in that forest six oaks fit for timber, of the king's
gift."[2] In 1278 a similar direction is transmitted to
the keeper of the King's forest at North Petherton.
The Friars are to have five oaks fit for timber for the
making of their dormitory. The town authorities, too,
welcomed them. A deed exists, dated January 21st,
1246, addressed to the bailiffs of Bruges Walteri. In
it the King, Henry the Third, ratifies the assignments
which they have made to the Friars Minor of a place
to build a church and necessary buildings in their
town.[3] As the brotherhood prospered, it became
usual for some of the great ones to seek spiritual
confraternity with them, and the right of burial in
their chapel. Thus in 1479 John Kendall, of Bridgwater, acquired a grant from Brother Robert, Warden
of the Friars, admitting himself, and his wife Matilda,
and William and Juliana, their children, to such
confraternity, duly set forth in a deed now enrolled
amongst the Bridgwater documents, and endorsed
with a form of absolution. In the same year, though
in a separate document, John Kendall is similarly
admitted to the benefits of the brotherhood. In an
earlier Latin document, written in 1409, Brother
William, the Warden, greets William Dyst and his
wife Joanna. "Through the merits of this life may
they attain everlasting joy." In recognition of their

[1] Dugdale's *Mon. Ang.*, Vol. VI, part iii. p 1531.
[2] Calendar of Close Rolls.
[3] Calendar of Patent Rolls, Henry III.

devotion to the Order and their benefits to the convent they are admitted to certain spiritual privileges, and after death they are to have the same benefits in the way of prayers as the brethren and benefactors of the Order. Sir Leonard Hakeluyt, Knight, and his wife, the Lady Margaret, both lie buried in the chapel. Moreover, as the rules of the Order became modified, as they eventually did, and it became permissible for the brotherhood to receive gifts of money, if not for themselves, yet for their house, many bequests were made to them from all over Somerset. Agnes Grene bequeaths "my best gowne"; Sir John Poulet, 20s.; Edward Grevylle leaves a bequest so that the brothers may celebrate for his soul; Bishop Bekynton, of Bath and Wells, gives 20s.; John Cammell, of Glastonbury, 6s. 8d.; Sir John Chokke, 3s. 4d.; Sir Richard Chokke, 6s. 6d.; Richard Burton, of Taunton, 6s. 8d.; and so on. At first it was amongst the laity, and notably with the poor, that the Friars' influence mainly lay, but it spread at length to layman and ecclesiastic alike. Probably the very real poverty in which the brotherhood began their mission formed a large factor in the influence which they acquired. Self-denial never fails to tell. A fragment occurring in a late fifteenth-century document might well have been the motto of the Franciscans.

If thowe be in povertie se patientlye that thow take it,
And thincke how into the world thou camest all naked.[1]

Yet there were weak spots in the Friars' armour. The chief one was that they were, if not entirely, yet nearly independent of episcopal control, and so frequently they became a thorn in the side of the vicar of the parish. They could act independently of him,

[1] Bridgwater documents.

84

acknowledging the Apostolic See as their supreme
guide. It is true that the bishop gave to them licence
to hear confessions (as was granted to the Warden in
the case of Lady Margaret Hakeluyt); and similar
permission was extended to another of their body in
regard to the Nuns of Cannington, as well as in other
cases. Yet in the main they were free lances, and as
such the parson of the parish was apt to look askance
upon them at times. They could perform many
religious offices; they could itinerate and divert dues
which might otherwise go to the vicar; the priests
could officiate at the burial of the dead, which might
take place in their own chapel or graveyard, paying
one-fourth part of the accustomed dues to the vicar.
They were free from the payment of tithe, either for
their house, garden, orchard, or herbage of their
cattle.

They were adepts at drawing up wills for the sick
and dying. Consequently the parish priests watched
them narrowly, and sometimes bewailed their intrusion.
When Archbishop Peckham directed the parsons to
welcome the brothers, the former felt it at times to be
a hardship indeed. Thus in 1462 a quarrel arose in
Bridgwater between two parties as to the possession
of certain deeds. A Bill of Complaint was laid before
Sir Richard Chokke, Justice, who proceeded to take
evidence on oath in the church of the Grey Friars.
A certified copy of this record is given by William
at Welle and John Walshe, Common Stewards of
the borough of Bridgwater.[1] Probably John Coswayn,
the Vicar of Bridgwater, would have preferred that the
inquiry should have taken place in St. Mary's. The
feeling, however, in Bridgwater never ran high. In
1502 Brother John Boldeheyter, a Friar Minor, was

[1] Bridgwater documents.

appointed to be a chantry priest in the parish church. He was *Sacrae Theologiae Baccalaureus.*

In one detail the Friars departed *toto caelo* from the direction of St. Francis. This was in regard to learning. Before the end of the thirteenth century they had gained immense influence in the University of Oxford. Their scholars multiplied apace, and could not be restrained. Throughout Europe they gained, deservedly, the reputation of being the most learned of the religious orders. Kilwarby the Franciscan became Archbishop of Canterbury in 1273; Bonaventura, their General, declined the great See of York; Bonaventura's successor in the Order filled the Papacy as Nicholas IV. Brother Alexander Barclay, a Devonshire priest, who was a Benedictine, and afterwards a Franciscan, became in the sixteenth century Suffragan Bishop in the diocese of Bath and Wells. He was "a good poet and rhetorician," who "wholly apply'd himself to read and write pious and historical Legends of Saints; some whereof he composed, but translated many more out of Latin into English."

Three famous Bridgwater Friars must be mentioned next. The Bridgwater House (or Friary) was, it should be said, in the custody or wardenship of Bristol. Thus Bristol, Gloucester, Bridgwater, Hereford, Exeter, Carmarthen, Dorset, Cardiff, and Bodmin all had Friars Minor foundations, and were included in one district, there being seven such districts in all England. Dugdale, quoting Leland, specially eulogizes Brother Henry Cross, a Franciscan, "famous in his age, not only for erudition, but also for piety."[1]

Nor did his virtue go without an honourable reward. He was made a sub-master of his order in England, which employment conferred on him he managed with so much

[1] *Mon. Ang.,* Vol. VI, part iii, p. 1527.

dexterity, that, what seldom happens, he gained much applause without envy. Nor did he, at his death, leave behind him any ill name, or small reputation, to learned posterity. For he writ some books which testify his good affection towards sacred literature; one of which was a commentary on Aristotle's Natural Philosophy, the other on the sentences of Longobardus. Witness the catalogue of renowned Franciscans. He was made Doctor of Divinity at Oxford, and the thirteenth reader in that house of the Friars-Minor. He died at Bridgwater, and was there buried among the brethren of that order.

Another eminent Bridgwater Franciscan was Brother John Summer. He too was an Oxford student, and made such great progress in philosophy and mathematics, that "there was scarce his equal at that time in England, but none exceeded him. He particularly apply'd himself to astronomy, and produc'd works in that kind which were highly commended, partly gathered from the most approved authors, and partly of his own wit and discovery; which, by command of Thomas Hiber, his Provincial, and at the request of Joanna, Princess of Wales, the King's mother, he finished, reduced into good order, and published."[1] About the year 1390 he was quite a noted person, and his books, *Canons of the Stars, Of the Quantity of the Year, Corrections of the Calendar*, with other works after the fashion of those days, made him eminent. A few years later William Auger, also from Oxford, came to settle in Bridgwater as guardian of the Friars' monastery. In that position he, "being quietly settled there, began to chew over again those things which he had often read, learnt, or disputed on in the schools; but he took most delight in reading and meditating on the Holy Gospels."[2] Brother Auger wrote some com-

[1] Stevens' *Abbeys*, Vol. I, p 101.
[2] *Ibid*, Vol. I, p. 102

mentaries on the Gospel of St. Luke, and then, his work finished, he passed away in the Friarn Street House, and was laid to rest in the little chapel. Brother Robert Cross, a Provincial of the Order, and a doctor of Oxford, lies there too. Although the site of the Friars' buildings is fairly easy to locate to-day, the exact position of their chapel has not yet been definitely ascertained. The length of it was 120 "steppys," its width 30 "steppys," and the width of the nave 14 "steppys."

The Friars' time in Bridgwater witnessed a whole catena of stirring events, and a development of thought in England which culminated in the series of upheavals and changes known as the Reformation. The Franciscans' advent was only shortly preceded by the Papal interdict which Pope Innocent III laid upon the kingdom in 1208, in the course of his quarrel with King John. This interdict was a monumental instance of Papal folly. It forbade the solemnities of public worship, and although its effects have been exaggerated, it practically closed all the churches. Baptism, confirmation and other sacred functions might be permitted in cases of urgency; marriage was allowed, though without the solemnities. Yet it barred all the usual worship of the people, and this, continuing for five years, might well have driven them into absolute alienation from the Church. King John, few will be found to deny, deserved excommunication or any other censure, for in spite of his *bonhomie* and his general popularity in Somerset—he was an excellent sportsman —it would be hard to exculpate him. He divorced his wife Hawisia, Countess of Gloucester, in 1189, and took to wife Isabella of Angoulême, but how lightly he regarded any such ties the stories of that day freely tell us. His reign was a miserable squabble with

Rome and with his subjects, ending in an equally miserable submission. However, he gave Bridgwater her first charter, and so started the town on a successful career. But this, in all probability, was due more to William Briwere than to the Plantagenet King. The Crusades had by this time well-nigh spent their force; England was developing her own resources and her trade. The constant irritation caused by the unwise policy of the Roman Church towards this country increased; it was not—certainly at first—a matter of difference of doctrine, but of policy. The Popes might coerce other countries; they coerced England too, somewhat, but it could not last. The independent spirit of Englishmen was bound to prevail, and it prevailed.

In 1349 the Black Death came; an awful pestilence which ravaged the land, and claimed thousands of victims in Somerset. So diminished was the population that the demand for labour rose by leaps and bounds, and in consequence labourers' wages rose too. The insurrection of 1381 was a consequence of this, and all our neighbourhood was for long in a very troubled state. In these crises the three religious forces in Bridgwater were the Parish Church of St. Mary, with its chantries; the Augustinian Hospital of St. John in Eastover; and the Friars. The time of religious intellectual and spiritual development was not yet. The discovery of the art of printing, the New Learning, the open Bible, the growing hatred of Roman political action, and Henry VIII's keen desire for a divorce from Katherine of Aragon and from the Pope, were the ultimate causes which led to the huge changes of the sixteenth century. Now the Friars, as has been seen, in spite of the excellence of their ideal—which on the whole was really well maintained in Bridgwater—had two weak points.  By the time the sixteenth century had dawned their system of mendicancy was bad and out of date ; their dependence upon the Apostolic See was now fatal.  The Act of Supremacy in 1534 placed the King, not the Pope, at the head of all persons and things in England, including the Franciscans in Friarn Street.  It was probably more from political reasons than from any delinquencies that Henry disliked them. He was a Catholic through and through.  But he must be master.  And this army of Friars in England, whom the common people dearly loved and trusted, who were sworn servants of Rome, must be done away with. The Act for the suppression of the smaller religious houses, passed in 1536, sealed their fate.  It was practically assured in 1534, when our Church's Con-vocation formally declared that " Romanus episcopus non habet majorem aliquam jurisdictionem a Deo sibi collatam in hoc Regno Angliae quam quivis alius extremus episcopus."[1]  The Franciscans had got on fairly well with the English bishops, but they always held themselves as ultimately bound in obedience to the Bishop of Rome.  Now, the declaration averred, that Bishop had no more power in England than any other bishop.  The difficulty, doubtless, might have been got over.  But Henry did not want to get over it.  He wanted the spoil of all these smaller houses, and his jackals wanted their share of it too.  The Friars had no lands, and almost no revenues ; there were only their houses, churches, and the beautiful ornaments and vestments which they loved to use for the services in their little chapel.  They were helpless. They could only bow their heads before the storm. Upon them first in England the blow fell, and in their

[1] "The Bishop of Rome hath no greater jurisdiction conferred on him by God in this kingdom of England than any other bishop."

utter helplessness they stood, as Cardinal Wolsey said to Cromwell, all naked to their enemies.

The wording of the surrender of the Friary is as follows :—

Memorandum ; we the Wardeyn and convent of ye gray Fryeres of Brygewater w[t] one assent and consent w[t]out any maner of coaccyon or counsell do gyve owr house Into ye handes of ye lorde vysytor to ye kinges use desyrynge hys grace to be goode and gracyous to us. In wytteness we subscrybe our namys w[t] owr proper handdes the XIII day of September In ye XXX yere of kynge Henry the VIII[th].[1]

per me Iohannes Herys gardi[m].
per me I. Thomen Howett.
per me Iohon Wake.
per me Richardum Harris, Sacerdotum.
per me Gerardum Morley, bachalaureum.
per me Iohannem Cogyn.
per me Andream Gocyt.
per me Robertum Olyver.

An inventory had been taken, in two parts. The first part enumerated "the housses of ffreres lately given up whiche have any substance of lead." Thus:—

The grey freres in brigwater one pane of the cloyster; two grete gutters bitwen the church and the batilment; diverse grete spowtes on both sides of the church w[t] an oryall in a chamber all leaded.

Lead was valuable, and must be seized. The second inventory is a long one:—

Thys Indentur makeythe mencyon of all ye stuffe of ye grey freeres of brygewatter receyved by ye lord vysytor under ye lord prevy seale for ye kynges grace and delyveryd to John Newport mayer ther and Rycherd Torell to se and order to ye kynges use w[th] ye howse and all ye pertenans tyll ye kynges plesure be forder knowyn.

<hr>

[1] Archbold's *Religious Houses*, p. 97.

The list is too lengthy to give. Almost all the items refer to ornaments and necessaries for the Friars' worship; very little for their private use.

In the choir were, a table of alabaster with 9 images; on the altar 4 altar cloths; 2 goodly candlesticks; a pair of organs; a leaden holy-water stoup and a sacry bell. In the church were 3 cloths before the altar, a frame of iron about a tomb, and an old coffer. No fewer than 22 copes are in the list, some of them evidently of exquisite workmanship. The vestments are very numerous. A suit of white silk for priest, deacon, and sub-deacon; 4 old tunicles, 7 old chasubles; many suits, of silk and damask, of all colours; altar hangings, cushions, silken palls, and other equipments for mediæval worship. At the end is a significant note. Memorandum: "Where the debts of the house drew about £18 or £19 the visitor hath delivered an old suit of vestments, with the cope and other small things, to the warden, and the warden hath undertaken to discharge all debts, and the visitor hath with him to the king's use in jewels and plate to the sum of 17 ounces and 18 ounces, and hath sold 2 old feather beds and 2 small pots and one pan for 17 shillings." Signed: per me Iohannem Newport; per me, Richard Tyrrell.

John Newport appears on Mr. Jarman's list as having been Mayor of Bridgwater in 1532; Richard Tyrrell in 1540.[1] The Friars' little property was sold to all and sundry persons, but it could not amount to much. The house and buildings had a value; the site went to one Emanuel Lucar. Very little, it is estimated, went into the King's pocket from the Brothers' property, save from the land and the Friary buildings standing thereon. The suppression was theoretically defensible, but the mode of carrying it out was, and is, abhorrent to every just mind. The Friars were mostly turned out into the world with nothing, and with their

[1] Jarman's *History of Bridgwater*, p. 269.

occupation gone. As Bishop Creighton once said, the Reformation suppressions had to come, but the King had to get the scum of the earth to carry them out.

When old, Leland visited Bridgwater he spoke of having seen "a goodly House wher sumtyme a College was of Gray Freres."[1] After giving a few memoranda upon it, he goes on to say, "the Accustumer of Bridgwater hath translated this place to a right goodly and pleasant dwelling House." His note is strangely appropriate. The old house, still remaining, has nothing but the memory of its former inhabitants. It is useful still, but in another way, and to a new generation. The Friars have utterly disappeared from English life. They vanished with even greater quickness than they at first took Bridgwater by storm with their burning religious zeal. No one has quite taken their place, and this is presumably because their work was over and done. It is not necessarily the unfit, in this throbbing world, who go to the wall; it is those who are no longer needed. The Brotherhood lived, prayed, and laboured; then they suffered and passed away like a dead man out of mind, as the Hebrew singer hath it. Yet one can hardly walk down Friarn Street without giving a thought to the noble and sainted dead who lie hidden away somewhere under the floor of the Brothers' chapel, and without half expecting to meet a Friar, clad in long grey cloak and cowl, walking barefoot to minister to some hapless soul.

[1] Dugdale's *Mon Ang.*, Vol. VI, part III, p 1531.

# CHAPTER VII

## THE AUGUSTINIAN CANONS OF
## ST. JOHN'S

WITHIN a short time after Innocent the Third's laying England under an Interdict, and thus depriving her people of the privileges of public worship, there was founded in Bridgwater an institution which flourished and did excellent work for more than three hundred years. This was the Hospital or Priory of St. John, in Eastover. The *ordinatio seu fundatio* of this Religious House is noted in Bishop Bekynton's Register at Wells,[1] beginning with the usual greeting to all sons of Holy Mother Church.

Let all know that the nobleman William Bruere has founded a hospital at Bruggewater, and has placed there clerical brethren (*clericos fratres*) who will serve God there, and has given possessions for their support and for that of Christ's poor (*pauperes Christi*), and promises to give more.

The gifts enumerated to begin with were the churches of Bridgwater, Northover, and of Ile Bruers, with all their rights and appurtenances, together with the chapel in the Castle of Bridgwater. The most important condition was "that the aforesaid hospital should be a free house of God (*Domus libera Dei*) founded in pure perpetual alms only for the poor of Christ and by no means for the rich or any others." The brethren were allowed to choose their Magister or

---

[1] See Archer's Account of Religious Houses.

Master out of their own body (*de gremio suo*); they
were to be free from procurations and all episcopal
burdens. The Magister was master in his own house
and could manage his own affairs, and appoint his
own officers and bailiffs outside as well as inside the
house. With regard to Mass and habit the brethren
were required to wear such clerical garments as suited
*Fratres hospitales* or those of a similar order, but,
as a distinguishing mark, with a cross of black or
blackish colour worked on their mantles and upper
cloaks (*cruce nigri aut nidii coloris in mantellis et in-
dumentis suis superioribus*). The brethren were also
required to live according to the regular rules and
constitutions of the Order of St. Augustine.

Also, that they should serve the parish church of Bruggewater where they live, and which they have for their own
use, by one of the aforesaid Brethren, and by a secular
Chaplain fit to hold the cure (*per alium capellanum secularem
idoneum pro cura supportanda*)

Also, that one of the Brethren or a secular chaplain should
daily celebrate one mass in the chapel of Bridgwater Castle;
and further, when the Lord of the Castle was at home and
should ask for it, the brother or chaplain should be bound
to minister at the canonical hours in a fit and becoming
manner. The Master and Brethren of the Hospital should
be entitled fully and without dispute to all the offerings and
oblations made in the said Castle. Also, the Lord of the
Castle for the time being shall find and in all future time
provide books, vestments, vessels, candles and everything
else either necessary or suitable for the said Chapel.

Also, that some fit or proper Brother should have the
charge and care of the poor, infirm and needy in the
infirmary, working under the Master, ministering to the
same according to the means of the House and his own
ability. Also, that two or three women not of gentle birth,
but still fit for the purpose (*non nobiles sed idoneae*), being of
good conversation and repute, willing and able to minister

to the poor and infirm there, should be duly admitted by the Master and Brethren. And these women should be always careful and ready both by day and by night to help the sick and to minister to them in all things, and further they should not turn their attention to any other acts and services excepting their due prayers and devotions.

It is expressly provided that no other women and sisters beyond the said number of two or three shall be admitted and kept on any pretext whatever.

Also, that no leper or lunatic, or any one having the falling sickness (*morbum caduum*) or any other contagious disease, or a woman in child, or a sucking infant (*infantulus lactens*), or any other unbearable (*intolerabilis*) patient shall be admitted into the aforesaid house, however poor and infirm. There were also many stringent conditions laid down to prevent the diversion of things given by the faithful "for the sustentation of Christ's poor people." There were to be no corrodies or free meals or boardings or pensions or chantries either to be sold or granted for money or favour (*prece aut pretio*).

Further, "We expressly forbid that either the rich or the powerful, whether of diocesan rank or ordinary people, or the ministers and stewards of the Patron of the House [Lord Briwere was the first Patron] should lodge, sojourn, or be entertained in the aforesaid Hospital and be a burden to the House and Brethren. Nor should they tax it by their frequent presence nor by feeding their horses nor by any costs of entertainment. If they do, let them be Anathema and lie under Divine vengeance. We, together with the aforesaid William Bruere, of our full episcopal authority approve, and for ever confirm the gift on behalf of ourselves and our successors and with the consent of the Chapter of Wells."

In testimony thereof are appended the seals of the Bishop and of William Briwere. Witnesses: William the Præcentor, William the Archdeacon, Alardus the Chancellor, Godfrey the Treasurer, Lambert the Subdeacon, Robert Succentor, Gilbert of Taunton, the Canons of Wells, and many others. Given at Woky xii Kal. Aug. in the fourteenth year of our bishopric. 1219.

This deed, it must readily be confessed, was drawn up in an admirable spirit, and with no little ingenuity. The Hospital of Bridgwater was eminently practical. Its object differed from that of the Knights of St. John of Jerusalem. It had a plain local object in view, i.e. to help the poor and afflicted, and none other. It more than anticipated the scheme of a modern infirmary, and combined with it the carefully regulated ministrations of religion.

A record,[1] dating from May 10th, 1286, throws some light upon hygienic arrangements in ancient days. It is a licence to the Master and Brethren.

Whereas they and the poor Christian sick there were in great need of running water they should be allowed to make a watercourse from the River of Parret on the South of the Great Bridge of Bridgwater, by means of a dyke three feet broad over their own land and the land of others, and of a depth according to the depth of the river, as far as the said Hospital; and thence along the causeway on the North side back to the said river so as to cleanse the privies of the said Hospital; the said dyke to be covered when necessary with stones and earth, so as to be level with the adjoining land and kept in repair by the said Hospital.

In due time other benefices and properties were allotted to the hospital, including, amongst others, the advowsons of Chilton Trinity and Wembdon. Some work in educating the poor was also laid upon the canons or brethren. There is no doubt that they did

[1] Cal. Patent Rolls.

it thoroughly and well. They were never a wealthy body, and frequently endured sore straits. Again and again the documents show how the Master and brethren appealed against this and that impost or due, upon the ground of their poverty. Their plea was usually allowed, which is tolerably strong evidence that the hospital was never well off. The number of documents and references relating to St. John's Hospital is very numerous indeed—relating to the election of a master or prior, to an appeal for the remission of a tax proposed to be laid upon the little society, to a petition asking that a poor clerk may receive preferment, or an ordination or regulation for the proper maintenance and support of a vicar serving one of the benefices of which the master and brethren were rectors. The regulation made for the vicar of Northover is an instance of this.

In return for the due performance of his duties the vicar was given "a house with a curtilage, 9½ acres of arable land, 2 acres of meadow, all oblations from whatever source, together with tithes of hay, ale, lambs, milk, wool, flax, hemp, pigeons, pigs, geese, apples, honey, wax, heifers, chicken, mills, leeks, garlic, and all other small tithes within the said parish whatever. The Vicar to find processional candles, bread and wine for the celebration of Mass, incense as often as required, and have the church clothes (vestments?) cleaned at his expense. The Master and the Brethren of the Hospital to sustain all other charges."

Certainly the master and brethren looked well after their duties in Bridgwater. They maintained the very high character which the Canons of St. Augustine gained, and deservedly gained, all over England. One might well have thought that the hospital and its brethren would have been free from envy or unpopularity. Yet, since any body which holds property runs the risk of either actively or passively offending other owners of property, so it was with the brethren of St. John's.

The Calendar of Patent Rolls records the issue, "on Feb. 6th, 1380, of a Commission of Oyer and Terminer to James (Lord Audley), Peter Courtenay, Henry Percehay, and others, on complaint of Thomas, Master of the Hospital of St. John Baptist, Parson of the Church of Bridgwater, that William Blacche, tanner, John Thomas, carpenter, John Kelly, hosier, and many others, armed, approached the said town, close, and houses, broke the doors and windows of his church, took food and £20 in money, closed and still hold the said door closed to the ministers and parishioners, assaulted his servants and so threatened them that they dare not come near the said Hospital." Another entry records that these riotous persons took away the master's goods and certain Papal Bulls touching the appropriation of the vicarage (of St. Mary's). Probably this was a quarrel, arising out of contested rights, between the master and William, son of William de Zouche, who was lord of two parts of the town of Bridgwater. The latter averred that the master, aided by his supporters, had prevented William's steward from holding his Court of Frank-pledge. William de Zouche was patron of the hospital and lord of the manor, and he was supported in his claim by many of the Bridgwater folk. The quarrel was purely local, and it was incidental, in those days, to most neighbouring magnates holding property or land.

A more serious riot occurred on June 19–20, 1381. The Patent Rolls record a pardon, " notwithstanding that in divers parliaments he was excepted as one of the principal insurgents, to Thos. Engilby, for the

THE ANCIENT BOROUGH OF BRIDGWATER

following treasons, trespasses and felonies with which he is charged, viz. . . . he went with Adam Brugge and others to the Hospital of St. John, Bruggwater, broke the house and seized and detained William Cammel the master until he delivered to him certain bonds between the men of Bruggwater and the said Master, released all his rights and profits to Nicholas Frompton, rector (*sic*) of Bruggewater, tithes of hay and corn excepted, and made fine in 200 marks for the safety of himself and convent. He also went to the house of John Sydenham and destroyed goods, and to the house where John was staying in the same town and burned writings touching his inheritance and court rolls of James Audley and John Cole, tearing off the seals. On the same day he also burned a tenement of Thomas Duffield in the town, value £20, and a house and goods of Walter Baron of Estchilton, causing the said Walter to be beheaded, and on the Friday following he went to Ivelchestre and made John Bursy, living in his house at Longesutton, to go with him; broke the gaol and took out Hugh Lavenham, there under a charge of felony, and made the said Bursy behead him, carry his head on a spear to Bruggewater and place it with that of Walter Baron on Bruggwater bridge."

Frompton was afterwards pardoned, with the conditional saving clause (usually introduced into documents at that date) that he did not kill Simon, Archbishop of Canterbury, or Robert Hales. He was in London at the time when the Archbishop and Hales were killed, in the famous Peasants' Revolt under Wat Tyler. Somerset, however, had nothing whatever to do with this revolt. Frompton, it is said, claimed the vicarage of St. Mary's from the master. He never got it. He may, of course, have utilized the prevailing excitement during the Peasants' Revolt, to raise a riot on his own account in Bridgwater. But there is no direct link between St. John's Hospital and the great peasant rising. A dissatisfied cleric made a fuss because a certain benefice was not given him. He was clever enough to take advantage of the unrest prevailing in other parts of England. That was all.[1]

These, however, are only passing incidents in the long and good career of the brethren. When they came to be suppressed, in common with the other religious houses, under Henry VIII, there was nothing to be said against them. It was in vain to resist the King—they acknowledged his supremacy. This, however, was of no avail; their time had come. Having been expelled, pensions were assigned to "the late master and Brethern of the surrendryde house of Seynte Ioones in Brydgewater. And they and every of theym to have their halff yeers pencion at Thanunciacon of oure Lady next comyng whiche shalbe in the yere of our Lorde godd 1539." Robert Walshe, the master, received a pension of £33 6s. 8d.; Thos. Coggyn, Richarde Kymrydge, John Colde, John Wyll, and Roberte Ffysher, £4 each; John Wood and John Mors, 40s. each.

---

[1] Professor Oman, in his interesting book *The Great Revolt of 1381*, in an incomprehensible manner connects the Knights of St. John, at Clerkenwell, with the St. John's Brethren at Bridgwater Hospital. There was no kind of connection between them The Bridgwater Brethren were Augustinian Canons of St. Augustine, living in St. John Baptist Hospital. The Clerkenwell Brethren were Knights Hospitallers of St. John, an entirely different foundation and Order Mr. Oman's suggestion that Frompton wished to avenge himself on the Bridgwater clerics because he had seen how the knights in Clerkenwell had been treated, falls to the ground. Frompton's anger with the Bridgwater men, whatever may have been its cause, had nothing in it to connect them with Clerkenwell. He was far too astute a man to make such a blunder. No one who had been, as he is said to have been, at Clerkenwell and in Bridgwater, could have made the mistake of supposing that the two religious communities were one and the same Order.

Of the masters or priors of the old hospital, of which every trace has now ceased to exist, the following names are known : Gilbert, 1281 ; Henry de Stanford, 1312 ; John Pathull ; William Cammel, 1381 ; Thomas Pulton, 1422 ; John Wemedon, 1423 ; Roger Cory, 1449 ; John Holford, 1457 ; Thomas Spenser, 1498 ; Richard Walsh, 1538.  Richard Walsh was one of the two clerics who were afterwards nominated to be Suffragan Bishop of Taunton.  As it turned out, however, he was not appointed.  Taunton and Bridgwater towns were both placed on Henry VIII's list, containing the names of places which were hereafter to be made the seat of a bishopric.  To neither, as yet, has this honour come.  Perhaps it may be so in the days before us.  Poor Richard Walsh's dream of being a bishop was never fulfilled ; he died a dispossessed prior.  But he did his duty well, and our old town, for many a day, must much have missed the kindly ministrations of the prior and canons of St. John's Hospital in Eastover, on the other side of William Briwere's great bridge.

BRIDGWATER PARISH CHURCH

NORTH PORCH

*Facing page* 10

# CHAPTER VIII

## THE PARISH CHURCH

### I

S T. MARY'S Parish Church has a long history, and
was here at the time of the Norman Conquest.
How long before that eventful period it was in existence is not at present known, nor does there appear to
be any great probability that the date of its original
foundation will ever be revealed. Merleswain the
Saxon, who was Lord of Bridgwater in 1066, no doubt
worshipped within its walls. Walter de Douai the
Norman,[1] who succeeded him, afterwards held the
manor, which passed in due course to his son, and
thence by marriage to Fulk Paganel, also of distinguished Norman descent. From the Paganels it
was transferred again, in 1180, to the great baron,
Lord William Briwere.

The church itself tells its own story well, by reason
of its varied architecture, but that story cannot be
traced—in the stones of the building now standing—
much further back than the end of the eleventh century.

---

[1] "Walcinus, or Walter de Douai, one of the chief landowners in
Som. in 1086, held Bathentuna or Bampton, in Devon, and lands in
Dorset or Wilts. The head of his barony was Castle Cary, where
Walter had his castle; it afterwards passed to the Lovells, probably by
descent. Bampton, and other of Walter's estates in Dev. and Som.,
descended to the family of Paynel or Paganell by the marriage of his
grand-daughter and heiress Juliana to Fulk Paganell, see Domesday of
Somerset, I, 61. 62. . . . Brigge, i.e. Bridgwater, another of Walter's
estates which descended to the Paganells." (*Bath Chartulary*, Som. Rec.
Society, p. 80).

Of the church which stood here in Walter de Douai's time scarcely any traces are left. The interior south-east corner of the tower certainly has some very early work, which some archæologists have pronounced to be Norman, and the crypt—were it accessible—would probably reveal more work of that period. But there is abundant evidence of much building having taken place herein soon after the year 1200, and it is most likely that the lines and dimensions of St. Mary's to-day do not vary greatly from what they were at that time. Quite early in the thirteenth century the church was, one may confidently say, very largely rebuilt, of course in the Early English style. Moreover, the documents exactly confirm what the church walls declare. It was early in the thirteenth century that William Briwere began to build the castle, and to bestir himself for the advancement of the town. There is little doubt that he largely modified the church which he found here, and rebuilt it, with infinite taste and skill, in the architectural style which was just then dawning in England. The story of the church walls, corroborated by the legal documents of that time, finds further confirmation in the unalterable tradition that William Briwere greatly beautified St. Mary's.

When Walter de Douai, who seems to have done but little for Bridgwater, took possession of the manor, St. Mary's was a purely parish church, a rectory, supported after the usual manner by tithes. In this way the rector was paid, and the parochial system maintained. But the monastic houses were then coming to be much in vogue, and it was getting to be the custom to subsidize these great houses with grants paid out of the parish rectories. St. Mary's quickly experienced this. The wife of Walter de Douai (probably it was the first Walter) after her husband's death granted the revenues

of the church to the monks of Bath.[1]  It was the first
alienation of the St. Mary's possessions, and that
alienation, in some direction or other, has strangely
enough never ceased unto the present day.  It still
exists; Walter's wife's gift of the advowson to Bath
Priory was the precursor of many subsequent grants of
the same property to other folk.  Thus Pope Adrian,[2]
in a document addressed to Robert Bishop of Bath
(1136–66), speaks of Bridgwater Church as belonging to the Priory of Bath.  When, however, the
Paganel family came to be lords of Bridgwater, there
were further developments in the history of the parish
church.  Ralph Paganel in 1086 had held five lordships
in Somerset, and many elsewhere.  The family came
from Moutiers, and they gave large grants of churches
and lands in England to the abbey of Marmoutier.
This was a Benedictine abbey not far from Tours, and
being the largest of the abbeys founded by St. Martin
was known as Majus Monasterium.  Lickford in Buck-
inghamshire, Cosham in Wilts, Trinity Priory at
York, and Allerton Mauleverer Priory were the English
cells to this abbey.  Henry II granted the manor of
Torvertone to the same house.

William Paganel, in a deed, confirmed his father

[1] Extract from *Bath Chartulary*, Som. Record Society, p. 38.  "Hæ
sunt res quæ dedit Walcinus de Duaio Deo et ecclesiæ S. Petri Bathoni-
ensis et Iohanni episcopo. . .   Et uxor ipsius Walcini cum filiis suis,
consilio baronum suorum, dedit medietatem decimæ de Careio et *ecclesiam
de Brigga* cum omnibus decimis et consuetudinibus quæ ad ecclesiam
illam pertinent."  John was Bishop of Bath from 1088 to 1122.

[2] He refers to "Ecclesiam de Brigga cum omnibus pertinentiis suis"
as Bath Priory property.  *Bath Chartulary*, p. 68.

Reginald, Bishop of Bath 1171–91, is most affectionately spoken of
by the Bath Priory authorities.  "Reginaldus, Episcopus hujus loci,
omnes terras nostras a prædecessoribus suis ad opus fabricæ ecclesiæ
nostræ diutius detentas, devote restituit, et quæ a prædecessoribus suis
nobis restitutæ erant, affectuosius ab ipso nobis confirmatæ sunt: . . .
ecclesias de Brugges el de Kary et de Rodestok nichilominus in usus
proprios nobis confirmavit," etc.  *Ibid.*, p. 154.

Fulk's grant of the manor of Bridgwater to William Briwere,[1] and his son Fulk Paganel, in a document[2] which has given rise t'o no little difficulty, granted Bridgwater Church to this same abbey of Marmoutier which his relatives had so richly endowed. But the church of Bridgwater had already been granted by the Douai family to Bath Priory. The advowson, of course, may have become separated from the manor, but this was unusual. It may be that the Paganels—some of whom were a bold and unruly set of men—set the Bath monks at defiance, and transferred St. Mary's to the great foreign abbey hard by their own old home at Moutiers. It may have been possible that Marmoutier held the advowson of St. Mary's for a few years, perhaps from 1187 up to the end of the century; or it may have been that the grant made on parchment was ineffectual in fact. Grants of property in those days, by deed, were ineffectual unless the grantee was given physical possession with proper formalities (livery of

[1] Carta Willielmi Paynel, de Manerio de Brugewalter:—

Sciant praesentes et futuri, quod ego Willielmis Paynel, filius Fulconis Paynell de Bamtone, concessi (etc.) Willielmo Briwere et haeredibus suis, donationem quam Fulco Paynel pater meus ei fecit de Burghwalteri, *scil.* totum manerium de Burghwalteri, integrè (etc.) Tenendum de me et haeredibus meis, per servicium dimidii militis, pro omni servitio (etc.) Testibus, Reginaldo de Mohun, Ricardo Briwere, et aliis.—Dugdale's *Mon. Ang.*, Add., Vol. II. p. 912.

[2] Carta Fulcodii Paganelli, de Ecclesia de Burgewalter:—

Ego Fulcodius Paganellus de Bahantune, omnibus qui praesens scriptum viderint vel audierint, notum esse volo, quod Ecclesiam de Burgewalter, de Sumersete, quae ad donationem meam pertinet, et me paternâ successione contingit, intuitu pietatis, et spe remunerationis aeternae, et pro saluta animae meae, et patris mei Willielmi Paganelli, et matris meae Julianae de Bahantune, et Alde (*sic*) uxoris meae, et filiorum meorum Willielmi et Fulcodii, filiarumque mearum Julianae et Christianae et ancestorum et successorum meorum animabus, donavi deo et beato Martino, et Monachis Majoris Monasterii in perpetuam elemosinam (etc.) Feci autem hoc donum assensu predictae Adae uxoris meae, et filiorum et filiarum mearum, praesentibus et audientibus testibus, quorum nomina subscripta sunt, Willielmo Paganello fratre meo, Stephano de Bahamtune, Alberto de Bahamtune, etc.—Ex dictis collect. *Rob. Glover Somerset Heraldi Miscel.*, lib. 5, f. 40a.

seizin). Many grants in old times were made by livery without any deed at all.

However these things may have been, William Briwere presently got possession of the church as well as of the manor, and there is every reason to believe that he restored and rebuilt the fabric in a magnificent way. After a few years he set to work upon his favourite foundation of the Augustinian Hospital of Saint John in Eastover, to which the tithes of several parishes afterwards became allocated, and one of the parishes thus allotted to St. John's was the parish church of Bridgwater. Briwere, no doubt, meant that the resources of St. Mary's should help the development of St. John's Hospital, and that the Augustinians there would provide in some measure for the spiritual work of the town and of the church. The ultimate arrangement was that the advowson should belong to the hospital,[1] saving the payment to Bath Priory of one hundred shillings a year.[2] This was afterwards regularly paid to Bath, or to those whom the Bath authorities appointed to be the recipients of the charge.[3] St. Mary's remained in the possession of the Augustinian canons until the suppression of their house in the sixteenth century. They were required to appoint a vicar who would govern the church, and be respon-

[1] " Request by R. Prior (of Bath) to J. (Jocelin), Bp. of Bath and Glastonbury, to confirm a grant of the church of Brug'Walter which the said Prior and his convent have made to the Hospital of Brug'-Walter, saving to the Priory of Bath one hundred shillings a year" (*Bath Cart.*, p. 14).

[2] "*Quit claim* by Robert, Prior, etc., *to William Briwer* of the advowson of the church of Bruge, saving 100s. yearly payable to the same Prior. Witnesses: Herbert Haweswia, Roger de Sancto Laudo, Roger de Monte, Forti, Walter de Wikes, Richard de Forda and many others" (*Bath Cart.*, p. 20).

[3] *Ib.*, II (Linc. Inn MS.), p. 103. "Letters of the Prior, etc., to the Master of the Hospital of St. John the Baptist of Bruggwalter, commanding him to pay to Brother Robert de Sutton during his life the yearly rent of 100s. due to the Prior from the church of Bruggwalter. Dated Monday next after the Feast of St. Martin the Bishop, 1332."

sible for its proper ministrations, and they had to see
that he received an adequate proportion of the revenue
for his sustenance. The position and duties of the
vicar of Bridgwater have not greatly changed, save in
scope, since William Briwere's day until now. Only
once, at the time of the Commonwealth, has the proper
*status* of the benefice been disturbed, and that was not
for long. St. Mary's was the centre of worship for the
town in the eleventh century, even as to-day.

The fabric is interesting as illustrating well the three
periods of architecture : Early English, Decorated, and
Perpendicular. Beginning westwards with the tower,
it is evident that this has seen many vicissitudes, and
has been greatly altered from its original form. Of
Norman origin, almost every Norman feature has disappeared. The arch leading from the tower to the
nave is Early English, of quite early thirteenth century.
Its apex indicates the height of the Early English nave,
and the height of the aisles can be seen from a carved
stone corbel at the west corner of the north aisle. No
windows with mullions of that date have been preserved, but later windows have been inserted in Early
English casings, notably at the west and north sides of
the nave. A beautiful Decorated window remains at
the west end of the south aisle, and a fine five-
light window of the same period is at the north-
west part of the north transept. The three windows
in the south aisle, between the porch and the west
end, are of the reticulated pattern of Decorated work,
very usual in the fourteenth century. All the remaining windows in the church are Perpendicular in style,
save one or two obviously modern ones. It will be
seen, therefore, that the Decorated builders, when
they came in, did not take away every trace of the
Early English work. They left the western arch,

some fine stonework within the north wall of the north transept, and some buttresses of quite early date, on the outer part of the church on its north side. The diagonal buttresses at the west corners of the tower are of fourteenth-century date ; doubtless they replace earlier ones. Portions of the tower date from quite early times.

It was the fifteenth-century architects, who brought in the Perpendicular style characteristic of Somerset, who left the great building almost as it now is. The pillars in the nave, chancel and south transept are all of this date, so are most of the windows that have not been mentioned already. The north transept contains two modern pillars, which take the place of an old wall running north and south, and which stopped somewhere in line with the north wall of the nave. There is a fine parvise, or priest's chamber, over the north porch, with the original winding staircase leading to it, and out on to the roof, quite unaltered. Here lived the priest whose duty it was to watch the lights burning before the various altars in the church in mediæval times. The transepts are very spacious, and any one standing at the mayor's place in the corporation seats, looking northward, has a splendid view of them, six arches in length, from north to south. It was in the north transept that the hagioscope, or squint, formerly was (referred to in Parker's *Glossary of Architecture*, and in other works), which passed through three walls in order to give a view of the high altar to those standing at the north porch.

At the base of the tower, at its south-east corner, is the doorway through which the Duke of Monmouth and Lord Grey passed on their hurried rush to the top of the tower, on Sunday, July 5th, 1685, when they went to look out for the Royalist troops on Sedgemoor. It was the last tower he ever climbed; it was the last church he ever entered; within eleven days he perished on the executioner's block. The tower might well be higher, but the exquisite spire surmounting it is a most wonderful specimen of fourteenth-century work, delicate and shapely, and exceeding in height anything in the county or in all the country round. There are few more beautiful spires in England than that which rises, in lines of intense simplicity and purity, over the old town of Bridgwater. From the top of it to the base of the tower is 174 feet. Half-way up the tower is the bell-chamber, containing its famous peal of eight bells.

Still keeping to the exterior of the church, it is evident that all the oldest work is on the north side. The buttresses, the walls, the stonework tell of very early date, mostly of the Early English style. Beneath the north transept is "le charnel-house," approached by a door cut in between the two recumbent stone effigies which lie beneath the great north window of this transept. The history of these effigies is entirely lost. Neglect by past generations has permitted them to be utterly defaced, and they are now unrecognizable. They date most likely from the thirteenth or fourteenth century. It is by no means improbable that they were erected to the memory of William Briwere and his wife, or possibly to his son and his son's wife. From their position they point clearly to being placed where they are in order to commemorate some great benefactors to the church. The north porch has been sadly and rudely dealt with by various ages, yet some beautiful thirteenth and fourteenth-century work remains. The two carved heads, one at each side of the doorway, are very quaint. The eastward one is excellent. It suggests a prior of St. John's, or a

bishop, but the head-covering—a mitre—is of an unusual pattern. Within the porch is an old font, broken
in two, built into the wall. The iron grille on the north
side is very old, and at the little wooden door on its
right may still be seen, every Sunday afternoon at
four o'clock, the giving away of thirty-one loaves of
bread to as many poor and infirm folk, under the terms
of the charity of Gilbert Bloyse. The bread is placed
on a stone shelf in the north transept on Saturday;
on Sunday afternoon the recipients appear, each one
coming forward as his name is read out, to receive the
loaf which is passed through the little charity door.
In spite of the vicissitudes which the porch has under-
gone, and its many alterations, its exterior is beautiful,
and some of its carved work is extremely good. The
west door of the church is an insertion of the fifteenth
century, very characteristic. The space beneath the
pointed arch and the hood moulding above it is filled
in with some bold foliage work, very deeply cut. On
the south side of the church there has been much restoration in the nave, although the chancel exterior,
and the south end of the transept, have been less
altered. The window at the east end of the chancel,
of Perpendicular pattern, was put up in the last century. During that period much restoration was
done: the old galleries were taken down, the roof
was thoroughly restored, the clerestory windows were
put in, the western arch (which had previously been
blocked up) was opened out, the tower was renovated,
and much of the stonework within and without was
thoroughly repaired. It is, indeed, a church which
needs constant and continual restoration. It needs
nothing new, but the careful preservation of the old.

The interior of the church needs some notice. On
the north side of the nave, towards the west, are two

quite old recesses covering the tombs of some great ones whose very names are now utterly lost. The lines of the canopies and the cusps suggest very early work indeed. Lying loosely within these recesses are two beautiful Early English stone grave-slabs, quaintly carved in great simplicity, with two outlines forming together the figure of a cross. Within the nave on the south side opposite are two modern recesses cut in the wall, which need no notice. The south porch has been restored almost out of recognition. Many Bridgwater worthies lie beneath it. It was a very favourite place indeed to choose for burial in mediæval times.

In the transepts and the chancel we come to the interesting part of the church which contained the chantries and the altars. The three endowed chantries —St. Mary's, St. George's, and that of the Holy Trinity —are, it would appear, not difficult to locate. The two latter most probably occupied the north and south chapels of the transepts (one of which now forms the organ chamber, and the other is known as the Sealey Chapel). Two such important chantries as these were bound to have prominent places. St. Mary's chantry (founded by Isolda Parewastel) was in all probability placed at the extreme east end of the chancel, close beside the very interesting and curious piscina and aumbry now to be seen on the south side, just eastward of the priest's door on the south. Thus the altar of St. Mary would be the easternmost within the church. The high altar stood in the chancel just opposite the aumbry at the south side, at the top of the third step leading eastwards. From the north porch the hagioscope which has been already spoken of gave a full view of this altar to those who from their position could otherwise not have seen it. This gives the position of the four chief altars in the church.

But there were other altars too. A will issued in 1533 directs that sundry small gifts should be made to "the hye awter of Bridgewater—our lady auter—trinite auter—St. George auter—holy roode auter—St. Katherine auter." This accounts for six. There was also an altar to St. Erasmus, to St. James, one for the Guild of the Holy Cross, and one to St. Gregory. This makes ten in all. The six altars not definitely located were placed in the transepts, although it is not possible now to give their exact position. The chapel of the Holy Cross was situate at the north side of the north transept, "super le charnel-house."[1] One altar was beneath the east window of the aisle now occupied by the corporation seats, and the piscina belonging to it still remains in the south wall. The remaining four were no doubt dotted about in the ample space of the transepts. Probably if the walls were stripped the remains of other aumbreys and piscinæ would be found. Above the chancel arch, at its apex, still can be seen the great iron hook from which the rood was suspended, above where the rood-loft used to stand at the entrance to the choir.

The church of St. Mary in the fifteenth century presented a very different appearance from that which it has to-day. The windows were all filled with painted glass, the walls were richly decorated with the most brilliant and tasteful colouring, and many frescoes were to be seen. The altars themselves were rich in carving, in costly decoration, in tapestries and needle-work, in splendid hangings, with embroidered work. Before them burned lamps or candles, glimmering softly in the dim light. It was a privilege and a great joy to devout folk, or to the members of the town guilds, to maintain a light before their favourite altar. Pictures

[1] Bridgwater documents.

and carvings abounded, most of these highly coloured. A mediæval Bridgwater inhabitant in his will directs that he shall be buried in St. Mary's Church "before the image (or painting) of St. Sebastian." There were no bare or whitewashed walls then. Colour abounded in every direction. Even the capitals of the columns were painted; hardly a space was left untouched. The font in St. Mary's still shows traces of the painted work it possessed in early days, when its vine tracery was all richly gilded. All the church, indeed, was then one blaze of colour. It appealed most marvellously to the sense of beauty in the worshippers, or, as others might say, it appealed powerfully to the senses. Our parish churches and cathedrals to-day are very impressive and singularly beautiful. But they are only the shells that remain. The brilliant interiors have all disappeared; the stone walls are content to appear in their native sombre hue.

In those times many interments took place within the church, whose crypt was ever looked upon as the fitting and honourable home for the dead. The practice, though less frequent, prevailed up to the last century. But then it was discontinued, and vast quantities of concrete were laid in the crypt both for purposes of stability and also of sanitation. The gravestones in the churchyard[1]—and, it is to be feared, within the church also—have been carelessly treated in the past. They have been taken up, broken, and laid down again, out of their place. Some beautiful Latin inscriptions are broken off midway. Many gravestones now form part of the floor of the nave.

The carved woodwork of St. Mary's is exceedingly fine. The sixteenth-century screen in front of the

[1] The following curious epitaph occurs on a stone in the pavement leading to the south porch of the church. First, in Latin and Greek, the

corporation seats is a splendid piece of work, very
richly carved. Formerly it ran across the church,
north and south, at the second pillar (going from east
to west) in the nave. In front of the choir and the two
transept chapels formerly was placed the old screen
now standing on each side of the chancel. Its date
is about 1420, and it is full of quietly tasteful work.
Between these two screens, at the early part of the
nineteenth century, sat the mayor and corporation in
the nave, facing west. Outside the screen, westwards,
was then the pulpit, which is now moved back to the
north pillar by the entrance to the choir, and is a most
beautiful piece of ancient wood-carving. Within the
altar rails are placed some old oak miserere seats, with
finely carved ends (fifteenth century), and some other
old bench-ends of the same date have been rescued
from oblivion to form a credence table. The altar
itself is Jacobean work, very gracefully treated.[1]

words: "Sacred to the memory of John Harvey, gentleman. A
remembrance "

> Vermibus esca licet mea putrida membra recumbunt
>   Exultans surgam victima grata Deo.
> Urna triumphali spoliatur turgida curru ;
>   Et Lethum stimulos perdidit aere suos ;
> Ergo ne detur mihi candida Palla quid obstat
>   Laeta resurgendi cum venit illa dies ? "

Perhaps we may offer the following translation.

> Though worms destroy my body
> I shall rise rejoicing, an offering pleasing to God.
> The advent of the conqueror deprives the burial urn of
>   loathsomeness,
> And death, though sharp, hath lost its sting.
> Why, then, should not the white robe be given to me
> When comes the joyful resurrection day?

The inscription ends with the following in Latin "My entrance on
the stage of this world was on the 20th day of July, 1623; my exit was
on the 1st of January, 1672; in the forty-ninth year of my age."

[1] Two fine oak screens have lately been given to the church. One
was the gift of the late Dr. Parsons, for many years churchwarden.
His screen is at the west side of the organ chamber, facing the north
aisle. The other screen, the gift of Dr. Axford in memory of his

Above the altar hangs the famous picture, concerning which so many legends are current. The story of its coming to Bridgwater is really a very simple one. It was the gift of the Poulett family, of which family Sir John Poulett, in 1627, was made Baron Poulett of Hinton St. George. The fourth Lord Poulett was made an earl in 1706. He held high office under Queen Anne, and was *Custos Rotulorum* of Somerset, and K.G. He died in 1743. He had four sons, John, the second earl; Peregrine; Vere; and Anne: also four daughters. John became second Earl Poulett; Peregrine, twin with John, was born in 1708, was member for Bridgwater, and died 1752. Vere was the third earl. He was born in 1710, and was elected one of the members for Bridgwater in 1741. In 1764 he was chosen to be recorder of the borough, and died April 14, 1788. Vere's son John, born in 1756, succeeded to the earldom in 1788.

Now in 1788 the picture was already hanging in the church. In that year the Rev. S. Shaw, Fellow of Queen's College, Cambridge, went on a tour through the west of England, and visited Bridgwater. He writes: "In the church is a fine altar-piece of Our Saviour taken from the Cross."[1] He describes the picture as being "a present from the late Mr. Powlett, uncle to the present Earl, of Hinton St. George, in this county." This "Mr. Powlett" was clearly Lord Anne Poulett, so named because Queen Anne was his godmother. For he was uncle to John, fourth Earl Poulett, the second and third earls having no uncles. John

father, who for many years was a resident in the town, is at the east end of the south aisle, leading into the south transept chapel. Miss Lovell Marshall has also decorated this chapel with oak panelling. The members of the choir and the congregation have panelled the chancel with oak, and have also restored some of the stalls in the choir.

[1] Shaw's Tour to the West of England. See Pinkerton's *Voyages,* Vol. II, p. 260.

was evidently in possession of the title when Mr. Shaw visited the church, which must therefore have been after April 14, 1788, when Vere died.[1] This Lord Anne Poulett, who never succeeded to the earldom, was born in 1711. He served in 1768, 1774, 1780, and 1784 as member for Bridgwater, and died July 5, 1785. The picture, therefore, has been in the church at least since this latter date, and thus has been on view there for a minimum period of a hundred and twenty-one years. Probably the period is a longer one, although there is no evidence to show the exact date when Lord Anne sent it. The Poulett family were thus intimately connected with Bridgwater by many and long-continued and close ties, and the gift of the picture was therefore a most natural thing for Lord Anne to do.

Whence did he get the picture? There are no written data to go upon, but the local tradition (rejecting certain incongruous variations, such as that he took it by conquest from a ship of the Spanish Armada, which feat, if he had achieved it, would have made him over two hundred years old) fits in so well with probabilities that it may well be accepted. The tradition is that, in the course of the interminable wars which at that time (*circ.* 1780) we had with France, an English man-of-war took captive a ship (French or Spanish), and brought her as a prize into Plymouth harbour. The prize and the cargo were sold by auction, and Lord Anne there purchased the picture, which was found in the cargo of the ship. Its subsequent arrival in Bridgwater was the outcome of the transaction. As concerning the artist, opinions have varied. *De gustibus non est disputandum.* It has been

[1] Pinkerton's extract simply states 1788, without giving the day or month.

assigned by various authorities to the Italian and to the Spanish school of painters. For reasons which it is not necessary to advance, the writer's belief is that it is the work of the great Spanish artist Murillo, who painted so many sacred pictures, and who died at Seville in 1682. It is, and has long been, one of the most highly-prized pictures in the west of England. It was painted, one would think, for what it now is, i.e. the altar-piece of an ancient parish church.

Since the first days when there was a vicar of Bridg-water the office has continued on the same lines, in theory, until now. The names of the earliest vicars have not been preserved. The earliest name which has yet appeared in the documents is that of one James, who witnessed a deed on May 12, 1245. It was a grant by William de Ferndon to Richard de Godyne-lande, son of Robert de Godynelande, of the moiety of his messuage in the town of Bruges, between the house of Robert de Varley and that of Stephen Tinctor, in free marriage with his daughter Dionisia. After the grantor's death and that of Alfreda his wife, the grantee was to have the whole messuage; in de-fault of issue the premises were to revert to the grantor, with other grants. Witnesses: Master Daniel de Weme-don; James, vicar of Bruges; Henry the Constable; Walter de Kentleshere; Roger Brun; Will. de Eve-mere; Will. Basset; Albinus de Godynelande; Robert of Dorchester, chaplain. Dated Bruges Walteri, 4 Id. Mai. Day of SS. Nereus Achilles and Pancratius, 1245. There is, however, a still more interesting deed amongst the archives of the town. It is a quit-claim by Juliana Manger, daughter of Clarina Manger, to the parishioners of Bruges Walteri, for the support of the Mass of the Blessed Virgin in the parish church, of her right in a burgage formerly belonging to

William Manger, for four marks and a yearly rent. Dated Bruges Walteri ; Monday after the Feast of the Purification of the Virgin ; 2 Henry III (i.e. A.D. 1218). This is evidence that the church was in complete working order, with all the ecclesiastical custom of that day in full activity, at the beginning of the thirteenth century. This document, it will be noted, is just after the removal of the Interdict of Pope Innocent III.

Another document of that period is instructive. It is in Latin, and the date is unfortunately gone (*circ.* thirteenth century). It is a grant by the whole of the burgesses of Bruges Walteri to Ffaramus Tinctor of a burgage in the town of Bruges which Richard Lupus formerly held in the North Street, between the house of Walter de Kentleshere and that of Walter Orlof, originally bequeathed by William, vicar of Bruges, to the service of the Virgin Mary (i.e. to the parish church) at a yearly rent of eighteen silver pence. Here, then, is another early vicar who may date even further back than James in the previous document. It is witnessed by some whose names have already appeared: Walter de Kentleshere, Walter Orlof, Laurence Wilde, Rob. Wilde, clerk, Walter Brun, Rob. Cissor, Henri Tinctor. It is sealed with an imperfect seal of Bridgwater Church, the Virgin and Child, in green wax; worded SIGILL: BEATE: MARIE: . . . Another thirteenth-century deed is an indented grant by the burgesses to J. W. of a stall in Bridgwater, between those of John le Hunte and Philip the Provost of Partone, at a yearly rent to the Proctors of St. Mary's Mass in the parish church of Bridgwater, of 10d., and to the chief lord of the town of 12d. The burgesses in another deed grant to J. half a burgage . . . between the half-burgage of J. M., held

of St. Mary, and the burgage which belonged to
N. F., which half-burgage A. L. gave, one moiety to
St. Mary's Mass in the parish church, the other half
to the great cross of the church, at a yearly rent of 12d.

Adam Lupus grants a stall in the High Street of the
town (between that of Walter Wodie on the west, and
that of Blessed Mary on the east) to Tho. Dodde, 12d.
yearly payable to the chief lord of the town, and a
premium of 24s. to be paid beforehand. Richard
Boye, in the middle of the thirteenth century, grants
a half-burgage, outside the East Gate (in Eastover)
towards Horsie on the west, between the burgage of
St. John's Hospital and the half-burgage of Richard
Boye, paying yearly a rose at Midsummer (St. John
Baptist's Day). How very closely, thus, in the
thirteenth century (none of the preceding documents
were of later date than that) the Church authorities and
the town-folk were bound together. These burgages
were stalls, held for the sale of goods for profit, in the
open street, and they were, it is clear, held by the
Church authorities (*vide* the above documents) as a
means of income. St. Mary's has a burgage ; William
the Vicar bequeaths one to the church ; St. John's
Hospital possesses one also. Mrs. Green, in her *Town
Life in the Fifteenth Century*, refers to this. "Monks
and heads of religious houses were, according to
Dr. Gross, excluded from citizenship, though given
rights of trade ; but from the Charter Rolls, John, 1215,
it appears that in Bridgwater the Brethren of the
Hospital of St. John were to be capable of taking up
burgages in the town and to have the same liberties
within and without the town as Burgesses. . . . In the
documents at Bridgwater there are many instances of
houses and market stalls being held by clergy. In all
the bills of sale stalls in High Street are named

burgages, and a lawsuit shows that a wool stall there was sold to the Abbot of Mulchelney." It should be noted that the brethren of St. John's Hospital were not monks; there were never any monks living in Bridgwater. But the point is, how curiously inter-mingled then were business matters and religious matters. The Church's interests were not forgotten, even when men sold goods at their stalls, and the stall of Blessed Mary took its place beside the rest.

# CHAPTER IX

## THE PARISH CHURCH

### II

THE documents which have already been quoted will sufficiently show how very much more the Church entered into town life, and the town into Church life, in mediæval days than is the case now. Religion was more *evident* then: its outer manifestations were everywhere to be seen.

"All the multitudinous activities and accidents of this common life were summed up for the people in the parish church that stood in their market-place, close to the Common House or Guild Hall. This was the fortress of the borough against its enemies—its place of safety where the treasure of the Commons was stored in dangerous times, the arms in the steeple, the wealth of corn or wool or precious goods in the church itself, guarded by a sentence of excommunication against all who should violate so sacred a protection. Its shrines were hung with the strange new things which English sailors had begun to bring across the great seas — with 'horns of unicorns,' ostrich eggs, or the rib of a whale given by Sebastian Cabot. Burghers had their seats in the church apportioned to them by the corporation in the same rank and order as the stalls which it had already assigned to them in the market-place."[1]

[1] *Town Life*, Vol. I, p. 153

# THE PARISH CHURCH

There being, however, in those days almost no literature save sacred books or manuscripts, the story of those times is really contained in the deeds or documents which were drawn up for the sale of houses, lands, or property; for proclaiming a gift or a legacy, for leasing property, making a will, gaining admission to a religious house, transferring possession to a church or a guild, or registering a mercantile transaction. The witnessing and sealing of these deeds was an important and solemn affair; responsible citizens who had a prominent share in the government of the town, or officers of some one of the guilds, were frequently chosen; also chaplains, vicars and ecclesiastics generally, as being able to read, though not always to write. It is only by sifting and analysing many hundreds of these documents that the history of the borough is evolved, and the process—especially in the case of an ancient town such as Bridgwater, so eminently rich in deeds and archives—is almost an endless one. Some specimens are here given, which will tell their own story, and will indicate the activities of the town in pre-Reformation days.

1. Lease by the burgesses of Bridgwater of five acres of land which M. bequeathed to the Mass of the B. Virgin Mary in the parish church. Dated Bruggewater, Sunday before St. George's Day, 1370.

2. Quitclaim by G. B. to R. P. of his right to a tenement which R. le M. formerly held . . . in the street between the parish church and the great bridge. Dated Sunday before the Epiphany, 1371.

3. Grant by Alice Frysell, daughter and heir of Adam Ebbott of Brughewater, to Thos. Wyldemersche, rector of the church of Chilton, of her tenement and garden in Orlones Strete. 1371.

4. Grant by L. H. and I. his wife to R. B. of rents, etc., which R. S. and A. his wife used to pay for three-fourths of a burgage in Pyneles Strete. 1371.

5. Quitclaim by G. B. and R. P. of three tenements in the borough, of which two lie near and within the west gate on the north side of the High St. between the town ditch and the tenement of Adam Leybourne, and the third tenement lies outside the said gate on the south side of the street as you go towards the park. Also two stalls in the said borough, one among the butchers' stalls and the other among the fishers' stalls. 1372.

6. Grant by Richard Cheselade and C. his wife to Richard Hyntelsham, clerk, of a half-burgage in the town, in Sainte Marie Strette, between the tenement of St. Mary and that of the Hospital of St. John the Baptist. 1372.

7. Lease by Walter Taillour and John Brouke, wardens of the goods and lights of Holy Cross in the parish church of Bruggewater, to J. R. and M. his wife and John their son, of a house in the street of the Friars Minor, at a yearly rent of 6s. 8d. 1373.

8. Quitclaim by Henry Rodmour; John Comyn, vicar perpetual of the church of Briggewater; Robert Northover and William Mareys, chaplains, to Rob. Plumptone of right to five acres of arable land in Donewere. 1373.

9. Grant by Isabella Ede, late wife of Thos. Ede, to Dominus Walter Toni and Dominus Robert the chaplain of Robert Plumpton, chaplains of Bruggewater, of all her lands and tenements within and without the town. 1374.

10. Grant on lease by Joan Hentylsham, widow, to Walter Keble and Edith his wife of a garden in Saint Marie Stret between the tenement of Wm. Cryche called "Jorgesen"[1] and that of John Payn, for their lives, at a yearly rent of 4d. Witnesses: Wm Cryche, John Lof, Hugh Mareys, Wm. Blacche. 1380.

11. Grant by Thos. Cronyle to the chaplain of the Blessed Mary of the church of Bryggewater of 2s. 4d. quit-rent out of his lands and tenements, for celebrating services for the souls of his father, and his mother, and his own soul. The rent to be held during the term of life of Margery his wife, and of Florence, Margery and Alice, his daughters; twenty-eight Masses to be said yearly. With power to distrain on eight acres of arable land at North Bowre. Easter Eve, 1380.

[1] The George Inn

12. Jordan Parmentar grants to God, St. Mary and All Saints' (i.e. the parish church) a yearly rent of 2s. from a house on the south side of St. Mary's Church . . . viz. 12d. for the Mass, 12d. for lights before the cross, for the souls of his relatives. Witnesses: Brother Geoffrey, master of St. John's Hospital, Brugeswalteri; Walter de Stocklinche, vicar of the church; and others. 1296.

O 13. Grant by the corporation to Richard Maidus of liberty to build over the west gate and the place thereto belonging, towards the east as far as the corner of the house late belonging to Roger le Seynmere, as may be best for his use and for defence of the town; with power reserved for evacuation thereof in time of war or need. Witnesses: Thos. de Morf, steward of the Lady Matillis de Mortimer, whose assent to the premises has been given; Dominus Walter de Stocklinche, vicar of the town; John Enesone, David le Palmere, provosts; Walt. Jacob, John le King, sergeants; etc. Feast of St. John ante Port. Lat. 1279.

14. Grant by Thos. Goldsmyth to David Kelyng, chaplain, of half a burgage in Seynte Marie Strete, between the house of the chaplain of the Blessed Mary of Bridgwater and the tenement of the master and brethren of St. John's Hospital. 1349.

15. Quitclaim by John de Chedesye to the custodians of the light of the B.V.M. of Bridgwater, towards the support of the Mass and the light of the B. Virgin in the parish church, for the salvation of his soul, the soul of Alice his late wife, and their ancestry, of a tenement in the town situated in Seyntmariestret, opposite the south door of the parish church.[1] Dated 1346.

16. Richard Maydous grants to his son John, a chaplain, a tenement in the town between the town ditch and a tenement of Richard, the grantor's son. Also all the grantor's goods, moveable and immoveable, in Bridgwater. Dated 1325.

17. In a document of the same date as the last is a curious phrase, where the River Parret is called "The water of Perred."

18. In a deed dated 1344 the witnesses are Robert de Boun, constable of the Castle; Ralph Pope, Edw. Babbe, provosts of the town; Gilbert Large, John Bosshel, bailiffs.

[1] This is where the vicar of Bridgwater afterwards lived.

19. A curious parchment. Edward Erl of Marche, Rich. Erl of Warewic, and Richard Erl of Salisbury, to all manner of men, greeting. We, on the King's behalf, charge and command you, and on our own desire, and pray you that ye neither hurt, vex, nor trouble, "pille, robbe, ne despoile, Johan Davy of Brigewater, marchaunte, ne eny of his servauntes or tenauntes, ne take eny of their goodes, whersomever thei bee or canne bee founde, as ye wol eschewe the Kyngges high displeasyd and our hevy lordshipe; but to suffre theim to peasably to ryde, goo, and abide in such places as may bee unto their ease and profit; for as mouche as we have takene the said Johan, as above, undre our tuicion and savegarde." Date between 1455 and 1460.

20. Perpetual lease or fee farm by the burgesses to William le Large of two seldae or shops in the High Street, which premises William formerly vicar of Brugeswalteri bequeathed to St. Mary's Mass in the same town, at a yearly rent of 10s., to the service of the Mass of St. Mary and of the Hospital House of St. John Baptist. This document is late thirteenth century, and bears the seal of the churchwardens.

21. A deed mentioned in Hugo's *Nunneries of Somerset* states that Robt. Hyll, late of the parish of Canyngton, tayllour, was charged before the King's justices for certain thefts. After a lengthy investigation before John Pykman, Archdeacon of Bath, and John Lugwardyn, Succentor of Wells, he was pronounced by a jury not guilty, and was declared to be restored to his former estate and good name. The Bishop issued a mandate to the Dean of Briggewater,[1] the curate of Canington, and John Bartilmewe, apparitor, for the proclamation of the purgation of the said Robert to be made in the parish church of Canyngton, and in the cathedral church and public market-place of Wells. Dated at Dogmersfield, 12th October, 1501.

22. The Archbishop of Canterbury issued his mandate, dated Monkton (in Kent) 20th November, 1331, that notice of his intended visitation should be given in the cathedral churches of Bath and Wells, in all conventual and collegiate churches, and in six of the most important parish churches

---

[1] This means that the vicar of Bridgwater was Rural Dean.

in the diocese. The Bishop remits a certificate of such publication in the churches ordered, and among them the conventual churches of Taunton, Athelneye, Canyngton and Barewe ; and the parish churches of Taunton, Bruggewalter and Pedyrton.

23. Note of the Assizes being held at Bruggewater, on Monday in the second week in Lent, 15 Edward III, 5th March, 1340-1.

24. A perpetual chantry was founded in the chapel of St. Peter in the court-house at Nyweton (North Newton). Certain possessions were granted to William de Hylpynton, the chaplain or chantry priest. A doubt arose touching the foundation and status of the chantry of Newton Plecy in the year 1418 on the appointment thereto of Richard Wyving. This resulted in the holding of an inquisition, in the parish church of Bruggewater, to determine the question. The inquisition was held before John Storthwayt, LL.B., Bishop's Commissary, and the following jurors : William Andergate, rector of Otterhampton ; Richard Lorgh, rector of Cherdelynch ; John Coors, vicar of Bruggewater ; Wm. Clyve, vicar of Canyngton ; John Obba, vicar of Leng ; John Hancock, rector of Chilton ; Robert Molang, rector of Enemere ; John Sliper, chaplain of the chantry of B.V.M. in the church of Bruggewater, and seven laymen. They returned on oath. that there was a chantry long ago erected in the chapel of St. Peter within the court-house of Newton Fforestars, otherwise called Newton Plecy : that it was a chantry, and not a free chapel or a parish church . . . that the chantry was not taxed, and was of the annual value of 100 shillings.

25. Memorandum. Taunton and Bridgwater were the chief of the disaffected districts (about 1498) "in the cause of the young Richard, styled an impostor, but more likely the veritable son of Edward IV." His cause was warmly espoused in the west counties of England. After his overthrow in 1498 a commission was sent to make inquiry. (This was Perkin Warbeck's rebellion.)

26. Commission of oyer and terminer to John de Stonore and others, on complaint of John Inge that Nicholas de Boneville, Lewis, parson of the church of Coumartyn, Adam de Leghe of Bruggewater, and others imprisoned him at Welynton, brought him so imprisoned to Stoweye, there detained him until he made fine with him by £50 in goods

and £500 in money by tale for his deliverance, and carried away his goods at the said town of Welynton. 1341.

27. Pardon, at the supplication of William, Archbishop of Canterbury, to Nicholas Frompton, chaplain, alias vicar of Brygewater, for all treasons and felonies committed by him in the late insurrection between 1 May and All Saints, provided that he did not kill Simon, late Archbishop, Robert Hales, or John de Cavendish, without prejudice to the recovery of damages against him by parties damnified in the said insurrection. 1382. (This refers to the murder of Archbishop Simon of Sudbury, under Wat Tyler, who led the peasants' revolt of 1381. Frompton was never vicar of Bridgwater.)

28. Grant by Thos. Fichet, Lord of Spaxtone, to the wardens of the light of the Blessed Mary of Briggewater, for support of the Mass and Light of the Blessed Mary in the parish church, for the health of his soul . . . of a tenement in Damyetestrete near the bridge called Vroggelandsbrigge, on the north side, between the tenements of John Purchatz and Thomas le Porter in length, and from the highway leading from another street called Vrogglane to the house which Walter de Eston holds of the grantor, in breadth. Witness, Henry, rector of Spaxtone, and others. 1344.

29. An attestation made by William Tredewyn, priest, of North Newton, within the parish of North Petherton. He declares that in his youth he was continually abiding in the vicarage of Briggewater, with one Sir John Wheler, parish priest of the said town (he was a chaplain), to learn, read and sing with the said Sir John Wheler, at the commandment of Mr. Sir John Colswayne, vicar of the said town. Date about 1480. (This document shows that the vicars exercised a wholesome discipline over the chaplains in requiring them to teach reading and singing.)

30. Decree of Thomas Overay, bachelor of laws, precentor of Wells Cathedral, stating that at a court held in Bridgwater church, over which, by the authority of Robert, Bishop of Bath and Wells, he was presiding, Edward Perys, of the parish of North Petherton, appeared and stated that he had been falsely accused of stealing a mare belonging to the abbey of Athelney, offering to clear himself of the charge ; that no one appeared for the purpose of contradict-

ing his statement, and that therefore the said Thomas Overay hereby declares and testifies that he is cleared, and restored to his former good name. 23rd November, 1475.

These deeds convey some idea of the various purposes to which a parish church was put in olden days, and they show that its use was by no means restricted to the holding of religious services. The town guilds had their chapels within the church, and frequently their special chaplains (*capellani annuellarii*) ministered at them. The guilds, religious as they were in spirit, were also in many cases great municipal institutions. In 1392 the seneschals of the Merchants' Guild of Bridgwater and of the community of the same town obtained a grant to assign certain lands in mortmain; and an indenture, which probably belongs to the beginning of the reign of Edward I, proves that there was a close relation of this guild on one side to the fraternity of St. Mary or of the Holy Cross, and on the other to the corporation of the town. The Brotherhood of the Holy Cross at Abingdon, which was established under Richard II, seems to have been practically the governing body of the borough, owned most of the land property in the town in the fifteenth century, and spent money liberally in the building of churches and the market cross.[1] The inhabitants were responsible for the maintenance of the body and tower of their church, and this was usually raised by a proportionate tax on the various properties in the parish. The bishops at that time possessed ample powers in the matter of church building, repairing, and even enlarging, and they could always at their visitations require that these things should be done. In the fourteenth century—a time of great prosperity

[1] *Town Life*, Vol. II, p. 214.

in Somerset—immense church building was undertaken, and many of the splendid towers in the diocese
were built then. A great deal of new work was done
in Bridgwater in 1366–7, probably including the building of the spire. Archbishop Walter Gray, of York,
*circ.* 1250, ordered as follows within his diocese.

We ordain and appoint that the parishioners provide a
chalice, missal, the principal vestment of the church, viz. a
chasuble, white albe, amice, stole, maniple, zone, with three
towels, a corporal, and other decent vestments for the
deacon and sub-deacon, according to the means of the
parishioners and of the church, together with a principal
silk cope for chief festivals, and with two others for the
rulers of the choir in the foresaid festivals, a processional
cross and another smaller cross for the dead, and a bier for
the dead, a vase for holy water, an osculatory, a candlestick
for the Paschal candle, a thurible, a lantern with a bell, a
Lent veil, two candlesticks for the taper bearers; of books,
a Legendary, Antiphonary, Gradual, Psalter, Topiary, Ordi-
nale, Missal, Manual; a frontal to the great altar, three
surplices, a suitable pyx for the "Corpus Christi," a
banner for the Rogations, great bells with their ropes,
a holy font with fastening, a chrismatory, images in
the church, and the principal image in the church of the
person to whom the church is dedicated, the repair of
books and vestments so often as they require repair;
and in addition to all the aforesaid things a light in the
church, the repair of the nave of the church, with its bell-
tower, internally and externally, viz. with glass windows,
with the enclosure of the cemetery, with other things belonging to the nave of the church, and other things which by
custom belong to the parishioners. To the rectors or vicars
belong all other things according to various ordinances, viz.
the principal chancel, with its repairs both in walls and roofs
and glass windows belonging to the same, with desks and
forms and other ornaments suitable.

That these directions were usually obeyed is shown
by a list of the Bridgwater churchwardens' possessions
pertaining to the church at the middle of the fifteenth

century.[1] It affords a fair idea of the gorgeous vestments, and the number of them, which were held to be
needful for worship in a large parish church four and
a half centuries ago.

On Sunday the services were, generally, three:
Matins, Mass, and Evensong. The first, answering to
our morning prayer, would usually be at about eight
o'clock in the morning. It was followed by the
Eucharistic service, more usually known to ourselves
as, and corresponding to, the office of the Holy Communion, most likely at nine o'clock. This latter
service was not solemnized after noon. Evensong, or
evening prayer, was held during the afternoon. Both
Matins and Evensong were accumulations of the monastic offices known as the Hours, just as our own
corresponding services at 11 a.m. and at 6.30 p.m.
are now practically a condensation of certain of the
"Hours" services. These services were well attended

[1] Churchwardens' lists of Church ornaments and vestments at St.
Mary's, 1447: "The delyverauns of the Goodys of the Chirchis of
Briggwater, by the Vycary William atte Well, Johan Sely, and others,
to Johan Martyne and William Snothe, Wardens of the seidechirche,
the yere of oure Lord MCCCCXLVII°, the IIII day off October·—In primis,
i crosse with II ymages of Mare and Johan, of sylvere and gylte. Item,
i ffote and i staffe to the same crosse, of coper and gylte. Item, i de-
monstracion [monstrance, or ostensory] for the Sacremente, off silvere
and gylte. Item, ii sensurys off sylvere, with II casis. Item, III chalys
of sylvere and gylte Item, II crewetes of sylvere Item, II candel-
stikkes of sylvere Item, i crismatory of sylvere gylte. Item, i schip
[incense boat] off sylvere. Item, II crossis of latone and gylte. Item,
vi corporas. Item, iiii. casis. Item, i rede purse of veluet with I
corporas ther in. Item, I relique of Seynt Stephyn, closed in sylvere.
Item, II coupis of sylvere for the Sacremente. Item, i box of latone for
the Sacrement. Item, II candlestikkes of latone. Item, broke sylvere
in a box. Item, i holy waterboket, with a spryngell of latone. Item,
iii massebokys. Item, a Grayles [Gradal]. Item, II Proceessionaries.
Item, i Pystolar [Epistolar]. Item, i Colitare [Collectary] Item, I Morty-
lage [Martyrology]. Item, I Antiphoner tofore Seynt Mare preste. Item,
i Portas [Portehors, or Portifory] of the bequest of Will. Hurste. Item, i
Antiphoner before the Dekyn Item, i Manuell. Item, I Ordynal Item,
i seute of vestements callid the gylte seute. Item, II copis, i chesepill
[chesuble], II tunyclis with other ornamentes of blew veluet, with lipardys
hedys of golde, that Alexander Hody yaffe inne [gave in]. Item, i cope of

131

in the main, partly from choice, partly from compulsion. Men at times were sentenced to perform penance for working on Sundays. One form of penance was that they should publicly precede the procession, barefoot, on the Sunday in church. It was a public punishment, and it had its effect.

The Bidding Prayer was usually said before the sermon. It was a compilation (in some ways) of great dignity and beauty, and was highly popular. One clause ran : "Ye shall make a special prayer for your fathers' souls and for your mothers' souls, godfathers' souls and godmothers' souls, brothers' souls and sisters', souls, and for all your elders' souls, and for all the souls that you and I be bound to pray for, and specially for all the souls buried in this church or in this churchyard or any other holy place ; and in especial for all the souls that bide the great mercy of Almighty God in the bitter pains of purgatory, that God for His great

white damaske with eglis of gold displayed, that Johan Cosyn yaf inne. Item, i hole seute of clothe of golde callid Boundys seute  Item, i seute of grene sylke, callid Hurstys vestementes. Item, ii rede copis for chauntours. Item, ii yelow copis for chauntours of borde Alexander [?colour of sandal-wood]. Item, i seute of grene sylke withoute cope. Item, iii copis, i chesepill, ii tunychs with sterris [stars] of sylke. Item, ii olde grene copis. Item, i olde pall of sylke. Item, i olde cope of purpur. Item, i auterclothe of rede damaske. Item, i veyle for Lente. Item, alle thapareyll for the hye auter of conterfet damaske, with lipardes of golde. Item, i clothe to hange aboue the hye auter with the xii Appostolis Item, ii dex [desk] clothis  Item, v auter clothis, with v ffrountelles. Item, i seute of ray [striped] grene sylke. Item, i Sepulcre clothe. Item, i peynted clothe of rede, with i ymage offe oure Lady. Item, iii coverlytes, bad and gode. Item, xvi pilowys of sylke  Item, x auter clothis of playne and napery. Item, xviii towelles playne and disperid. Item, ii auter clothis dysteyned, of the Assumpcioun offe oure Lady. Item, i auter clothe of the Passioun ; i peyre of white vestementes for Lente ; i white cloth for the hie auter for Lente, with ii curteyns of bustian to the same ; i white tynacle of fustian , i white cloth for the high auter, with a crosse of blew bokeram , i stenyd cloth to hang by for the auter, yn the rode lofte. Item, there lackyth iii towellys ; i white cloth to hang by fore the crosse yn the rode lofte ; i old Lent cloth to be put uppone Sent George."

Endorsed—"Bonorum Ecclesiæ de Brigwater" (Bridgwater documents).

mercy release them of their pain if it be His blessed will. And that our prayers may somewhat stand them in stead, every man and woman of your church help them with a Pater Noster and an Ave Maria." Connected with the Bidding Prayer was the recitation of the Bede Roll, when the priest read out the names of those who had lately died, and commended them to the prayers of the people.

Popular, also, from a spectacular point of view, was the Litany. It was recited in Latin, frequently in the afternoon. The priest and clerks, preceded by cross and censer, marched in procession round about the church, while one would sing the petitions. The response, *Sancte Maria* (or some other saint), *ora pro nobis*, was at least understanded of the people, and was highly appreciated by them. If it chanced that some penitent should be sentenced to walk in front, clad in penitential garb, it may be that additional zest was given to the occasion.

At St. Mary's, where there were many altars, chantries and chaplains, the services on Sunday—other than those conducted by the parish priest or his assistant—might be numerous. One or more of the guilds might attend at their own altar, ministered to by their own chaplain. The chantry priests would certainly have to recite the Mass for the founder of their chantry, and some of the members of his family, or his friends, would be very likely to be present. Thus various services of this nature would be proceeding in different chapels and at various altars in the church all the morning, save that on Sundays and festival days no priest might begin his service until the gospel of the principal service, at the parish altar, was concluded.[1]

[1] There is no reason to think that simultaneous services at various altars in the church were not held (as in continental churches to-day)

There was certainly less preaching then than now, and it was of a different scope. Abundance of instructions were issued to the clergy for their sermons, many of which consisted of analyses of sin, of direct and plain exhortation to their flocks to abstain from certain vices, with a full statement of the consequences which would follow upon impenitence. The Lambeth Synod of 1281 says: "We do ordain that every priest who presides over a people do four times a year, that is, once in each quarter of a year, on one or more festival days, either by himself or by another, expound to the people in popular language without any fanciful subtlety, the 14 articles of Faith, the 10 commandments of the Lord, the 2 evangelical precepts of charity, the 7 works of mercy, the 7 deadly sins with their progeny, the 7 principal virtues, and the 7 sacraments of grace. And in order that no one may excuse himself from this on account of ignorance, though all ministers of the Church ought to know them, we have here with great brevity summed them up." Then follow the particular directions. The preaching was at times sparse; it tended to become the one thing left out. Education was at a very low ebb; the people knew very little; the litanies and Masses were more popular than sermons, even if these were delivered "without any fanciful subtlety." The time of sermons was not yet; it came later. Nevertheless the authorities continually urged them, and sometimes the bishop would send a great preacher round the diocese to preach. All persons who were of age, and not under sentence of excommunication, were communicants, and the great Mass of the year was on Easter Day. Every one was

subject to the restriction about the parish altar. It is probable that groups of worshippers in the different chapels were hearing Mass at the same time.

CORPORATION SCREEN, ST. MARY'S CHURCH

*Facing page* 134

expected to communicate then, and to confess at the least once a year before Easter. The devout did so more frequently.

By the time the sixteenth century had come it was evident that there were many abuses in the Church system, as, indeed, there are in every system. But the Papal supremacy was an intolerable yoke; it had to go. Rome had too much to say in the matter of appointments to offices in the English Church; her officials swarmed everywhere. Nevertheless the Reformation was far more a political than a doctrinal movement at the outset. Henry VIII had many schemes of his own; some were wise and some were vastly foolish, but his determination to be master within his own realm was necessary. Out of it all the rest sprang. Friars, monks, chantry priests—all had to go. But the parish priests could not be turned out. English people had borne much; they would not bear that. They were religious folk after their kind; to have no religious services in the beautiful parish churches which their forefathers had built, and which they had known from infancy, would have been abhorrent to them. So in the great upheaval—some of which was moral, some of which was doctrinal, and most of which was political— when every religious institution in England was shaken to its foundations, the parish priests retained their position in the churches of the land.

In Bridgwater they were quiet and good men on the whole. Frail, no doubt, with all the frailty of erring human nature, but yet popular. They were continually in touch with the people. The vicar's house was in St. Mary's Street, opposite the south porch, very near to that of the chaplain of St. Mary's Chantry. In fact, the four groups of men who represented the officials of the church within the town—the Friars, the Augustinian Canons, the Chantry Priests and Chaplains, and the Vicars—fraternized thoroughly and well. It is a popular delusion, frequently advanced, that it was otherwise, yet it *is* a delusion. There was greater religious unity before the Reformation than ever came after it.

Of the vicars of Bridgwater, those who were here after the founding of St. John's Hospital were appointed to their office by the master and brethren of that house. After the Reformation (with a significant exception at the time of the Commonwealth, of which more anon) they were nominated by the reigning sovereign. This is still the case, save that the appointment, which yet runs in the King's name, is by law vested in the Lord Chancellor. The names of the original rectors of the parish have not been preserved, and it is not definitely known who acted as patrons of the living in the days from Walter de Douai to William Briwere.

Thus the parish church is the oldest and most venerable building and institution in the town. It was here when first we hear of Brugie under Merleswain; it has maintained its offices ever since. It came, and saw the town and castle grow up all around it. The town has expanded; the castle has gone. The thoughts of men have widened with the process of the suns, and religious thought has grown, as everything else has grown. There is an evolution, not in the revelation of things divine, but in men's apprehension and conception of them. Hence the presentation of religious truth, in its outward manifestations, changes with the stride of the passing years.

The following is the most complete ascertained list of vicars of Bridgwater now available. The term vicar is not necessarily used technically, but as the *Vicarius* of a rectory which subsidized, first, the priory of Bath; secondly, as is supposed, the abbey of Marmoutiers; and thirdly the Augustinian House of St. John in Bridgwater. Ordination of vicarages did not as a rule take place until the thirteenth century was well advanced, and sometimes even later. The Lateran Council of 1213 decreed that all appropriators should appoint, and competently maintain, perpetual vicars.

| | | | |
|---|---|---|---|
| Ralph, the Clerk of Bruges | 1170 | Henry Willes . . . | 1594 |
| William . . . | | John Devenish . . | 1605 |
| James . . . . | 1245 | George Wotton (Canonical | |
| Walter de Stocklinche . | 1296 | Vicar) . . . | 1644 |
| Walterus . . . | 1309 | John Norman (Minister under | |
| John Paris . . . | 1316 | the Commonwealth) . . | |
| John de Torrebrian . | 1340 | George Wotton (restored to | |
| Richard de Exbrugh . | 1348 | his benefice) . . . | |
| John Bodeley . . | 1373 | William Aleyn, A.M. . | 1669 |
| John Comyn . . | | Benjamin Bulkley, A.M. . | 1720 |
| Wm. Hurst . . . | 1389 | Laurence Payn . . | 1723 |
| John Cors . . . | 1415 | Moses Williams . . | 1732 |
| John Coswayn . . | 1423 | John Coles . . . | 1742 |
| John Coswayn . . | 1431 | George Rawley . . | 1785 |
| Richard Croke . . | 1474 | William Wollen . . | 1785 |
| Frater Thos. Spencer . | 1498 | James Wollen . . | 1822 |
| Robt. Mitchel (in decretis bac.) | 1499 | Daniel Nihill . . | 1844 |
| John Hooper, A.M. . | 1520 | Thomas George James | 1848 |
| Olyver Smyth . . | 1522 | Michael Ferrabee Sadler | 1856 |
| Thomas Strete . . | 1528 | William George Fitzgerald . | 1864 |
| Edward Craftes . . | 1571 | William H. H. Bircham . | 1896 |
| Cadwallader Hughes . | 1593 | Arthur Herbert Powell . | 1901 |

# CHAPTER X

## THE CHANTRIES AND CHANTRY PRIESTS
## OF ST. MARY'S

### THE CHANTRIES OF ST. MARY'S

IN the fourteenth and fifteenth centuries it became greatly the fashion in England to found chantries. Nearly all the mediæval towns shared in this custom, and Bridgwater formed no exception to the rule. The immediate purpose of the founder was that he should receive the special prayers of the Church for his soul, the souls of his family and ancestors, and generally speaking for the souls of all Christian people. In order to secure these benefits he would provide the maintenance for a priest, or for two priests, who should continue their good offices for him after death, and if the chantry were endowed *in perpetuam* it was intended that these religious intercessions should continue to be offered. When the chantry priest died, the heir or representatives of the founder would appoint some priest as successor, and so the prayers would be perpetuated. This idea of establishing religious foundations for the special purpose of securing the constant prayers of those who were to minister thereat was not the original ideal at all. If a man, say in the eleventh century, built and endowed a church, he would naturally expect to have the good offices of its ministers, and this would not be denied him. But this was implied rather than expressed; it was the pious and general feeling of the time. The foundation deeds of earlier churches and institutions, indeed, mostly stated that the founder had established them for some such purposes, but they were general rather than particular. The chantry founder, on the contrary, intended that the chantry priest for whom he made provision should regard it as his first and supreme duty to pray for the souls of the founder and the founder's kith and kin. Thus a strong element of individualism crept in : a method of securing special spiritual privileges as a consequence of certain endowments supplied.

Other ideas were mixed with these ; notably the desire not to be forgotten on earth after this life was over. This feeling was intensely strong ; it lasted for many centuries in England. For this purpose, amongst others, obits, anniversaries and trentalls were established. An obit was a religious service held every year to commemorate the founder's death, when alms were distributed and petitions were offered up for the soul of the deceased person. It partook of the nature of a private service, usually taking place at a side altar, or at the special altar of the chantry itself. An obit might last for a term of years, or, as the wills sometimes stated, for ever. Anniversaries were magnified obits, more sumptuous in their surroundings, more public in their character, and more costly. They, too, were yearly commemorations of the founder's death, and it was permissible to celebrate them at the high altar of the church. Trentalls were thirty Masses for the deceased, one Mass to be said every day for thirty days consecutively.

These chantry services were secured not only by wealthy individuals, they were frequently supplied at the instigation of the great town guilds or fraternities.

Some of these guilds were purely religious, others were not. But they all provided that Masses and prayers for the souls of deceased brethren should be said after their death, and the attendance of members of the guild at the funeral was encouraged. Thus the poor had their chance as well as the rich ; hence the great popularity of these guilds. Some of the Bridgwater guilds had their own chaplain, whose duty it was specially to carry out these duties. These varying plans and purposes may serve to account for the fact that two thousand chantries were founded in England between the thirteenth and the sixteenth centuries.[1]

Connected with the chantries were lights, lamps and oratories. An oratory was usually a small domestic chapel attached to (or within) a manor-house or castle (specially, though not always, when the house was far away from the parish church). They were for the use of the family and household, the rights of the parish priest being always carefully preserved. Lights were usually placed before the image of some saint (either a picture or a carving in wood or stone) in order to honour the saints, and generally as a pious act. Lamps were more permanent and more important than lights, and frequently had small endowments to maintain them. Chedzoy had a light in the parish church, maintained by lands and tenements "in the tenure of sondery persones," of the annual value of 6s. 2d. ; North Petherton had the same ; Stokegurcy had a light and obit maintained at the annual cost of 10s. 2d. ; and Lilstock Chapel possessed lights maintained by cattle given, value 13s. 4d. East Quantockshead and Kilve both were provided with lights, and Goathurst with an endowment for an obit.

[1] Dr. Cutt's *Parish Priests and their People*, p. 442.

# THE CHANTRIES AND CHANTRY PRIESTS

Bridgwater possessed three endowed chantries within the parish church, that of St. George, of the Holy Trinity, and of St. Mary. St. George's Chantry was fairly well endowed. Its rental (according to Edward's VI's Commission of 1548) coming from twenty-seven items of property—land, houses, workshops, burgages, and other property in Bridgwater and Chilton—amounted in the gross to £7. 4s. 8d. From this gross value three deductions had to be made, thus: Rent resolute to the king as of the monastery of Athelney, per annum, 4s.; to a certain Mr. Michell, per annum, 4d.; paid to the bailiff of the borough of Bridgwater, 17s. 10d. Thus the net annual value came to £6. 2s. 6d.

Holy Trinity Chantry had even more possessions. Forty-four items of property yielded a gross annual rent of £10. 18s. 7d.; net £9. 14s. 8d. St. Mary's Chantry yielded a net rental of £8. 0s. 8d. Allowing for the change in the value of money, St. George's Chantry had an income of about £122; Holy Trinity of £195; and St. Mary's of £160. 10s. This is reckoning the shilling of that day as being equal in value to £1 of our money. The three chantries together thus possessed an endowment of about £477, which, be it remembered, came from the free gifts of churchpeople. There never was any sort of compulsion about founding a chantry. The stipends of the then chantry priests would amount (in our money) on an average to £159 each per annum, which cannot be put down as a very exorbitant sum. They were secular priests (not professed, as monks), and there is evidence to show that they were popular men. It was their duty to minister at the altars in their respective chantries, and to observe all obits, anniversaries and other religious services appertaining to the founder's scheme, or to

any subsequent benefaction. As well as the three
chantries, the Commission takes account of "an annual
rent given as well to the use and observance of an
anniversary held in the parish church there, as to the
use and maintenance of a light there perpetually burning." For the maintenance of these the mayor, bailiff
and burgesses of Bridgwater aforesaid render annually
from the profits and revenues of "certain their lands
lying in Stower Estover in the county of Dorset in the
tenure of Thomas Bolston,[1] per ann. xiii shillings."[2]

St. Mary's Chantry came to be founded by a Bridgwater lady in a really romantic way. There was living
in the town, in the fourteenth century, a family named
Parewastel, whose name is fortunately preserved in the
documents. A member of this family, named Isolda,
went out to the Holy Land upon a pilgrimage. Such
pilgrimages were not unusual—as, for instance, to
St. James of Compostella,[3] in Spain; to St. Thomas'
shrine at Canterbury; or to Our Lady of Walsingham.
Few, however, went to the Holy Land; it was too
great a journey. But Isolda went, and for three years
"she daily visited the Lord's sepulchre, and other
holy places of the Holy Land." Alas! a sore trial
overtook her there. She was "stripped, and placed
head downwards on a rack, and beaten; then, half
dead, she miraculously escaped from the Saracens."
Happily, she at length got safely back home, and then
she petitioned the Pope to be allowed to build a chapel

[1] The Balston family is now settled in Kent. Mr. R. J. Balston was
High Sheriff of Kent a few years ago.
[2] Somerset Record Society, Vol. II, p. 237.
[3] Thomas de Stanton, clerk, going a pilgrimage to Santiago,
nominates Thomas de Heppeworth and John de Bruggewater, clerk, his
attorneys in England for one year. Oct. 7th, 1331. (Bridgwater documents ) Gilbert Russel (A D. 1317) leaves to the man who shall make a
pilgrimage for him to St. James of Compostella, and to Rochemadour,
40 shillings. Historical MSS. Commission, 1872, p. 315

at Bridgwater in honour of the Blessed Virgin, and for
her soul's health, and for those of her ancestors; and
to endow it with a yearly rent of 36 florins. "She
therefore prays for licence to found and endow the
same, and to reserve the right of patronage to herself
and her heirs." Urban V, who was then at Avignon,
returned answer, "Put up an altar in the church of
the parish in which you wished to build and found the
chapel." Isolda at once set about founding her chantry,
and presently completed it. Later she urged yet
another request, viz. that relaxation of a year and
forty days of enjoined penance should be granted to
such penitents as should visit the altar of the chantry
of St. Mary at the time of the feasts ordered by the
Chancery. This petition was also granted. The
incident casts an interesting side-light upon mediæval
life. One wonders if the fair Isolda had been crossed
in love, or what it was that sent her out to Jerusalem,
the land of the dreadful infidel and Saracen? Her
secret is safe now, and the chantry she so loved to
found passed out of existence three hundred and fifty
years ago.[1]

Two Bridgwater documents exist which refer to the
Parewastels. One, dated 1321, is a grant by Nicholas
Prymeson to John Parewastel and Isota (Isolda), his
sister, of two parts of a third part of a burgage in
Horlokestrete, between the tenement of the master of
St. John's Hospital, on the south, and that of John de
Cloteworthi, on the north. The other is a grant by
Isolda to Robert Croyl of the same property. The
date is torn off: it is some time in the reign of
Edward III. Her plea to Rome was favourably
answered in 1366, and so the grant she made to
Robert Croyl may have been part of her financial

[1] Papal Registers, 1342-1419.

143

arrangements for her new chantry. Isolda probably sleeps beneath the pavement of St. Mary's Chantry, very likely under the very place where the altar once stood.

Chantry priests were not necessarily obliged to assist the parish priest in his work; this depended entirely upon the terms of their appointment. Frequently they did so, becoming an addition (in large town churches) to the parochial staff; sometimes they helped in out-lying districts. But their own special duties implied constant services, which might not be omitted. The following document well illustrates the position and duties of a chantry priest, and the great care which is evident in its construction shows how thoroughly the entire system was planned out.

To all the sons of the Holy Mother Church to whom the present letters shall come, John Sydenham and Walter Holmour, Seneschals of the Merchant Guild of the town of Bridgewater and the commonalty of the same town, in the diocese of Bath and Wells, greeting in the Lord everlasting. Know all of you that, by the special licence of our most illustrious prince and lord the lord Richard the second by the grace of God King of England, to us granted in this behalf, the statute of mortmain notwithstanding, we John and Walter, Seneschals, and the commonalty abovesaid do give, grant, and by this our present charter confirm to Sir Robert Northovere, chaplain of the chantry of the Blessed Mary in the parish church of Bridgewater aforesaid, who now is, and to the successors of the said Sir Robert Northovere, chap-lain in the chantry aforesaid, in aid of their maintenance for ever, and to perform and celebrate services or divine offices, and to sustain the other charges below-written in the aforesaid parish church every year for ever—10 messu-ages, 5 acres of land, 3 acres of meadow, and 40 solidates of yearly rent, with their appurtenances, in Bridgewater. To have and to hold to himself Sir Robert Northovere, chaplain of the chantry aforesaid, who now is, and to his successors chaplains of the said chantry in aid of their maintenance for ever, to perform and celebrate offices or divine services in the aforesaid parish church, and to maintain the other charges, as is abovesaid, for ever. Rendering therefor yearly to the chief lords of that fee the services therefor due and accustomed. And we John and Walter, Seneschals, and the commonalty abovesaid, our heirs and successors, are bound to warrant, acquit, and defend the aforesaid 10 messuages, 5 acres of land, 3 acres of meadow, and 40 solidates of yearly rent with the appurtenances in Bridgewater aforesaid to the same Sir Robert Northovere, chaplain, and his successors chaplains of the said chantry against all men under the manner and form aforesaid for ever. Reserving to us the Seneschals and to our successors for ever the faculty of presenting a fit chaplain confirmed in the holy order of priesthood to the said chantry as often as and when it shall be void for a chaplain. And the charges which the chaplain of the said chantry who for the time shall be ought to sustain and support, and the offices which he ought to celebrate or perform, whereof mention is made above, are these.—Namely, that the chaplain of the said chantry whosoever, who for the time shall be, ought to reside therein continually, and unless he shall be hindered by infirmity of body, as frequently as he is able, saving his honour and due devotion, to celebrate the solemnities of masses, and to be present in his surplice in the choir of the said parish church daily at all canonical hours together with his clerk fitting therefor, whom the same chaplain shall provide for this at his own costs and expenses only and entirely. And therefor the same chaplain shall have and also occupy the place on the north side of the same choir next the entry of the same choir, that is to say, where the deacon of the church aforesaid formerly used to stand. And the same chaplain shall be obedient and reverend to the vicar of the said church according to what becomes his state and office. And the same chaplain shall also provide one lamp day and night for ever continually burning in the aforesaid choir, (and) thirteen tapers burning in the choir aforesaid to be renewed yearly on the vigil of the Assumption of the Blessed Mary. And the tapers aforesaid shall weigh, as often as they shall be so renewed, thirty-three pounds of wax.

*Item :*—two torches to be lighted up and to burn every day at the elevation of the Corpus Christi in saying the mass of the Blessed Mary in the aforesaid choir, of the weight of sixteen pounds, to be renewed on the vigil aforesaid every year.

*Item:*—two tapers burning at the daily mass of the Blessed Mary.

*Item:*—one wax candle burning every night whilst the antiphons are sung before the image of the Blessed Virgin Mary in the church aforesaid.

*Item:*—one attendant to watch and regulate the clock, unless he shall be willing to watch and regulate it himself; and he shall provide and maintain all the lesser or little things necessary, brass and iron, pertaining to mending and maintaining the said clock at his own costs and expenses alone and wholly. And the said chaplain shall reside where the chaplains of the said chantry in former times were wont to reside: namely in the house next the vicarage house, on the west side. And because one moiety of the wax carried down with the bodies of the dead into the parish church aforesaid and placed upon such bodies at the obsequies and on the day of their burial with small candles by an ancient laudable custom heretofore observed, from a time and by a time of the contrary whereof the memory of man is not, pertained to the vicar of the aforesaid church, and the other moiety, all small candles altogether excepted, to the chaplain of the aforesaid chantry by the disposition of us and of our ancestors parishioners of the aforesaid parish church,—we give and grant the said moiety of the wax, small candles altogether excepted, which of old pertained to the chaplain of the aforesaid chantry, as is aforesaid, to the chaplain of the said chantry who for the time shall be and to the said chantry, by the tenour of these presents, for ever, in aid of the support of the charges aforesaid.

In witness of all and singular which things we have caused our common seal to be set to these.

Dated at Bridgewater the fourth day of the month of May in the year of our Lord 1393, and in the 16th year of the reign of King Richard the second after the conquest.

In the Bridgwater documents the names of various chaplains to the chantries are scattered up and down, showing that they mixed freely in the life of the people. In the middle of the fifteenth century Thomas Hardyng, William Mersshewyll, William Cary, John Grenow (a *canonicus regularis*), Richard Smith, Richard Jarscomb, John Spenser, priests, were all familiar names in the town. In 1463 Thos. Burgeys was chaplain of the Fraternity of the Holy Trinity. Their names might be largely multiplied, but it is scarcely necessary. To St. Mary's Chantry, from 1406 to 1464, the chantry priests were appointed by the two seneschals of the Merchants' Guild of Bridgwater, whose names appear as patrons. From 1484 and onwards the patrons were the mayor, two bailiffs, and other burgesses of the town. The regular chantry priests held their office for life; the *capellani annuellarii*, of course, were chosen from time to time. Some of the chaplains were promoted to the rectory of Chilton Trinity, then entirely separate from Bridgwater. At Chilton there were parish devotions to St. Mary and St. Katherine. In 1414 Johanna Fote left to the wardens of the goods of the light of the Blessed Trinity her best brass pot, "that her soul may be had in everlasting remembrance by the brethren and sisters of the said Guild." To the same wardens she leaves as much linen thread as will make an altar-cloth for the altar of the Holy Trinity, and some property for the maintenance of a chaplain there. There were also wardens of the light of the chantry of St. Mary, and the lights of Holy Cross.[1]

There is an interesting document of Edward I's reign, written in Latin, which throws some light upon the Bridgwater guilds. It makes known—

unto all the faithful in Christ to whom these present letters shall come, that all the burgesses and the commonalty of the Burgh of Brugewater, for the promotion of love and charity,

[1] Bridgwater documents.

and the repression of strife and rancour, have ordained that they will choose yearly two Seneschals of their Guild, and one Bailiff, to attend on them; such Seneschals to have power to punish those offending against these ordinances. If any one among them shall maliciously impute to another a charge of theft, forgery, neifty ["nativitatis," the being a born bondman], murder, adultery, or excommunication, and be convicted thereof before the Seneschals aforesaid, he shall be amerced and bound to the commonalty in the sum of 12 pence, and make satisfaction to the other, at the award of his peers. No one shall implead another without the burgh, under pain of amercement. If any one shall be summoned by the bailiff to appear before the Seneschals, and neglect to do so, he is to be amerced. Those opposing execution or distress, made by the bailiff by order of the Seneschals, are to be amerced and bound to the commonalty in 40 pence, besides making due amends by award of their peers. No one in the burgh is to buy flesh or fried fish before the third hour [9 a.m.] for the purpose of regrating [retailing], under pain of becoming bound to the commonalty in the price of the flesh or fish so bought or sold. If any one is elected to the office of Seneschal of St. Mary's, or of the Holy Cross in the Church of the said burgh, or to the wardenship of the bridge of the said burgh, he shall render account for the moneys arising therefrom to the said Seneschals, whenever summoned so to do. Any person refusing any one of those offices, if elected thereto, is to be bound to the commonalty in the sum of 6s. 8d. All penalties and amercements are to be duly levied by the bailiff. The Seneschals are to render account for all moneys received by them, each year, upon the morrow of the Circumcision of our Lord.[1]

Thus were intertwined, in mediæval days, the sacred and secular interests of life.

A few miles from Bridgwater, between Cannington and Stogursey—situate within the borders of Cannington parish—stand to-day the ruins of a little chantry, which possess a most real interest for all lovers of ancient times. This is Idstock, Edstock, or

[1] Bridgwater documents. See His. Com., p 316.

THE RUINED CHAPEL OF IBSTOCK

Facing page 148

Ichestoke. The manor of Idstock, in the time of King Edward the Confessor, was held by one Ulf. A certain John held it at the time of Domesday Book, of Roger de Curcelle. It passed to the Bonvilles, and thence to the Duke of Suffolk. At the adjoining manor of Bere lived Sir William Paulet, who in 1416 founded at Idstock, "in a new chapel there erected (on the north side of an old one to the honour of the Virgin Mary), a chantry," to be served by one priest. The purpose of the chantry was the usual one, "for the health of his own soul, and the souls of his ancestors and successors"; and it was duly endowed with lands. Probably the original chapel, officially called a free chapel, was so named by reason of its having been built on what was then royal demesne. The names of thirteen successive chaplains of this remote chapel of Idstock have been preserved; Thomas Spreth, the first, in 1427, and Thomas Shakyll, who was the last, appointed in 1524.

How strangely calm and peaceful were the lives and the duties of the chaplains of Idstock! They ministered to the handful of country folk living around, and to the occupants of Bere manor. Day by day would the prayers be said for the souls of the founder and his family; day by day, in the tiny chantry whose walls still stand on the north side of the older chapel, would the chaplains kneel and intercede for their little flock. They lived far from the busy haunts of men, out of the main line of roads; a veritable hermitage.

The ruins of Idstock chapel are very humble, and they are sadly dilapidated, yet they possess an intense fascination for us. In the north wall still remains a beautiful little Early English window, but it will soon fall down. The walls are crumbling to decay; the pillars lie around; the building is roofless, and huge tendrils of ivy twine in fantastic shapes about the stones. It is almost hidden away in a wood. It bursts suddenly upon the traveller like an enchanted ruin ; one expects to hear music, and the ringing of the bell. Thomas Shakyll lived here twenty-four years, and was expelled—when chantries were dissolved—in 1548. He was then fifty years of age, and was a devoted churchman. Glastonbury Abbey, the glory of Somerset, had just fallen, and poor Thomas, out of his tiny savings, left something to build up the ruined walls. Now Glastonbury and Idstock—the great abbey and the tiny chapel—are sisters in ruin and in desolation. Yet thousands of people from all parts of the world visit the gorgeous ruins of Glastonbury : no one comes to peep at little Idstock. Few people know where it is, and Thomas Shakyll's lonely chantry has almost passed out of the ken of men.[1]

An entry in the church registers of Stockland parish, not far from Idstock, shows the confusion that arose after the Reformation, when so many chapels and chantries had been destroyed. It is a baptismal entry. "1621. Lancelot : ye son of Nicholas Burnard of Edstock Chapel in ye parish of. . . . Baptized Oct. 28." Even the name of the parish in which Idstock Chapel was situated had come, in eighty years' time, to be a matter of doubt, and so the place is left blank in the entry.[2] Yet in spite of all, the old sanctuary has not entirely lost its influence. An

[1] I carefully measured the ruins in 1904. The length of the chapel, from the east chancel wall to the west end of the nave, is about 45 ft. The chancel is 12 ft. wide ; the nave 16 ft. The chantry is a separate adjunct to the chapel on its north side, like a tiny transept. Its dimensions are 15 ft. by 9 ft. The Early English window in the chapel is 4 ft. 6 in. high by 11½ in. wide. One column from the ruin is now placed in Bridgwater Church.

[2] I am indebted for this note to the Rev. Charles W. Whistler, vicar of Stockland, who kindly sent me the extract from the registers.

inhabitant of Bere relates the finding of the dead body of a poor little child, some sixty years ago. What was to be done with it? They remembered Idstock Chapel, standing, albeit in ruins, hard by. So the little waif was laid to rest in the ground close to the old chapel walls, under the shadow of Thomas Shakyll's much-loved chantry, which had then stood desolate for three hundred years.[1]

It was in the first year of King Edward VI, 1547, that the final Act was passed which dissolved the chantries, and which gave their possessions to the Crown. Henry VIII had previously secured the passing of a similar statute, but that, characteristically enough, made its basis the consideration of property rather than of religious representation. That was Henry VIII's way. Public opinion, however, had advanced a little, and it was felt necessary to give some colour of a reason—considering what enormous sums of money had already passed from the Church to the King and his agents—for putting an end to the chantry system.

"Consydering," the Act recites, "that a greate parte of superstition and errors in Christian Religion hath byn brougt into the myndes and estimacon by reasone of the ignorance of their trewe and perfect salvacon throughe the deathe of Jesus Christ, and by devising and phantasinge vayne opynions of Purgatorye and Masses satisfactorye to be done for them which be departed, the which doctrine and vayne opinion by nothing more is mayntayned and upholden then by the abuse of Trentalles, Chauntries and other provisions for the continuance of the saide blindness and ignorance; . . . it is now ordeyned and enacted that all manner of Colleges, Free Chapelles and Chauntries, having been within five yeres next before the firste day of this present parliament[2] which were not in actuall and real possession of the late King . . .

---

[1] This story was given to me, at first hand, in 1904.
[2] The first day of Parliament was November 4th, 1547.

shall, immediately after the feast of Easter next cominge, be adjudged and deemed and allso be in the verie actuall and reall possession and seisin of the King our Soveraigne Lord and his heirs and successors."

Promises were held out in the Act that the proceeds were to be devoted to the founding of grammar schools, "and other godly purposes," excellent enough in their way. But these promises were very rarely redeemed. The property, vested nominally in the King, suffered frantic leakage. Lands were administered by certain receivers, and a vast number of private grantees became much the richer. Subtle individuals—they abounded at this period—pressed their claims, and not in vain. Some educational foundations were indeed made, but the bulk of the property—which in the case of land was not infrequently charged with periodic sums for the relief of the poor—was absorbed in other ways, entirely alien to the original purpose of the monks.

The plate and ornaments were not of very great value. St. George's Chantry at Bridgwater yielded one silver chalice, weighing seven ounces. The chantry was served by "John Saunders, clerke, of the age of 50 yeres, of honest conversacion, incumbent there." The chantry "of oure lady within the same paryshe churche" possessed a chalice of eight ounces, and the priest was "John Tollor of thage of 40 yeres incumbent ther." Trinity chantry had one chalice weighing eight ounces, and was served by "John Jugker clerke of the age of 63 yeres, compotently lerned incumbent ther." An interesting note follows. "The Vicarage ther is of the yerely value of £12. 6s. 8d." (about £246 of present money) "wherof Thomas Strete, clerke, is now incumbent, and findeth one priest under hym to mynister, and helpe to serve the cure ther, which priest celebrateth every sonday at a Chapell annixed called Horsey distant a myle from the paryshe churche. The parsonage is impropriate, and is in the kinges majesties handes. Partakers of the lordes holy sooper ther eleven hundred persones." Taking into account

# THE FOUNDATION WALLS OF
# HORSEY CHAPEL
### EXCAVATED IN 1903.

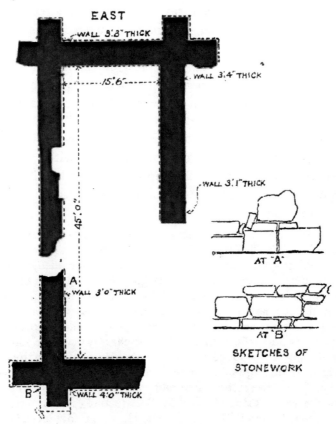

EAST

WALL 3'3" THICK

WALL 3'4" THICK

15'6"

WALL 3'1" THICK

45'0"

AT "A"

A

WALL 3'0" THICK

AT "B"

SKETCHES OF
STONEWORK

B

WALL 4'0" THICK

## PLAN.
### SCALE - 12 FEET TO ONE INCH.

that in those days all persons of age (say over fourteen years) were obliged to communicate, it is estimated that the total population of Bridgwater then would be about 1900 persons.[1]

Horsey Chapel, mentioned above, was a very ancient building, probably of the thirteenth century, and was served by the vicars of Bridgwater. It perished soon after the Reformation, and was entirely lost sight of. Three years ago, however, its site was discovered, just out of Horsey Lane, on the Bath Road. Its foundations were laid bare, and were carefully sketched and measured, as on the accompanying plan.[2] Horsey was said (by tradition) to be the mother church of Chilton, and again Idstock and Huntstile are both in Chilton parish. Chilton being now united to Bridgwater, the entire group, Chilton, Idstock, and Huntstile, have all fallen within the jurisdiction of the vicar of Bridgwater.

On the whole the chantry priests were well liked, and they enjoyed constant intercourse with the people, who frequently made them the channels for conveying alms to the poor. There is no doubt that the poor suffered for a time by their disappearance from English life. It was far more to their loss that the chantries and town guilds were swept away, than the suppression of the great abbeys. In Edward VI's reign, after all the old religious and social systems had been so ruthlessly abandoned, and nothing whatever had been devised by the State to take the place of these charities,

[1] See introduction to Vol. II of the Somerset Record Society, where the subject is considered, p. xviii. At Taunton there were 3000 communicants, corresponding to an estimated population of 5000 people This is only an estimate, but it is the nearest result obtainable.
[2] The foundation walls of Horsey Chapel were discovered and laid bare by my friend and colleague the Rev. W. M. K. Warren, who, with the aid of some of his friends, undertook the work of excavation and carried it to a successful issue.

there was great poverty in England. So much might have been done with all the proceeds ; so many excellent schemes might have been set on foot and endowed. Unhappily it was mostly frittered away, or went towards the great enrichment of noble families, and families not noble. "Edward was not so rapacious as his father," writes Mr. Archbold, "and he was but little kinder. From the chantries (of Somerset) he secured a revenue of £900 a year, while £25 would cover the total annual value of all his Somerset educational foundations."[1]

The chantry priests of St. Mary's were pensioned off with the sum of £5 each per annum, which, if the pensions had only been regularly paid, was as much as could have been expected. Thomas Shakyll received the same sum. But the after-story of many good men who were presumably granted pensions by Henry VIII and Edward VI is a very sad one, and will not bear close inspection. Too frequently the word of promise was kept unto their ear, yet broken to their hope.

For the rest, it was eventually inevitable that a system which paid men who should be employed mainly in saying so many Masses for the dead, must pass away. It was the prostitution of a noble ideal. In effect—had it not been for the guilds, who numbered many poor amongst their members—it permitted or tended to permit the wealthy to acquire, *ex hypothesi,* greater spiritual privileges than others, and to acquire them vicariously. But just as men frequently are better than their creeds, so the chantry priests were better than their system. They became excellent neighbours, kindly men, always about the town, and helpful persons generally. Public opinion was largely

[1] *Somerset Religious Houses,* p. 292.

with them, seeing that they could not be bundled out, as the Friars were, with nothing in their pockets. At least they got something with which to start life afresh, and they ceased from their work, at that fateful Eastertide, 1548, with the goodwill of many and many a household.

When the Bridgwater chantries were suppressed, and the spoils were being gathered in, the Commissioners' Report says "the inhabitantes ther make their most humble peticion to have a free grammer scole erected ther." Their humble petition was ignored, or conveniently forgotten. It was not until 1561 that a grammar school was established in the town, two reigns later, by Her Most Gracious Majesty Elizabeth, the reforming Queen.

# CHAPTER XI

## REFORMATION CHANGES

THOMAS STRETE was instituted to the vicarage of St. Mary's on August 11th, 1528, and he retained his position until 1571. He must indeed have witnessed the most remarkable changes in Bridgwater. He served under four sovereigns : Henry VIII, Edward VI, Mary, and Elizabeth ; he was there when mediæval religious customs were in full power and possession ; he lived to see them all swept away. There was grumbling and muttering in various quarters as to certain prevalent abuses, even at the time when he was instituted, but no one could have foretold what was coming. The mills had been grinding slowly for years ; at the end their speed was vastly accelerated, and they ground swiftly and exceeding small. It is nearly always so in all great movements. The pent-up forces seek an outlet, and tarry long. Then comes the opportunity. In England the opportunity arrived with the King's personal quarrel with the Pope. That was the fulcrum on which the lever rested ; all else was but contributory. Thus Thomas Strete served quietly in his parish, as a young man, during the Reformation Parliament (from 1529 to 1536), which legalized the changes which the King had in view ; he saw the Friars and the Augustinian Canons turned out in 1539 ; he saw no more of the chantry priests after 1548. The Cannington

nuns no longer walked about the streets; Athelney,
Glastonbury, and all the great religious houses had
gone. He lost many a friend, one may be sure, in
those saddening times. He must have been continually in contact with the Brotherhood at St. John's
Hospital in Eastover; and the Friars, of course, were
always in evidence in the town. The chaplains and
chantry priests he met every day, and he must have
known them intimately every one. How utterly desolate the Bridgwater streets must presently have
seemed to the poor vicar! How, when he officiated at
the services in his church—it is not clear whether
he had an assistant or not—he must have missed the
Masses, the obits, the trentalls, the anniversaries, the
bright altars gleaming in the transepts and chapels,
the lamps and the lights of a few years ago! His
fellow-priests all gone; St. Mary's now the only
church left within the town, for the others had been
desecrated and sold or given to those who chanced to
be in power and in favour then. It was trying to
many people; devout and good people too, as we
know from the letters and memories of those times; it
must have been grievously trying to Thomas Strete.

William Pole's "chapelle of St. Salviour," which
Leland noticed in his visit to the town, near to the
south gate, had disappeared; the oratory at Ham,
which was an offshoot of Athelney Abbey, had ceased
to be. The Lepers' Hospital of St. Giles, also noticed
by Leland, had passed out of activity; Idstock Free
Chapel was dismantled and unused. But perhaps the
most striking and terrible proof to those who loved
the old order of things was the mutilated quarter of
the body of Abbot Whiting of Glastonbury, which,
when the great abbey was seized, was brought to
Bridgwater in a cart and stuck up contemptuously

upon the east gate, close by where the Queen's Head Inn now stands. That grim relic was an instance and example to men of the foul deeds done by the emissaries of Henry's agents, who had no scruples and no conscience. Whiting was a lord of Parliament, and a man wholly devoted to his abbey and its work. Upon a preposterous charge of having stolen some of the sacred vessels of his own Benedictine house, he was condemned to death, and was barbarously murdered on Glastonbury Tor. History has shown to us that he was innocent of all save his enthusiasm for the old faith, yet the old man of eighty years was not spared. It was a horrible incident even in that day of horrors. People knew when they looked up at the east gate, that a new era had indeed come. But O, the pity of it all ! They might have pensioned the abbot with some trifle out of the vast spoils of their robbery ; they might have saved the splendid abbey for other generations to see ! But other counsels prevailed ; the comely place was dismantled, and the contents were sold. The meagre ruins which remain even yet call forth the admiration of the visitor ; they give a hint and a suggestion of what the place once was.

Yet there were vast compensations. Had there not been some widely-felt desire for reformations, even Henry VIII could hardly have done all that he did. His greatest service of all was that he rid England of every shred of Papal domination. The new Prayer Books appeared ; the services were rendered in the English language, they were simplified and made more edifying for popular use. The Mass was altered to the Communion Office ; the Bible was made more accessible ; it was ordered that Erasmus' paraphrase of the New Testament should be placed beside the Bible in every parish church. There was a tendency, mainly owing to foreign influence, that change and alteration would be pressed too far, notably in Edward VI's reign. This, however, was checked by the violent reaction which ensued in Queen Mary's time, and which will always be remembered by reason of the terrible religious persecutions which disgraced that period. It was not until Elizabeth's long reign set in that peace was ultimately restored, slowly and deliberately, and the more sober elements of the Reformation were quietly allowed to bear fruit. Bishop Barlow, who held the see of Bath and Wells, was obliged to flee the country owing to the Marian persecution, but he returned in time to be one of the consecrators of Archbishop Parker in 1559, under whose primacy the Elizabethan religious settlement was mainly effected. Meanwhile Gilbert Bourne had entered upon Barlow's see at Wells, and Barlow, upon his return to England in quieter times, was made Bishop of Chichester. In 1559 the second Prayer Book of Edward VI, with some alterations, was accepted by Parliament, and was incorporated into an Act of Uniformity. Only 189 of the clergy refused to accept it. The last great Papal blow at an English sovereign was attempted by Pope Pius V in 1570, when he excommunicated Queen Elizabeth, and absolved her subjects from their allegiance. It was a bold and clever bid for power, but it failed. Three and a half centuries earlier Innocent III had excommunicated King John, and had, after a long struggle, brought the wily Plantagenet prince to his knees. But things had greatly changed since then. If Pius V needed a test case, he had it. There was a Papal party remaining in England, active and watching. But the Pope's thunderbolt fell harmless, and added nothing to his power. His Bull declared Elizabeth to be an illegitimate usurper,

BRIDGWATER PARISH CHURCH

WINDOW AT WEST END OF SOUTH AISLE

*Facing page* 160

who had tried to destroy Catholic faith and practice;
it declared her to be *ipso facto* deprived of her throne,
and her subjects liable to excommunication if they
continued to obey her. One enthusiastic servant of
Rome had the audacity to affix a copy of the document
upon the door of the Bishop of London's palace. But
he was arrested, and was executed as a traitor to the
Queen. The great question was settled at last; Rome's
power in England was mortally wounded. The Bull,
instead of injuring the Queen, caused her people to
rally around her with greater zeal.

A year after this Thomas Strete the vicar died. He
had had a long vicariate of forty-three years, and so
crowded with events and with fateful changes that the
experiences of no vicar of Bridgwater, before or since,
could ever compare with his. He came to his benefice
when the Reformation struggle, outwardly, was only
dawning. He left it when the reforming principles
were accepted and settled. The services in the parish
church were changed in his time from the full pomp
and ceremony of the old religion to the simpler and
more edifying modes of worship of that same religion
reformed in its practices and purified from its abuses.
The ceremonial change was great; the doctrinal change,
which was a reversion to far more ancient and pure
principles of the Faith, was necessary. He must have
been a brave man to bear it all; to pass from the
waning splendour of the old to the simpler and truer
beauty of the new; from customs and services which
as a child he had been taught and had learned to love,
to the Book of Common Prayer as set forth by the ablest
minds of the realm. If he had been able to write down
all that he saw and did, his book would be one of the
most valuable treasures that Bridgwater could possess.
Had he lived but three years longer he would have

used the same Elizabethan chalice which is used in
St. Mary's Church to-day (it was provided by Archbishop Parker's order in 1574), and our link with the
pre-Reformation time would have been, in that detail,
absolutely complete.  He found his church brilliant
and ornate with the most costly and beautiful ornaments and decoration which that period could provide;
he left it exquisitely beautiful still, but putting on a
newer mantle of simplicity.  If ever parish priest lived
and toiled through an age of transition, violent, painful,
distressing at times, yet hopeful in its ultimate issue,
Thomas Strete was that man.

Other changes followed.  In 1596 an order was made
by John and Alexander Popham, George Sydenham
and seven other justices named, at the Bridgwater
sessions, that no church-ale, clerks-ale, bid-ale, or
tippling be suffered, and that such only be suffered
to tipple as be or shall be lawfully licensed according
to the orders made at those sessions.  These ales had
been a cause of trouble for some time.  They originated
in quite early times, and are frequently referred to in
the visitations of ecclesiastical authorities.  People who
were in financial straits would hold a bid-ale (*biddan*
to beg), which was a species of revel where ale was sold
at a profit, and frequently a collection of money was
made.  Bride-ales were favourite means of starting
newly-married couples on their domestic career.
Church-ales were gatherings of a kindred nature, where
conviviality, sometimes of a rather boisterous sort, was
indulged in, and the profits of the entertainment were
devoted to some Church purpose.  A church in Berk-
shire in 1449 records in its books a payment of four-
pence " for making the church clean against the day of
drinking in the said church."  This may have been an
extreme case.  But one of the Canons of 1603 directs

162

that the churchwardens shall permit no plays, feasts, banquets, or church-ale drinkings to be kept in the church, chapel, or churchyard. That such a mandate was made shows that there was need for reform, and that—as indeed is very well known—grave irregularities had accompanied the celebration of these quasi-social, quasi-religious assemblies.

Social changes are hard to follow, and especially in so complicated a movement as the English Reformation. Beyond all doubt, the poor suffered most grievously after the dissolution of the religious houses. St. John's Hospital in Eastover did good work for the poor and the infirm; nothing took its place. The Friars had done their share of such ministrations, and no body of men has replaced them from that day to this. St. Mary's Church had at least ten priests working in connection with its various organizations, and most of these were channels of what we should now call poor relief. Even the mediæval funeral was an immense boon to the poor, seeing that the well-to-do would generally direct in their wills that alms should be given to those who would attend their obsequies, and say a prayer for the deceased man's soul. At the obits and anniversaries, too, there was frequently some little gift for the poor. These Church channels of aid to the miserable and the outcast were summarily closed, and great sufferings and privation ensued in consequence. The rich benefited by the suppressions of the monasteries and chantries; the indigent were left lamenting. Of the vast sums of money which fell into the hands of the State and the servants of the State, scarcely any driblets trickled back into the possession of the needy. This was the appalling blot upon the escutcheon of the Reformation, or rather upon those who rode forth to wage its battles. It squandered its huge wealth; it wasted its precious opportunity; it let the day pass by when it might have founded the most magnificent system of poor-relief that any nation ever possessed.

This sordidness, moreover, brought its dire spiritual consequences. Whatever religious principles might lie underneath the great movement—and no doubt there were many such—they were soon covered up under a load of purely secular bargainings. It was impossible to destroy such a mass of churches and chapels without harming religion itself. It could hardly promote reverence and godliness to see the lead stripped from church roofs, the contents of abbeys sold to any passer-by, and the sacred vessels and vestments tossed about like the very riff-raff at an auction sale. Reverence is a tender plant, easily bruised. The men who carried out the great spoliations bruised it sorely, with lamentable results. It is not easy to acquire precise knowledge of Elizabethan days, but it is hardly denied that crime and evil increased. How could it do otherwise? The moral restraints of the old system—a system which in spite of all its faults exercised great moral influences—were suddenly removed, and nothing was substituted. Chaplains and priests wandered about, their occupation gone, looking for some post wherein they could earn a morsel of bread. The very bargaining for the spoils was harmful. It suggested that Church property was made to be bandied about. It introduced a haggling spirit which was unlovely. This was the darker side of some Reformation consequences.

There was a gain in another direction, which was that the thoughts of men were less confined in ecclesiastical channels. There was room found for expansion, and expansion was needed. It was not that the New

Learning greatly influenced Bridgwater; it did not.
It was working its way quietly yet surely in London
and in great centres such as Oxford and Cambridge,
but it was long before it greatly influenced Somerset.
Here men accepted the Reformation consequences very
much as a matter of course, just as they acquiesced
tacitly in Abbot Whiting's murder. There is a huge
force in the mere inertia of things; in the acquiescence
of men in things of which they may even strongly
disapprove, but which they do not know how to
prevent. Moreover there soon came to be abundance
of events to claim their interest. The Spanish Armada
sent a thrill through England, and it made Rome more
hated than ever. Philip II of Spain declared that
Pope Sixtus V had formally made England over to
him, and so sent his fleet of 129 vessels, manned by
8000 sailors, carrying 19,000 soldiers, with provisions
sufficient to feed 40,000 men for six months, to claim
the Pope's gift. It maddened Englishmen, and it
gave an immense impetus to sea-going enterprises,
such as then were becoming very general. The
Armada expedition was a total failure. The triumphant motto which was inscribed upon the medal
which the Queen caused to be struck greatly delighted
the people: *Deus flavit, et dissipati sunt.* Every one
knows of the famous Elizabethan sailors and expeditions. Bridgwater, as a port of some consequence,
had her share in these voyagings. It has been stated
that it was a Bridgwater man who first gave warning of
the approach of the Armada, but it is difficult to
discover any proof of the assertion. Yet the new outlet for men's thoughts and ambitions in this love of
sea-expeditions, either for discovery or for trade, was
excellent. Badly and cruelly as many of the Reformation acts were carried out, the movement led to an

emancipation of thought which was entirely healthy and good.

Bridgwater was badly dealt with in the matter of education. St. John's Hospital had done a little in that direction. It was not much, but it was all there was to be had, and it was better than nothing. The inhabitants' petition to the King when the chantries were dissolved, that the people should have a grammar school given them out of the property of which the town was then mulcted, was scandalously ignored. In 1561 Queen Elizabeth (out of the great and small tithes which she granted to certain persons, and which she ought to have restored to the parish church from which they had been stolen) endowed the free grammar school at Bridgwater with an annual payment of £6. 13s. 4d. for providing education facilities for the youth of the town and of neighbouring parishes.[1] Richard Castleman in 1633 added to this endowment, which received a further bequest from George Crane and Mrs. Brent in 1699. The appointment of the master rested with the Bishop of Bath and Wells. Much more help should have been given to Bridgwater in the sixteenth century for educational work. The town has never entirely recovered from the penurious way in which it was treated when the dissolution was effected, and when a school was, with great humility and courtesy, asked to be granted to the people to whom, and to no other, the very property of right belonged. Richard Holworthie, a merchant and alderman of Bristol, in 1643 bequeathed "to the Mayor and Commonalty of Bridgwater, where I was born," the sum of £52, but it does not appear that the grammar school shared in the benefaction.

[1] "Uni Pedagogo sive Ludimagistro ad Pueros et Juvenes ibidem et oppidis vicinis adjacentes et ad illam confluentes erudientium et bonis literis instruendum."

## REFORMATION CHANGES

At the end of the sixteenth century, therefore, there was some instruction provided for the town children. It was an important time. Bearing in mind what Bridgwater went through in 1645 and 1685, a severe trial was coming upon those who were being taught as boys early in the seventeenth century. The siege would test their mettle in 1645, and their sons' mettle, at Sedgemoor, twenty years later.

Meanwhile the Puritan tide was steadily rising. It rose in spite of Roman activities here and there, but still it rose. Sir Edward Waldegrave of Chewton was a leading Somerset Romanist. In 1562 he, his wife, and his priest, with some others, were imprisoned for having the Mass celebrated in his house. Robert Parsons, of Nether Stowey, was a vigorous seminary priest who had to flee the country in 1574, but who returned to pursue many plots, and was a tireless advocate of the Papal cause. John of Bridgwater was a canon of Wells and rector of Porlock, and he also held the rectorship of Lincoln College, Oxford. He, with some students, also became an ardent Romanist, and fled to Douay in 1577. But these men, and others who sympathized with them, suffered severely, and scant mercy was meted out to them. When James I came to the throne he wished to show some favour to the Puritans, but the Hampton Court Conference caused him to change his mind. Matters came to a sharper crisis under Archbishop Laud, who held the see of Bath and Wells for two years, without ever residing within the diocese. He succeeded to the throne of Canterbury in 1633. Laud's want of tact, his dominating nature, and his rigorous enforcement of disciplinary measures hastened the crisis. He was a man of high ideals, and he hated Puritanism. His life was truly sacrificed for the Church's sake, yet a

prelate of calmer mien might have achieved his purpose where Laud failed. Bishop Piers, who held the
Bath and Wells bishopric for thirty-eight years,
witnessed the full force of the great storm which was
coming. Laud was executed, Charles the First's unhappy policy embroiled the nation in civil war, and the
Puritans, who had employed every effort and skill to
gain power and influence in every part of the realm,
gained an ascendancy which lasted for many years,
and which brought severe persecution upon the Church
of England.

Then there appeared upon the scene that vigorous
and masterful man, of immense power and insight,
who was destined to make and to leave his indelible
mark upon English life. Oliver Cromwell rose to
power, and with him the Puritans. It is necessary to
inquire how Bridgwater fared at this time.

In 1643 an assembly of divines was directed to meet
at Westminster in order to advise Parliament upon
matters of religion. The majority were Presbyterians,
some were Independents; a few Churchmen were
placed upon it, but seldom attended its meetings. At
first the Presbyterians triumphed, for the Scots had
bargained that they would only send an army into
England against the Royalists on condition that
Parliament would accept the solemn League and
Covenant, which meant the Presbyterian form of
religious government. But Cromwell was not a
Presbyterian, he was an Independent. He was content to bide his time; at last entire power came to him.
Then Independency rose to be the supreme form of
religion. Presbyterianism was tolerated with other
Christian bodies; it was necessary to do this. The
only men who were not to be tolerated were members
of the Church of England, Quakers, Roman Catholics,

and Unitarians. The Prayer Book had been forbidden to be used. "The said book of Common Prayer shall not remain or be from henceforth used in any church or place of public worship in England or Wales; the Directory shall henceforth be used." Any minister neglecting to use the Directory was for such omission to forfeit 40s. To speak or write against it involved a fine of £5. If in any public or private place, or in any family, the Prayer Book was used, each person so offending was fined £5 for the first offence; for the second £10; and for the third they were to suffer one whole year's imprisonment, without bail or mainprise. This law came into force on St. Bartholomew's Day, 1645.

But there was worse to come. The Long Parliament appointed a Committee of Religion, who undertook to search out and deal with scandalous ministers. "It is found," said the ordinance, "by sad experience that parishioners are not forward to complain of their ministers." Those who were appointed to seek out such were very successful. Any clergyman who was a Royalist was guilty of "malignity"; he had to go. If he used the Church of England service, or taught its doctrines, he had to go. Orthodoxy and loyalty were thus severely dealt with. A third charge was that of immorality, but this was a blind which deceived no one. The first two offences were the vital ones; the third was thrown in as a make-weight. Any one could give evidence against a clergyman. There was no evidence on oath, no fair trial, no attempt at justice being done. By these means some of the ablest and most learned and devout clergymen in the Church of England were expelled from their benefices under the Commonwealth. Many died in prison; some fled abroad; some eked out a precarious existence in any way they could devise. It was proposed in the House of Commons that the prisoners should be sold as slaves. There was, indeed, an ordinance that the expelled minister should have one-fifth of the value of his benefice to support himself and his family. In some cases, no doubt, this was done. But in the majority of instances it was not done, and the greatest sufferings ensued. Sad stories, very distressing to read, are the miserable conditions which at that time were forced upon the rector of Yeovilton, and the vicar of Ilminster. The President of Trinity College, Oxford, was driven out, but he managed to get the curacy of Broomfield, worth £25 or £30 a year. Some eight thousand clergymen were cast forth by this enactment. Amongst them was the vicar of Bridgwater.

Now some time before, in 1592, the aldermen of Bridgwater had very properly felt that more preaching was needed in the town. Accordingly they appointed the Rev. Cadwallader Hughes to be preacher in St. Mary's. He sought for and received confirmation of his appointment from the Bishop. In the next year he appears in the lists as vicar of the town, and he was succeeded in 1594 by the Rev. Henry Willes. After him came the famous John Devenish, in 1605. Devenish was one who strongly favoured the Puritan position, which was then very acceptable in Bridgwater. He was a man of great activity, and was an indefatigable preacher and lecturer. The Bishop of Bath and Wells of that time, William Piers, had been irritated by the lack of due conformity by some of the lecturers in the diocese, and he went on to develop a dislike to lectures and lecturers *per se*. Devenish had lectured in the church on market-days, and Humphrey Blake, his churchwarden, had been reprimanded for not presenting his vicar to the authorities for censure. In due time

Mr. Devenish passed away, and George Wotton was nominated by Charles I to succeed as vicar of Bridgwater. This was on January 15th, 1644. What offence Mr. Wotton committed is not known. Whether he was a Royalist, and thus hateful to the Cromwellian party, or whether he was a loyal churchman and preached and ministered according to the rules of his Church, is not told us. At any rate he was obnoxious to those who disliked the Church of England, and in common with thousands of other clergymen he was expelled from his living. The Presbyterian Directory was ordered to be used in the churches in the year succeeding Mr. Wotton's institution to the living. If we allow a little time to elapse in order for the Commonwealth agents to see if he used the Directory, we arrive at the time of his expulsion. Probably, therefore, as with a great company of his fellow clergy, he was driven out for using the Prayer Book and for conducting the usual services of the Church. It was the year 1645, the year of Bridgwater Siege.

Wotton having been got rid of, some one had to take his place. By a deed dated January 1st, 1646, the mayor, aldermen, and burgesses appointed Mr. John Norman to be minister of Bridgwater, at a yearly salary of £110, free of rates, taxes, or assessment. Humphrey Blake was mayor. Seeing that at that time the monarchy was practically in abeyance, although the King was still at large, the Commonwealth was all-powerful, and could do pretty well as it liked. It could, and did, thrust in all sorts of people to the livings thus vacated. The Assembly of Divines had already matured plans for licensing and ordaining men who seemed to them to be fit to fill the places of the ejected clergy. That is to say, men (many of them, no doubt, excellent enough in their way, but many also who

were very much the reverse) who held doctrines quite
alien to Church doctrine, who accepted the Directory,
who were not churchmen, but anti-churchmen, were
thrust into the Church's benefices. A hundred years
before Henry VIII had turned out the chantry priests;
now Cromwell turned out the vicars. Mr. Norman
took possession, but St. Mary's from that time until
the Restoration ceased to be ministered in accordance
with Church order and rule. It was a ministry; but
not a Church ministry. He was minister, not vicar.
He was there by the power of the sword of Cromwell's
well-trained Ironsides, and the power of the Parliament, but not by the bishop's fiat, which alone holds
force in the Church of England.

Mr. John Norman is reported to have been an excellent man, and to have done good work. His position
must have been exceedingly painful to him; for the
man whom he ousted had a wife and six children, and
was in dire poverty. Moreover he had done no wrong
save in obeying the recognized law of his Church.
Poor George Wotton! He obtained a wretched post
as a teacher at Williton, and his wife had to spin in
order to get bread for the children. Yet he fared far
better than some of his fellows, for he was neither
imprisoned nor killed. The Rev. Richard Powell,
rector of Spaxton, when he repaired to his own
house at the time the Parliamentary army possessed
Taunton, had to get people to watch whether any of
the soldiers were coming, seeing that they had often
searched his house and thrust their swords through his
beds, to find him. When Bridgwater fell, after the
siege, those clergy who would not take the Covenant
were driven on foot to Portsmouth, and there put on
board ship to be taken to London. Mr. Powell was
amongst them.

# REFORMATION CHANGES

Amongst other clergy who were in the siege was the unfortunate Dr. Raleigh, Dean of Wells. He was also rector of Chedzoy, and on the breaking out of the war was very barbarously used. After the surrender of the town he was made prisoner, and taken out, contemptibly tied to a wretched horse, to Chedzoy. He was allowed to remain a captive in his own rectory, but the man who wished to have Chedzoy benefice for himself, and who afterwards got it, carried him away prisoner. His wife and children were turned out. The dean was sent, a prisoner, hither and thither, and ultimately to Wells. Being placed in the charge of one Barrett, the latter stabbed the dean to death. No punishment was inflicted; the times were too brutal and too lawless.

When Charles II became king the intruded ministers were treated (in some cases, not in many) as hardly as the clergy whom they displaced had been. Reprisals took place. It was all horrible enough, yet it was the anti-churchmen who were the first assailants. The eight thousand clergymen who were ejected by the Parliamentary edict suffered fearfully. When their day of exile and of misery was past, only eight hundred survived to come to their own again. George Wotton was one. He came back to St. Mary's a shattered man, but with strength enough left to live on for a few years. He died in peace at his vicarage in 1669.

An Act of Uniformity was passed in 1662, requiring the intruded ministers to retire from the churches in which they had ministered, unless they were willing to conform to the Church's rules. The great majority conformed and remained where they were. About eight hundred felt unable to do so, and were compelled to retire. Seeing that they—not being churchmen— had enjoyed the Church's emoluments for sixteen years,

though preaching doctrines quite foreign to Church
tenets, the hardship was less severe by far than that
which the clergy had endured in 1646. Eight thousand
clergymen were turned out then; happily only one-
tenth of that number of ministers had to undergo
ejectment in 1662.[1]

Yet some angry feelings were left behind. The
Conventicle Act and the Five-Mile Act were harsh,
and most people would now think them unwise. They
were on a parallel with the tyranny which enforced the
use of the Directory, and which imprisoned men for
using the Prayer Book even in family worship. Yet
they were none the less regrettable. Among the
Reformation consequences the doings of the years
between 1644 and 1662 are sadly painful to remember,
seeing that they deal so very largely with religious
strife. The Church of England suffered by far the
most severely, and suffered, in the main, in silence.
But the Puritans suffered too in their turn, as seems to
be the fashion in this rough world. *Hinc illæ lachry-
mæ.* The tears came to George Wotton and to John
Norman alike.

[1] Calamy says that two thousand ministers were ejected, naming,
however, only 523. But Curteis, who is the most careful of all the
authorities, puts the number at eight hundred

# CHAPTER XII

## THE VOYAGE OF THE *EMANUEL* IN 1578

EXPLORATION by sea was from early days a
characteristic of the British race. Two causes
led up to this: the love of adventure, and the love of gain.
Trading voyages obviously were intended to reward
the merchants who initiated them, and, to some extent,
those who shared in their perils. Bridgwater was
influenced, at various times, by both these motives.
Her shipping trade with foreign trading ports is elsewhere spoken of, and it is known that it brought no
small gain to the craftsmen. The sailors who lounged
about the great bridge were men who could take and
give hard knocks, and who had sailed many a time to
French, Spanish, Irish and other ports, well able to
give a good account of themselves. The Parret, as
being their highway to the outer world, and as the
channel of much of their prosperity, was as much
revered and valued by the great and little folk of the
old town as was the Tiber by the Romans, the Liffey
by the Irish, the Thames by the great merchants of
London, or the Tagus by the Portuguese. It took
them to the Severn Sea, which was a place generally
bristling with adventures; it was the waterway which
carried their exports and which brought in their commodities from foreign shores. All Bridgwater men
loved their river, and regarded it as being in no small
degree the mainstay of their fortunes and of their town.

Voyages of adventure became more the fashion in England in the fifteenth century. The famous Christopher Columbus, by his well-narrated expeditions, added zest to the growing appetite for voyaging. His son describes him as being "a person worthy of eternal memory." "The Admiral Christophorus Colonus," he writes, "imploring the assistance of Christ in that dangerous passage [to the New World], went over safe himself and his company, that those Indian natives might become citizens and inhabitants of the church triumphant in heaven; for so it is to be believed, that many souls which the devil expected to make a prey of, had they not passed through the waters of baptism, were by him made inhabitants and dwellers in the eternal glory of heaven."[1] Tales about him were circulated everywhere, of his bravery, his enterprise, his religious fervour. When about to write he would first test his pen by writing the words, *Jesus cum Maria sit nobis in via.*[2] He died on Ascension Day, 1506, at Valladolid in Spain, and his body was afterwards removed for magnificent burial in Seville Cathedral, with the epitaph, "Colon gave Castille and Leon a new World." Other great seamen had aroused the popular imagination. Stories of the voyages of John Cabot and of Sebastian Cabot were in the mouths of every Bristol man. Sir Francis Drake's tales of his marvellous discoveries delighted every one. Sir Humphrey Gilbert, a Devonshire gentleman, was busily engaged in framing plans for making acquisitions in America, and for gaining very full letters patent from Queen Elizabeth. Raleigh was soon to follow suit in similar ventures. There were many

[1] Life of Colon, by his son Don Ferdinand Colon. Pinkerton's *Voyages*, Vol. XII, p. 3.

[2] May Jesus with Mary be with us in our journey.

others. Voyages of discovery were becoming the vogue; the notion was in the air.

About this time the brave mariner Master Martin Frobisher, one of the greatest of the Elizabethan seamen, born in Yorkshire in 1535, was pondering over his pet project, the discovery of a north-west passage to Cathay, the great Empire of China. Already, in 1576, he had set out with the two ships *Gabriel* and *Michael*, and a pinnace of ten tons, on a northern journey around the Shetland Islands, towards Labrador. His pinnace was lost, and the *Michael* went astray, but he managed to return, bringing with him some earth which was supposed to contain gold. In the following year he started on a second expedition, from Blackwall, with one of the Queen's ships, the *Aide*, and with the barks *Gabriel* and *Michael*. In this voyage the region about Hall's Island, at the mouth of Frobisher Bay, was taken possession of in the Sovereign's name, and was afterwards designated *Meta Incognita*. More earth—also supposed to be auriferous—was brought home. Still dissatisfied, however, the undaunted sailor determined to embark upon a third voyage, and to set about raising and equipping a well-appointed expedition with which to carry out the great purpose of his life. It was this expedition which was shared in by Bridgwater men.

Thus, in the year 1578, Her Most Gracious Majesty Queen Elizabeth having reigned over England for twenty years, Nicholas Chute being mayor of Bridgwater, Edward Popham and John Edwards members of Parliament for the borough, and Edw. Craftes vicar of the parish, Frobisher's famous third voyage began. Hakluyt's testimony to Frobisher and his plan is interesting enough. "Captain Frobisher, being thoroughly furnished of the knowledge of the sphere,

and all other skills appertaining to the art of navigation, as also of the confirmation he hath of the same
by many years' experience both by sea and land,
and being persuaded of a new and nearer passage
to Cataya [Cathay] than Capa de Buona Speranca,
which the Portugals yearly use; he began first with
himself to devise, and then with his friends to con-
fer, and laid a plain plot unto them, that that voyage
was not only possible by the north-west, but also he
could prove, easy to be performed. And further he
determined and resolved with himself, to go make full
proof thereof, and to accomplish or bring true certificate of the truth, or else never to return again; knowing this to be the only thing of the world that was left
yet undone, whereby a notable mind might be made
famous and fortunate. But although his will were
great to perform this notable voyage, whereof he had
conceived in his mind a great hope, by sundry sure
reasons and secret intelligence, which here for sundry
causes I leave untouched, yet he wanted altogether
means and ability to set forward and perform the same.
Long time he conferred with his private friends of these
secrets, and made also many offers for the performing
of the same in effect unto sundry merchants of our
country, above fifteen years before he attempted the
same."[1] The merchants, however, appeared obdurate
to Frobisher's allurements, and held their hand. He
then appealed to the Court, and was encouraged by
Dudley Earl of Warwick, and others. When his
second voyage was ended Frobisher hastened to the
Queen with the joyful news of the discovery of abundance of gold ore, and Elizabeth was not proof against
the prospect of gaining untold wealth. "Preparation
was made of ships and all other things necessary, with

[1] Pinkerton, Vol. XII, p. 511.

such expedition as the time of the year then required."
The scheme certainly promised well. Fifteen good
ships were supplied, bravely equipped and well manned.
Moreover valiant preparations were made for procuring
and storing more gold ore, which would surely, it was
believed, pay for the whole charges of the fleet, with
something handsome to spare. Plans were schemed for
letting some discreet soldiers and others stay in Meta
Incognita, in order to guard the treasure which would
be stored up. A cunningly devised timber-house was
made, conveyed in pieces which could be joined together, to be erected with sufficient accommodation and
comfort to protect the custodians of the treasure from
frost and tempest during the long winter sojourn
which would be theirs in the northern land. The
following ships made up the fleet.

| | |
|---|---|
| The *Aide*, with the Admiral . | Captain Frobisher. |
| The *Thomas Allen*, with the Vice-Admiral . . . . . | Captain Yorke. |
| The *Judith*, with the Lieutenant-General . . . . . | Captain Fenton. |
| The *Anne Francis* . . | Captain Best. |
| The *Hopewell* .. . . | Captain Carew. |
| The *Beare* . . . . | Captain Philpot. |
| The *Thomas*, of Ipswich . | Captain Tanfield. |
| The *Emanuel*, of Exeter . | Captain Courtney. |
| The *Francis*, of Fowey . | Captain Moyles. |
| The *Moon* . . . . | Captain Upcot. |
| The *Emanuel*, of Bridgwater . | Captain Newton. |
| The *Soloman*, of Weymouth . | Captain Randal. |
| The bark *Dennis* . . | Captain Kendal. |
| The *Gabriel* . . . | Captain Harvey. |
| The *Michael* . . . | Captain Kinnersley. |

The last two of these ships had, as we have seen, been
in the 1576 and 1577 expeditions; the *Aide*, a powerful
vessel of 180 tons, in the expedition of 1577 always
acquitting herself well. Captains Fenton, Best, and

Philpot were all tried men, highly experienced mariners.
One hundred men offered, and were to stay in Meta
Incognita all the year, of whom forty were mariners for
the ships, thirty miners for gathering the gold ore
together for the next year, and thirty soldiers for
guarding the rest. Twelve ships were to return with
cargoes of gold ore at the end of the summer, three
ships remaining behind for the use of those captains
who should inhabit the distant land. All being prepared, Frobisher, the general, with all his captains,
appeared before the Court, then situate at Greenwich,
where Her Majesty graciously bade them farewell.
Upon Frobisher a fair chain of gold was bestowed ; the
rest of the captains kissed the Queen's hand. On May
27th, 1578, the fifteen ships met together at Harwich,
where the captains mustered their companies. Four
days later the fleet set sail. Captain Newton, of our
good Bridgwater ship *Emanuel*, otherwise known as
the *Busse* of Bridgwater, had also a master on board his
vessel, one James Leech. There was with them too in
the ship a passenger, Thomas Wiars, who afterwards
wrote a brief but interesting report of the *Emanuel's*
journey home.

Before starting, each captain received from Frobisher
certain articles for the direction and management of
the men on board, and these have peculiar interest as
showing to us the way in which a great sailor in
Elizabethan times ruled his crews.

Swearing, vice, card-playing, and filthy communication were to be banished. It was to be the rule to serve
God twice a day, with the ordinary service usual in the
Church of England, and to clear the glass, according
to the old order of England. The admiral carried the
light, and when this was put out no man was to go
ahead of him, but each was to set sails to follow the

admiral's ship as near as may be. Either by day or night, the ships were to keep within a mile of the admiral. Every night all the fleet was to come up and speak with the admiral, and if weather forbade, then some must speak with the vice-admiral, and receive the order of their course from Master Hall, the chief pilot. If mischance happened to any man by day, they were to shoot off two pieces, and if by night, to shoot off two pieces and show two lights. If any man in the fleet come up in the night, and hail his fellow, knowing him not, he was to give the watchword, "Before the world was God." The other (if he were one of the fleet) must reply, "After God came Christ his Son." In foggy weather every ship was to keep up a reasonable noise with trumpet, drum, or otherwise, in order to keep clear of one another. If land were discovered by night, due warning was to be given to the admiral, and if the ships chanced to lose company by force of weather, they were to get into a certain latitude until they made Friesland, and being once entered within the straits every ship was to shoot off a good piece every watch, and look out well for smoke and fire, until all the fleet be come together. Should any enemies be encountered, four ships, viz. the *Francis*, of Fowey, the *Moon*, the *Dennis*, and the *Gabriel*, were to attend upon the admiral; four others were to wait upon Lieutenant-General Fenton in the *Judith;* and the remaining four, viz. the *Anne Francis*, the *Emanuel* of Bridgwater, the *Thomas*, and the *Michael*, were to follow Vice-Admiral Yorke in the *Thomas Allen*. Lastly, any man in the fleet behaving disorderly was to be kept in custody until such time as he could be taken before the admiral to be punished as his offence should deserve. Such were the rules of sea-going expeditions from England two and a quarter centuries ago.

# THE ANCIENT BOROUGH OF BRIDGWATER

On May 31st the ships left Harwich, and sailing along the south coast of England westwards, came by Cape Clear, off the south-west coast of Ireland, on June 6th. Here chase was given to a small bark supposed to be a pirate, but which turned out to be manned by some unfortunate men of Bristol who had been sorely mauled by Frenchmen, who had spoiled and slain many of them. The general came to the help of his countrymen "with surgery and salves to relieve their hurts, and with meat and drink to comfort their pining hearts," and bade them farewell. Pursuing their journey, Frobisher and his ships sailed north-west from Ireland—being carried somewhat out of their way by a strong current from the south-west—and after sailing for fourteen days without sight of any land, or any living creatures save the sea-birds, made West Friesland on the 20th of June. Friesland is the group of islands now known as the Faroe Islands, belonging to Denmark.[1] Frobisher promptly landed and took possession of them in the name of his Sovereign, and there is little wonder that "the savage and simple people," as he termed them, "fled fearfully away." After three days at the Faroes[2] the fleet left for Frobisher's Straits, looking tenderly back, as they sailed away, at a high cliff which was the last land in sight, and which "for a certain similitude," they named Charing Cross. Bearing in a southerly direction, through driving ice, and meeting in one place with many whales, they came in

[1] See note in Rear-Admiral Collinson's *Three Voyages of Frobisher*, p. 125.

[2] AUTHOR'S NOTE — Hakluyt speaks (in the account of Frobisher's second voyage) of Friesland as being a ragged and high land, having the mountains almost covered over with snow, and the coast full of drift ice. This was on the 4th of July. I was myself in the Faroe Islands in June 1896, and saw no trace of either snow or ice. It was warm, and no sign of frost was to be seen. But the climate may have changed there since 1577.

sight of the Queen's Foreland on the 2nd of July, and
by nightfall had entered into the Straits.

From this time the troubles of the expedition began.
The ships were greatly hindered by ice which drifted
hither and thither by reason of the continually shifting
winds, and the first misfortune was the sinking of the
hundred-ton bark *Dennis,* which was shattered by an
iceberg and sank in sight of the whole fleet. Unfortunately the *Dennis* had on board part of the timber
house which was to have been erected on Meta Incognita for those sailors who were to winter there.
This accident greatly depressed the men. The bad
weather continued, and the admiral, baffled by fogs,
got some of his vessels into the "Mistaken Straits,"
believing them to be Frobisher's Straits. But, wisely
concealing his error, he induced the fleet to follow
him, declaring that all was well. His crew afterwards
reported that " he hath since confessed that if it had
not been for the charge and care he had of the fleet and
fraughted ships, he both would and could have gone
through to the South Sea, and dissolved the long
doubt of the passage which we seek to find to the rich
country of Cataya." Poor Frobisher! His faith in the
existence of a north-west passage to the golden East
was strong ; he could not let it go. And, luckily for
the sailors and for discipline, they believed in the
passage-way too, because their master did. Like all
true leaders, he gained their obedience because he led
captive their imagination, and then dominated their
will.

There was considerable scattering of the fleet. Towards the end of July the Bridgwater ship *Emanuel*
was missing, and it was not until the 27th that she got
out of the ice, and met with the fleet under Hatton's
Headland. Their ship, the crew pleaded, was so leaky

that they must of necessity seek harbour, and her stem
was so beaten in that she could scarcely keep afloat.
They had had 500 strokes at the pump in less than
half a watch ; they were so worn out that they had to
appeal for help from the crews of the other vessels.
Considerable murmuring arose at this time amongst
some of the crews, but Frobisher was able to allay it.
Would that he could equally well have controlled the
weather ! The storms increased, with snow and bitter
cold, and the fleet was separated. When three of the
ships, the *Aide*, the *Michael,* and the *Gabriel*, chanced
to meet in the Countess of Warwick's Sound, the
rejoicing was most heartfelt. "They highly praised
God, and altogether upon their knees gave Him due,
humble, and hearty thanks ; and Master Wolsall, a
learned man, appointed by Her Majesty's Council to
be their minister and preacher, made unto them a
godly sermon, exhorting them especially to be thankful
to God for their strange and miraculous deliverance in
these so dangerous places." Master Wolsall was a
well-beneficed English clergyman who had volunteered
to sail with the expedition, and whose ministrations
the sailors received with abundant gratitude.

By the time that August had well set in it became clear
that no habitation could be put up on Meta Incognita
that year, and the fleet, with all the crews, must fain
return home in due course. Meanwhile ore in considerable quantities was dug, and placed in the ships. The
*Emanuel* had put on board from the Countess of
Sussex mine, 30 tons ; from Dyer's Passage, 20 tons ;
from Bear's Sound, 60 tons. This work filled up
the days until September. On September 2nd the
*Emanuel* again got into trouble. Some sailors on
board one of the pinnaces reported that as they came
out of Bear's Sound they "did see the *Emanuel* in

great danger to be lost to the leeward of the Sound,
and did strike their sails upon the last of the flood,
to anchor as they did judge among the rocks, and then
it was not likely they should ride to escape all the
next ebb, the wind at N.N.W. and a very great gale:
God be merciful unto them." Ultimately the general
set out to sea in the *Gabriel* to seek the fleet, leaving
the *Busse* of Bridgwater and the *Michael* behind in
Bear's Sound. The *Michael* followed, leaving our
Bridgwater ship, " which was doubtful of ever getting
forth." So the captains of the great expedition turned
the bows of their vessels toward English shores. It
was a long voyage home, as voyages reckoned in
those days, and there was no lack of perils right
up to the end. The *Emanuel* had a terrible time.
" Among other, it was most marvellous how ye *Busse*
of Bridgewater got away, who being left behinde the
fleete in great daunger of never getting forth, was
forced to seek a way northward, thorowe an unknown
channel full of rockes, upon the back side of Beare's
Sound, and then by good hap found out a way into
the North Sea (a very dangerous attempte) save that
necessitie which hath no law, forced them to try
masteries. This foresaide N. sea is the same which
lyeth upon the back side of all the N. land of
Frobisher's straits, where first ye Generall himself in
his pinnesses, and some other of our company have
discovered (as they affirme) a great foreland where
they would also have great likelihood of the greatest
passage towardes the South Sea, or *Mare del Sur*."[1]
Thus nearly, as the old chronicler tells us, did the
Bridgwater mariners come to threading the mysterious
sea-passage to Cathay !

On the *Emanuel's* homeward voyage, however,

[1] Hakluyt, in Admiral Collinson's *Three Voyages of Frobisher.*

Thomas Wiars the passenger tells us of further glories gained by the Bridgwater captain and crew. They were now quite alone on the high seas. Leaving Bear's Sound, they set sail, and fell in with the shores of Friesland on September 8th at six of the clock at night. Leaving the south-west point of Friesland, they encountered shifting winds, but these at length abating, and they steering south-east by south, kept their course until September 12th, when at about 11 a.m. they descried land some five leagues away. This new-found island they accounted to be twenty-five leagues in length, and the longest way of it south-east and north-west. The southern part of it was in the latitude 57° and one second part, or thereabout. They kept the island in sight from the 12th, to the 13th of September at 3 p.m. There appeared to be two harbours upon the coast, and great quantities of ice abounded, from which, indeed, they did not get clear until September 15th. Continuing their journey, on the 25th September they sighted the welcome coast of Galway, thence along the south coast of Ireland, and home. By the 1st of October, we are told, all the ships of Frobisher's fleet—save the ill-fated *Dennis*—arrived safe in various ports. Not more than forty men lost their lives in the whole expedition, which number, as the writer says, was not great, considering how many ships were in the fleet, and what strange fortunes they passed.

The ore, alas! was useless, and contained no gold. But it was safely stored, some in London, some in Bristol town, no doubt to the great admiration of the people of those famous ports. Glad and thankful indeed must Captain Newton, and Master James Leech, and Thomas Wiars, and all the Bridgwater sailors have been as they sailed up the winding River Parret, with the tall spire of St. Mary's getting clearer and

clearer to their view. How many were the greetings
on the quay, how eager were the congratulations of the
townsmen, how for many and many a day would the
sailors on the old bridge talk of the glorious voyage
of the *Emanuel!* The inscription beneath the statue of
the old sea-hero Blake, now standing in the centre of
the town, indeed applies well to those sturdy sixteenth-
and seventeenth-century men who went down to the
sea in ships, to do business in the great waters of the
outer world.

Sleep after toyle,
Port after stormy seas ;
Ease after war,
Death after life,
Doth greatly please.

# CHAPTER XIII

## TRADE AND TRAFFIC

GERARD in his particular description of Somerset remarks that the building of the bridge at Bridgwater by William Briwere meant the downfall of the ancient Saxon borough of Langport as it stopped all ships at the Castle. In old days there might have been considerable traffic, perhaps, of pilgrims going to Glastonbury, but the great movement was to come in Norman times. The conquest of Glamorgan and of ancient Caerleon was made from the North Somerset coast and Parret waters, and this would mean traffic at Bridgwater. Further, all the Severn ports looked towards Ireland, and in his wars with Ireland Henry II constantly requisitioned men and supplies from North Somerset. In the archives of the city of Dublin we meet with such names (1172–1320) as John of Taunton, Thomas of Quantock, Hugh Pollard, Walter of Petherton, Roger of Comwych, Adam Malet, Ralph de Falaise (probably of the Stoke-Courcy family), pointing to early communication between Somerset and Ireland. John de Courcy, together with the Poers and Barrys and Percevals, probably enlisted many stout West-Countrymen for their campaigns in Ulster. [1]

Elsewhere, Bridgwater vessels plied far up the Severn valley and past the forest of Dene. In 1233 (Close Rolls) the constable of Bridgwater Castle had orders to assist the abbot and monks of Tewkesbury

[1] See Greswell's *Land of Quantock*.

188

in shipping timber and lead from Bridgwater "for the repair of their church." At Caerleon there must have been a notable landing place, and every creek and pill of the Severn was familiar to Bridgwater sailors.

From a notice in the Patent Rolls dated February 7, 1277, and written from Woodstock, we learn that the sailors of Bridgwater were summoned to assist Edward the First in his Welsh campaign. A safe-conduct was given that year to Eudo la Zouche (who had inherited by marriage part of the Briwere property in Bridgwater), conveying by water corn and other victuals by his own sailors of Brugeswauter, Totnes, and Dartmouth to Pembroke, Pembrokeshire, Kaermardyn (Carmarthen), Kedēvelly, and Sweyneseye (Swansea) for the support of those people who were then on the King's expedition against Llewellin son of Griffin and his accomplices in rebellion.

Here are one or two entries to show how Bridgwater and its sailors were required to take part in the Scotch wars of Edward I (1302). "August 10. Westminster. Appointment of Thomas de Werbelton and Peter de Donewyco to punish at their discretion the commonalties of the town of Briggewauter (with others) who promised to send a ship well armed in aid of the Scotch war and took no measures to do so, to the retardation of that expedition." This was followed by a milder order dated November 10, 1302, by which Peter de Donewyco, King's clerk, was appointed to act in conjunction with the sheriffs of Somerset (and other counties) to induce the bailiffs and good men of Briggewauter to send one ship furnished with men and necessaries in aid of the Scotch expedition so as to be there by the Feast of the Ascension ready to set forth against the Scots at the King's charges. In the following notice of the appointment of Nicholas Fermband in 1307, there is a distinct Protectionist flavour. Together with the sheriff he is ordered to see that a recent proclamation prohibiting any one from taking out of the realm corn, animals or other kind of victuals, horses, armour, money, gold or silver plate, or silver in mass (except corn and victuals destined for Gascony) be strictly observed by the bailiffs of Bridgwater.

In 1311 (May 23) the mayor, bailiffs, good men and commonalties of Briggewauter with Ilfardcumme (Ilfracombe) and Bardestaple are ordered to provide three ships, with Thomas de Kirkeby as clerk, in aid of the King's service in the war against Robert le Brus, fully armed and provisioned for seven weeks. The vessels are to be at Wolrikeford near Carrickfergus in Ulster by the morrow of midsummer-day. The mariners and men are to obey the orders of John de Ergardia as admiral and captain ; Thomas de Kirkeby to superintend the fitting out of the vessels. This aid is not to prejudice them nor to be drawn into a precedent. This last clause is instructive as showing how the ports and boroughs were acquiring power and were already in a position to make terms for themselves.

In 1322 there are two orders (Close Rolls) to the mayor, bailiffs and men of Bruggewauter, the first dated March 1, in accordance with which they were ordered to prepare ships against the Scotch rebels, the second dated April 3, 1322, by which they were ordered to fetch men from Ireland to Carlisle.

In an order dated August 12, 1326, there are signs of the French war, when all owners of ships of burthen of fifty tons and upwards were required to come from Briggewater to Portsmouth with ships, arms and victuals to start in the King's service against the French. On June 28, 1328, an order was sent through the mayor and bailiffs of Briggewater to all shipowners to be prepared to repel an attack of the French.

The following orders in the Close Rolls are also instructive : April 25, 1330. At Woodstock. To the Sheriff of Somerset. Order to cause the wheat lately ordered to be carried to Plymouth to be carried to Bruggewater and delivered to whom the King shall depute. Ships to come to Bruggewater to carry the victuals to Bordeaux. February 18, 1331. At Windsor. Protection until Michaelmas for David le Palmer and Hugh le Mareys, merchants of Bruggewater, and their servants trading in corn and other victuals within the kingdom, on condition that they do not transport the same to foreign parts contrary to the late proclamation. By another entry in the Close Rolls it transpires that the King, "compassionating the estate of the people of Wales where there is a great scarcity of corn," granted leave to these Bridgwater merchants to take 500 quarters thither. England, in those days, was looked upon as a corn-exporting country.

In 1331 there was a notice of the appointment of Thomas Boy on the nomination of Arnold Nicol, chief butler of the King, to collect during the said Arnold's pleasure a custom of 2s. on every tun of wine imported by merchant strangers into the port of Bridgwater and Lyme, which the King has granted to Arnold Nicol until Michaelmas for a sum to be paid by him into the exchequer. This entry throws light upon the wine trade of the port, the customs, and also the method of nominating the "costumer." The chief butlership was an ancient, and in old days, no doubt, a very lucrative appointment, and the perquisites of the chief butler were considerable if levied in the same way as indicated above. Originally the office was claimed as hereditary in certain families.

## THE ANCIENT BOROUGH OF BRIDGWATER

There is an allusion to the departure in 1386 of John of Gaunt with an English expedition to Castille, amongst whom, we know, was the famous Simon de Raleigh, of Nettlecombe, to assert his claim to the Castilian throne. "March 28, 1386. Westminster. Appointment of Wm. Whitbread, John Polyn, and John Hayly of Bristol to provide ships and arrest mariners in ports of Bristol, Briggewater, Chepstow, and Axwater for the passage of Robert de Veer [Vere], Marquess of Dublin, for the Duke of Lancaster's expedition to Spain." Robert de Vere, Earl of Oxford, was one of the King's (Richard II) chief advisers, against whom there was a formidable party of baronial opposition. However, John of Gaunt's designs upon Castile ended in the marriage of his daughter Katharine to Henry of Castile, bringing the thrones of England and Spain together by a matrimonial alliance—as it has recently by the marriage of King Alfonso to the Princess Victoria.

In the Charter of Edward IV the bounds of Bridgwater (apparently enlarged) are thus described both by land and along the river (June 18, 1468):—

"That the Liberties and Franchises of that Town or Burrough shall extend themselves out of the same Town or Burrough by the Limits, moots and bounds following :—To wit by Land : on the east part of the said town to a certain Cross called Kelyng Cross: and from thence to a certain field called Matthews Field on the west part of the same town : and from thence to a certain place called Cropill on the north part of that town: and from thence to the said Cross called Kelyng Cross :

"And by water from the Bridge called Lymebridge to Heuclyve [Leuclyve?] and from thence to Brendown [Breandown] together with the Rode called Seynt Andrew's pole [pool]: from this pool to Highbregge:

the Head of Comwiche, wijn penyes dokke [?] mill pille, prioraspill [Prioress of Canington's pill?], Harfullpille, Saxpole, Pauletpille, Downendepille, Pegenspille, and Crowpille with all other pools, creeks and places in the same water for ships and other vessels to lie and rest in."

Some of these local definitions appear to be lost, but the coast and river jurisdiction of the town of Bridgwater would seem to have taken in the sixteen miles of the Parret windings and the littoral of Burnham and Berrow. Heuclyve may have been some point of the Polden ridge, where of old the loop of the Parret used to run towards Cranebridge. "Wine penny dock" tells its own tale, and here the duty on imported wine may have been levied. The "Head of Comwich" is so far interesting as it points to the old-world importance of Comwich or Comwith as a terminus or *head* of navigation. St. Andrews pill preserves the name of the apostle known at St. Davids and also at Banwell and Stoke Courcy, and may have been at Burnham where the church was dedicated to St. Andrew. It was a favourite Somerset dedication along North Somerset. The word "pill" is Welsh, as in Coganspille across the channel: "Creek" appears surely in Creech St. Michael and elsewhere in the Parret valley.

The port and landing places of the Parret mentioned in the Charter of Edward IV were difficult to reach from the Severn Sea, and the windings of the tidal river itself formed a considerable obstacle to an invading foe. The distance by river between Bridgwater and the mouth of the Parret is sixteen miles. Sir Walter Raleigh in a Report on the sea defences of the western counties (Sherborne, 25 November, 1595), wrote: "Somerset is sealed from danger having Devon towards the south, and on Severn side it hath not ports capable of any ships of burden and the indraught is long and dangerous." He notices that Dunster, Minnett (Minehead), and Bridgwater are ports "into which small barques cannot arrive without precise observation of tyde."

To come up the Parret in ancient times vessels had to wait at a place called "Botestall," marked on old maps as off Stolford, and so watch their chance. This place belonged to Stoke Courcy Castle. In Speed's map (1610) under Botestall the following sailing instructions are given: "To sail into the River Parret from the westward for the Port of Bridgwater you will first make a high round hill called Brent Knoll, nearly over Burnham Church, which you must keep due east, and then sail along till you open Bridgwater Steeple. And then you are to keep the north side of Burnham Church, just opened, till you open the river to the eastward of the Warren House of Steart Point."

To avoid some of the perils of Parret navigation it was proposed (1 January 1723) "to make a new cut through a narrow neck of land about three-quarters of a mile from and out of the Parret to empty into Stolford Bay" (Gough MSS., Somerset 7. Bodleian).

In connection with the waterways of the Parret the question of inland public roads and tracks was an important one with the trader. Sometimes they were in a bad state, and on March 27, 1326, Bishop Drokensford issues an Indulgence "pro Calceto de Brugg," i.e. a ten days' indulgence to all those who might charitably aid in repairing the "causey" or causeway between Bridgwater and the Polden Hills. It was not till 3 George II that, in consequence of an Act for repairing several roads going into Bridgwater, short and level communication between Puriton and Bridgwater, almost touching the bank of the Parret at one place,

was made. From the west the most important pack-
road must have been that which can still be traced
along the present high road leading to Durleigh,
Enmore, and so to "Travellers' Rest" and Bun-
combe Hill. These deep tracks bear witness to centuries
of traffic, but not wheel traffic. The usual traveller was
either a packman or a drover, and this primitive state
of communication lasted longer in the West-Country
than elsewhere. In the Brendon districts wheel traffic
was hardly known in many places till the nineteenth
century.

Here is an extract throwing light upon the state of
the roads nearer Bridgwater in 1737: "We, Jos. Taylor
and John Mounsher, surveyors of the highways of the
Parish of Bridgwater, do hereby present that the highways leading from Bridgwater to North Petherton, to
Wembdon, to Bawdrip, also to Durleigh, are very bad,
out of repairs and dangerous to all travellers who pass
these roads. This is a great detriment to the parish.
Sworn before me Thomas Yeates, Mayor, 27 April, 1737.
Samuel Smith, Alderman."

It is clear, however, that a continuation of water
carriage from the borough boundary of Bridgwater to
North Petherton and so to Taunton was always an
important matter. In 1382 (Patent Rolls, 6 Ric. II) it
was complained that owing to the erection of Bathpool
Mills, one and a half miles from Taunton below Creech-
bury hill, by the Abbot of Glastonbury, obstruction
was caused to river traffic. "The boats," it was said,
"which used to carry merchandise from Briggewater
to Taunton could not go as formerly." Again, "The
fish which used to swim from Briggewater to Taunton
were so hindered by the aforesaid mills that they could
not swim as they were wont." "The bank of the
river which used to be thirty feet wide was then not

more than ten or twelve." We are informed also that there was a place in the lower part of the said mills, called Bathpolecrosse, up to which all boats came from Briggewater towards Taunton, and, time out of mind, were there discharged and unladen. The river craft were called botes and trowys with their various freights, to wit, firewood, timber, charcoal, pitch, salt, iron, lime, grain, ale, wine, etc.

More than a hundred years later (1498–1500) there was another complaint about a mill at North Curry belonging to the Dean and Chapter of Wells. The men of Taunton alleged that "time out of mind they have had free passage upon the waters of Tone, Bathpole mill and Brigewater. This was now stopped, and in the winter season, as the ways, i.e. roads, were so foundered by the overflowing of the waters they had no carriage." This was, no doubt, set forth as a great grievance, but the Dean of Wells, interviewing my Lord of Winchester, as the lord of the manor of Taunton, thought fit to traverse it. "And as for bote passage, your said officers know right well that in all the said season the water was so low and with so many shallows [?] and bays in the river between our mill and Taunton that it was not possible to convey any bote that way. And in the wynter season the meadows be so filled and replenished with water that the botes may go over at any place, so that they shall not be let [hindered] by the mill " (Wells MSS.).

In the other direction Bridgwater was connected with Glastonbury via the River Brue, which falls into the River Parret, and the River Brue was linked with the Axe by the canal or waterway that passed Rooks Mill. In the church accounts of St. John's, Glastonbury, the seats for the church are described as being made in Bristol (1500). "David and six men accompanied the carved work, which was shipped in two great boats from the Back near the Temple Friars, at Bristol. These boats were brought to Rooks Mill (on the Pill-row Cut) in S. Brent. Thirteen boats hired at Meare brought part of the work by water from Rooks Mill to the bridge at Maydelode (i.e. near Glastonbury station). Other parts were conveyed by land in thirteen wagons. John Pederam with one carriage and horse brought the carved work from Rooks Bridge to the church, and the whole transit took a week." Rooks Mill figures very early in Glastonbury history as the place whence each tenant of the abbey was bound to carry "vina et victualia Domini apud Rokys myll de batellis." Rokes mylle was a kind of port of entry, and here, according to John of Glastonbury, a curia was held by the abbot in Henry VII's time to judge a case according to maritime law.

Modern canals supplemented these ancient water-ways. In 1827 the present canal linking Bridgwater and Taunton was cut, in spite of much opposition, and in 1828 the Glastonbury Canal was united with the Brue, capable of carrying 'vessels of fifty to one hundred tons burthen, and able to navigate the Bristol Channel. The River Brue is navigable to Cripps House, a distance of four miles.[1] Other more ambitious schemes have been broached in the cutting of a canal between Bridgwater and Combwich Reach, and also the cutting of a trans-Somerset canal from Stolford to Seaton. It is clear, however, that in a smaller way Bridgwater has always been in trading communication with the various parts of the great Parret valley by means of primitive waterways and artificial canals.

William of Worcester (1415–82), chronicler and

---

[1] Phelps, *Hist. of Somerset.*

traveller, son of William of Worcester, a substantial burgher of Bristol, gives some useful information about the Severn ports at this date. Axwater, he says, is the first port down the coast after Bristol. Comwych is described as three miles from Bridgwater, and is a "portus navium Brygewater." Myned (Minehead) is the next port towards Devonshire beyond Bridgwater, then "Combe Portus, id est Ilfercomb; Barstable portus sequitur."

Ships (naves), small ships (naviculae), and boats and "naviculae vocatae Anglice wodbryshys, cacheys, pycardes," coming from the ports of the towns of Wales and of the towns and havens of Tynby, Myll-ford-havyn, West-Horford, Lawgker-havyn, Lanstefan-havyn, Kedwelly-havyn, Swansleg-havyn, Neth-havyn, Kerdyff-havyn, Newport-havyn, Usque-havyn (Usk), Kerlyon-havyn, Tyntern Monasterium super flumen de Wye, Chepstow-havyn, Betysley water super aquam de Wye, and of other ports *sive homones* (?) of the comitates or counties of Cornwall, etc. These ships were laden *stango et piscibus*, i.e. stones and fish.

Elsewhere William of Worcester says that all the ships lying "apud le hollow bakkys" at Bristol and hailing from Hispania, Portugallia, Bardegallia, Bayona Vasconia (Gascony?), Aquitania, Britannia Islandia (Brittany?), Irlandia, Wallia and other parts drop anchor at Blackstone. From this description it is possible to infer both the countries with which not only Bristol but Bridgwater men traded and also the kind of ships in which they sailed. The coast traffic would require smaller vessels than the continental.

In addition the old chronicler gives us a list of the familiar islands and landmarks of the Severn Sea beginning from the west, viz. Insula Lastydenale, Insula de Meulx, Scopeholm, Stalmeys (four miles from Scopeholm), Grasholm, Shepesland, Rupis de Crowe, Insula Caldy, Insula Wormeshede, Le Holmys, Insula Barry, Lindey, Syllay (Sully?), Flatholm, Stepeholm, Insula Donye, Englysh Stonys, Insula St. Tryacle.

In an old letter written by Sir Edward Stradlynge of St. Donat's Castle in 1581, the whole haven of Aberthawe, and the government and appointing of all passing boats using the same haven, the granting of all "cockettes," i.e. "counterparts of the King's seal," and all other money for kyllage (keelage), shippe money, and all customs, commodities and royalties whatsoever were claimed by the writer as having belonged to his ancestors since the conquest of Glamorgan as "lords of the manor of East Orchard." He claimed also to be lord of the manor of Sully, which originally belonged to the kings of England (Stradling Letter). From the same letter it appears that the haven of Barry—that very ancient landing place—belonged absolutely to Lord St. John of Bletsoe. The above extract is interesting as illustrating the claims of feudal lords over sea ports and havens in former days. Bridgwater was fortunate enough in securing borough privileges to itself at an early date, thanks to its early charters. It secured also all the pills and landing places along the Parret from Lymebridge to Breandown as part of its port. It was, therefore, more independent than Barry, for instance, or Dunster, which were simply baronial landing places. The Bridgwater skippers and merchants had to pay king's dues and customs and, before the time of Edward IV, acknowledgments to the Mortimers and Brewers. But they were practically self-governing men. Henry VIII is supposed to have conferred the peculiar honour upon Bridgwater of making it a distinct county so that the king's sheriff could not send a writ there. This gift, which has certainly never been used to the full, gave occasion for the following doggerel (Jarman, *History of Bridgwater*, p, 37) :—

> Then Harry the Eighth (there may be odd views of it)
> Made the Boro' a county, tho' we never made use of it.
> This shows how kings play fast and loose with their bounties,
> Now beheading of wives, now retailing of counties.

In Tudor days there was a trade depression in Bridgwater, much in contrast with its prosperity in Plantagenet times. Leland, visiting the town in 1538, noticed two hundred houses in a decayed state, and this is borne out by a notice in the Plymouth Municipal Papers of an Act (32 Henry VIII) for the re-edifying of houses in the borough and towns of Bridgwater, Taunton, Somerton, Ilchester and elsewhere. Was it that the town guilds were becoming too greedy and monopolist, driving trade into the villages? The principle of *co-optatio* would work inside these guilds almost by a natural law.

In Queen Mary's reign (1555) there was the following protest made by the representatives of the cloth industry in Somerset: "Whereas, before this time the borough towns of Bridgwater, Taunton and Chard in the county of Somerset have been well and substantially inhabited, occupied, maintained and upholden for the most part by reason of the making of woollen clothes, commonly called Bridgwater, Taunton and Chard clothes, which in time past were much desired as well beyond the seas as in the realm of England, and thereby the inhabitants and poor people of the said borough or towns and of the country thereabouts were daily set on work and had sufficient living by the same. . . . Forasmuch as certain persons dwell-

ing in villages and hamlets, not being prentices, have
of late days exercised, used and occupied the mysteries
of cloth-making, weaving, fulling and shearing within
their own houses," etc., the petitioners beg for an act
for the sealing and viewing of it to stop the village
industry.   Herein lay the spirit of Monopoly!

In 1592 the ships of Bridgwater were catalogued
thus: one ship of 30 tons, two of 25 tons, two of
20 tons, one of 16 tons, one of 10 tons.   These diminished quickly, and on December 11th, 1596, Christopher
Salmon, mayor of Bridgwater, and four aldermen
recommended William Wallis as "searcher" to Lord
Burghley in place of William Hoskins, deceased,
"the appointment being of small value and trade
having decreased so that only one barque of any
account belonged to the town."   This was shortly after
the Armada and England's successes against Spain.
It is possible that although much privateering was
done and many ducats taken from Spain, this very
success caused legitimate trade with Spain to dry up.
Spain, moreover, recovered her naval power, and in
1597 a bark from Brittany was boarded by a Spanish
vessel which, with three others, kept the Channel.   The
captain threw overboard letters of intelligence he had
from Thomas Chaplyn, merchant, of Bridgwater.

In the reign of King Charles the Bridgwater merchants objected to the King's taxation (1629) in consequence of the decay of the town, and certain remissions
of sums assessed upon the hundred of North Petherton
were granted them, as hereafter noted (Chapter XIV).
In 1631 wheat was very dear, viz. 8s. 3d. a bushel;
times were bad generally, and letters were addressed
by the mayor of Bridgwater to Sir F. Dodington,
then sheriff of the county, about measures to be
taken for the relief of the poor.   Similar letters were

addressed to Thomas Luttrell, the sheriff in 1632. No doubt this local distress and general feeling of "bad times" added fuel to the political animosities of the day. There were not wanting in those days certain selfish merchants who conspired to make capital out of the general scarcity and distress. There were the evils, also, of piracy at sea, which were very great until dealt with by the Commonwealth admirals. These were always most formidable and existed all round the English coasts. Every hand was against the merchant venturer when he started on his travels, and the Algerine pirates were not the only offenders.

In 1630 there is an official letter of Thomas Wyndham to Edward, Earl of Dorset, describing how a certain Derrick Popley of Bristol tried to "corner" all the salt of commerce in the Severn Sea. He sent down one Yeomans of Bristol "along Severn on the English side" to buy up all the salt he could get. 'At Barnstaple Yeomans pretended that he had a fishing voyage in view and went from merchant to merchant and bought up above 700 bushels. At Watchet he and Jacob Andrews of Bridgwater bought up the lading of two French ships. Salt therefore rose from 4s. 8d. to 15s. the bushel, much to the great grievance of all people and the ruin of many poor fishers for herrings, such as we may suppose to have plied their trade from Minehead.

Under the Hanoverian dynasty the trade of Bridgwater revived again. From a note in Bowen's Map, c. 1720, we learn that Bridgwater was a large and populous borough town well frequented by merchants and traders, "that ships of 100 tons often ride in the Parret, there being upwards of forty sail belonging to the town." About 1750 the customs amounted to over £3000 p. a. clear of salaries, a good coast trade being carried on with Bristol and the Severn ports. Twenty colliers brought coal from South Wales. Abroad the foreign trade was with Spain and Portugal, as of old, with Newfoundland and sometimes with the Straits, Virginia and the West Indies. Large quantities of wool were brought from Ireland and sold in the markets.

In 1889 Mr. Jarman wrote: "As a seaport Bridgwater has some claim to importance, its home and foreign trade being considerable. Vessels of 300 tons can be navigated as far as Bridgwater, and goods can be conveyed by barges elsewhere as far as Langport and Creech St. Michael. The navigation dues amount to about £1000 yearly, and the number of vessels entering the port yearly is 3000–4000 with a tonnage of 200,000–250,000. The chief imports are coal, grain, timber, linseed, valonia, gypsum, esparto, hides and potatoes, etc." In these days of steam and motor traffic the advantages of Bridgwater as a centre of river communication, aided by canals, are surely very great. It might be made the collecting centre of all agricultural and farm produce, with a view to further distribution by steamer to South Wales and by rail elsewhere.

NOTE.—In the MSS. of the Plymouth Corporation (Ninth Report Hist. MSS. Commission) there is a letter from Sir Ferdinando Gorges, the famous American colonizer and lord-proprietor of "New Somersetshire," written to Mr. Robert Trelawney, Mayor of Plymouth, inviting the shipowners of the West-Country to co-operate with the shipowners of London to put down piracy on the high seas which, in the last few years, had deprived England and Scotland of 300 ships with lading and merchandise (1617). The merchants of London were willing to subscribe £40,000. At Barnstaple there were the same complaints.

# CHAPTER XIV

## ADMIRAL BLAKE

ROBERT BLAKE, the famous "General-at-sea,"
as he and other great leaders in Commonwealth
times were called, is *the* great Hero of Bridgwater. So
much so that, if the old "Bridge of Walter" were
ever to be re-christened, it would be called "The
Bridge of Blake," the true eponymous hero. For, if
it be necessary to cast up accounts, Robert Blake did
more for the lasting fame of Bridgwater than the
Domesday Walter de Douai or the great Baron
William Briwere, the author of so many of its original
privileges and ancient endowments. The bridge and
the shipping and the restless ebb and flow of the tidal
Parret itself call up the picture of that bold and ever-
active seaman, one of a great family and clan, whose
outlook was down those long muddy reaches, past its
little landing-places, creeks, and "pills" to Bridgwater
Bay, to the Severn Sea, and thence in the *crescendo*
scale of enterprise to lands washed in the Occident and
Orient by the mighty Ocean itself. The seeds of
enterprise, like the famous *coco de mer* itself in the
Seychelles, were carried down the Parret and deposited
on far distant shores almost, it would seem, by random
agencies and by cross currents. Unless, indeed, we
discern in such masterful minds and such indomitable
perseverance as that displayed by our West-Country
mariners, the purposeful intentions and fixed ideas of
men now recognizing for the first time the new des-

tiny of a free and awakened England, and the trumpet-call to fame. Surely the call came not only from the *mare clausum* of Selden and the narrow seas around England's cliffs, but from *oceanus circumvagus*, a wider sphere and a more mighty heritage. And so Blake and his compeers fought for the honour of the flag not only with the Dutch along the North Seas and the Dogger Bank, but with the Algerine ships of North Africa, the French in the Mediterranean, and with the Spanish in the Canaries and the West Indies and, indeed, wherever they could meet them. Their wonderful maritime and naval activity was a contemporary feature of the Commonwealth, and Robert Blake was, first and foremost, the head figure of it. It was the day of small things, as far as comparisons with modern developments are concerned, and both Bridgwater, Bristol and the rest of the Severn ports seem muddy creeks and ditches, but in the seventeenth century the Avon and the Parret could find a berth for stout British-built vessels manned by hardy sailors (every one of them a trained man), who served the occasion well when the first blows of the great naval duels had to be dealt.

Robert Blake's father, Humphrey, was a merchant of Bridgwater of great note, and had amassed by trade £8000, a large sum in those days, and he had amassed it chiefly by trading with Spanish ports. This Spanish connection is worth noticing as it meant much to the Blake family, not only so far as trade was concerned, but because of certain influences which its members imbibed from a first-hand knowledge of Spain and of Spanish ways. It is said that the first news of the sailing of the Invincible Armada from Spain to England was brought by a Bridgwater ship belonging to Humphrey Blake.[1] Far back in the

[1] *Life of Admiral Blake*, by one bred in the family.

centuries Bridgwater was often a starting-place for a pilgrimage to the shrine of St. James of Compostella. Robert Blake made it the starting-place of a new kind of pilgrimage altogether, not wholly consonant with the old.

St. Mary's Church, with its historic parapets and far-reaching steeple dominating Sedgemoor and all the lowlands round, was the church where at the old font, still surviving, Robert Blake received his Christian name, and the baptismal entry is there for all to see.

It is said that the infant was carried to the mother church from a little house of a somewhat dark and dingy appearance in Blake Street, where certain ancient features are still pointed out. It seems clear enough that this house really had the honour of first sheltering one of the greatest of England's naval heroes.

Blake's christening robe, described as a very handsome one of coloured silk, edged with silver filigree, as well as his christening cap, of silk and velvet, are in the possession of his descendants, the Ruddock family, a name that figures amongst the recent mayors of Bridgwater. As a boy Robert Blake received the first rudiments of his education at King James's Grammar School in Bridgwater, an institution of good repute in its day. It has long since disappeared, but, by a curious coincidence, was replaced by another school of similar aims which was conducted in the house in which the Admiral was born (Jarman's *Bridgwater,* p. 64). Being fond of books young Blake looked to Oxford and, at the age of sixteen, went to St. Alban's Hall. Here he tried for a Christ Church scholarship, but failing in this attempt he shifted his abode from St. Alban's Hall to Wadham College, an institution just founded by Nicholas and Dorothy Wadham, Somerset benefactors living at Merrifield near Ilton and friends of Robert Blake's father.

# ADMIRAL BLAKE

Few details are known of Blake's undergraduate days, and one old story goes that in his frolicsome mood he was "addicted to stealing swans," but if such were ever the case the permanent result upon his understanding and character was not worse than that left upon the great Shakespeare by his inroads upon Sir Thomas Lucy's deer park.

Robert Blake made an unusually long stay at Oxford, remaining there nine years. This was chiefly owing to his great love of the classics, which in his case seemed to work the best results and to show how true may be the maxim of the Oxford schools: "Emollit mores, nec sinit esse feros." We are told that "he intended to put himself on some Faculty line for a profession, rather for the increase of knowledge than of fortune." The ambition of being a quiet man of academical research comes to us as a revelation and perhaps betrays by a flash one of the deepest springs in Blake's nature. That he would try to increase the world of knowledge without increasing his own fortune we can well believe, for the trend of Blake's life was to amass glory and riches for his country but to gain little for himself personally. However, he showed his bent for the classics by writing in 1623 a copy of verses on the death of the great antiquary Camden, a feat which argues a strong sympathy with England's history and archæology. Throughout his life Blake kept up his classics, and gave point to his occasional pleasantries by quoting Latin phrases and introducing apt sayings from the classics which he knew *ad unguem*.

From Oxford Robert Blake was summoned back to Bridgwater by the death of his father (1625). Towards the end of his life affairs had not prospered with Humphrey Blake, and it was rather a heavy burden that he bequeathed to his son, to look after the future of a large family which originally numbered fourteen, of which twelve were sons. Humphrey Blake's failures may have come from bad debts or through the fluctuations and uncertainties of Spanish trade. Or it might have been owing to the pirates that swarmed everywhere, from whom there was no protection at that date.

Here is a significant letter from the Commonwealth Admiral the Earl of Warwick to John Pym living at Cannington (*Bouverie Papers*, Hist. MSS. Commission).

"A bark of Blakeney in Norfolk has told me that divers Irish pirates are abroad well manned, and that they have taken a Yarmouth man and hanged all the English and their dogs also. None escaped but a French pilot of S. Malo. They lie about Ushant, Conquet Road, Belle Isle, Croisie and Nantes. If they be not prevented they will take many of our merchantmen who have no defences." This disgraceful state of things lasted till Robert Blake took up the whole question of piracy and settled it.

Robert Blake has been described by one who was bred in the family as a man of about five feet six inches in height and a little inclined to corpulence, "of a fresh sanguine complexion, his hair of the frizzled kind, as was then the mode. He wore whiskers (moustaches) which he curled when he was anyways provoked. He was commonly very plain in his dress, but when he was abroad and appeared as General he was always dressed as became his rank, with a reserve of moderation." In a word, he was a plain stalwart Englishman without pretence or ceremony when ceremony was out of place, a far different character from the more picturesque cavalier, but a more terrible foe to meet. Place one of Goring's rascally troopers alongside of Robert Blake and you have the contrasts of the age illustrated as in two portraits. Like other born leaders of men by sea and land

HEAD OF ECCLESIASTIC

CARVED ON NORTH DOOR OF NAVE OF BRIDGWATER CHURCH

*Facing page* 208

## ADMIRAL BLAKE

Robert Blake proved that it was not by the standard of his inches but rather by his bold and unquenchable spirit that he was to be measured. When at Oxford in 1619 Blake stood for a fellowship at Merton College, and the only reason why Sir Henry Saville, the warden of the college, objected to him was that he was not quite tall enough. It happened well for his country that Robert Blake was "ploughed" on this score for the Merton fellowship. The vigour of that manhood and versatile talent that displayed itself in the sieges of Lyme and Taunton, fought the Dutch for the mastery. of the seas, humbled to the dust the Sallee rovers, forced the harbour of Santa Cruz at Teneriffe, where even Nelson failed—might have withered away in the monotonous and colourless round of an Oxford tutor and don.

In addition to the town of Bridgwater there were three places in the neighbourhood with which Robert Blake and his family were closely associated, namely, Planesfeld or Plainsfield Court in Over Stowey parish under the Quantock Hills; Knowle manor in Puriton parish at the foot of the Polden Hills; and Tuxwell manor in Spaxton parish. Of these places Tuxwell, or Tocheswelle, as it was anciently written, seems to have been the first manor which the Blake family held. In Queen Mary's reign Tuxwell was in the possession of George Sydenham, a member, probably, of that family which took its name from Sydenham close to Bridgwater and was represented by so many branches at Stogumber, Dulverton, and elsewhere. In Elizabethan days the Sydenhams figure prominently in the muster rolls of local levies ready to fight against Spain. From a manuscript in the possession formerly of Humphrey Sydenham we are told that George Sydenham had licence to alienate the manor of Tuxwell to Humphrey Blake in 1555. Far back in the history of Bridgwater there was a certain William Blaccke who, in 1380, together with many others, laid violent hands upon certain Papal Bulls belonging to St. John's Hospital, and possibly this Blaccke may have been an ancestor.

Tuxwell, however, as a kind of *incunabula gentis*, claims more than a passing attention. It is a quiet retired farm-house close to a moorish bit of ground called Radlet (Radeflot) Common, and together with a place called "le morland" belonged formerly to the Duchy of Lancaster. In 1550 a rent resolute was paid to the Duke of Somerset as of his manor of Tuxwell. It is difficult now to guess the original size of the manor, but in 1829, when Tuxwell farm was sold by the trustees of Lord Egmont to Henry Labouchere, Lord Taunton, it consisted of 329 a. 3 r. 25 p. and had a "Blake's orchard" and a "Blake's Eight Acres," keeping alive the name of the original owners. Inside the house—now completely modernized—are a few old oak beams across a parlour, and underneath the room itself is said to be a well, probably the well which attracted the first settler to Tuxwell. Quiet and remote as the little Quantock village of Spaxton now seems to be, nestling in a peaceful landscape, it used to boast of stirring memories in Elizabethan days. Here was the home of the Elizabethan admiral, Sir Robert Crosse, whose exploits in helping to capture the *Madre di Dios*, as commander of the *Foresight* in 1592, must have been handed down to young Robert Blake and bruited abroad over the whole of Quantock land as well as Bridgwater. The tale of the capture reads like a romance. Sir R. Crosse's share of the plunder was £2000, no inconsiderable sum in those days. Of spices alone the *Madre di Dios* had, at her sailing, no less than 537 tons and of ebony wood 15 tons. The tapestries, silk stuffs and satins of the rich carrack were worth a king's ransom. The gentry and merchants of the West-Country were fired by constant tales of ocean adventure and enterprise. Had not one of the Palmer family of Fairfield near Stoke Courcy accompanied the famous Sir Francis Drake round the world? Many of the old Somerset manor-houses such as Dodington Hall, Fairfield, Nether Stowey and others were re-edified and enlarged by their owners about 1580 as if the times were good and Spanish doubloons were enlarging their revenues.

The acquisition of one piece of landed property very often leads on to another, either by purchase or by marriage. Close to Tuxwell, just outside the boundaries of Spaxton parish and within Over Stowey, lies the manor of Plainsfield Court, apparently a more important manor than Tuxwell. In the Over Stowey tithe map Plainsfield figures as a separate section of the parish, and has separate entries of its arable ground, woods and pastures. In 1829 the manor is described as lying partly in Spaxton as well, with an acreage of 274 a. 1 r. 9 p., Plainsfield Park covering 35 a. 2 r. 26 p. Humphrey Blake, the Admiral's father, married the heiress of this adjoining property, Sara Williams, of a knightly family that had been already settled at Plainsfield for a hundred years. There is good authority for saying that Plainsfield Court was the dower of Sara Williams, and that it had been granted first to Sir John Williams by Henry VII, descending from him in turn to Reginald Williams, John Williams and Nicholas Williams. In the Herald's Visitation of Somerset, 1623, the Admiral's father is styled Humphrey Blake of Plainsfield, son of Robert Blake of Bridgwater.

As at Tuxwell, so at Plainsfield the name of Blake has been preserved in a field-name, viz. Blake's Close Orchard, 3a. 1 r. 0 p., and in one of the lower rooms of Plainsfield Court itself there is still to be seen a plaster moulding or panel, seven feet long and two wide, with the arms of the Blake family, a chevron between three garbs, dated 1663, and with the initials E.B. in the centre of the foliation. The influence of the Blake family was great at this time in the Quantock villages of Over Stowey, Spaxton, and Aisholt, and in course of time there were many ramifications of the clan elsewhere, for they were a prolific set. They became allied with the Perry family at Halse, the Sealy family of Bridgwater, the Crosse family of Blackmore in Spaxton, the Selleck family of Over Stowey, the Upton family of Fitzhead, and so on. The old biographer of the Admiral, who had been bred in the family, writes thus : "There is at Padknoller [Charlynch] a family of the same name and of the same blood as I was assured on the spot, but when I desired further satisfaction concerning it of the master of the family, he, to my very great surprise, seemed willing enough to shuffle off any relation to Admiral Blake, on account of his being a Puritan and a Commonwealth's man, that person being an utter enemy to the principles both of one and the other. And, to show how whimsical Party is, there is a family of the Blakes, about twelve miles from thence, who have lived long in the profession of those [Puritan and Commonwealth] principles, and who cannot make out any relation in blood to Admiral Blake's family." It may be noted as a wholesome sign of the times that there is now a laudable, if not a feverish, anxiety, not only on the part of the Padnoller branch, but also of all others descended from the Blake stem, to claim affinity with the great Admiral, and their name is legion. If the clan be really devoted to this hero-worship, it is clear that they can not only satisfy a legitimate pride when the family connection is established, but that they can learn much from their hero in whatever sphere of action he was engaged. More especially is this the case because Robert Blake stands for character rather than state honours. Yet upon whom could the title of the "Earl of Bridgwater" have rested better than with Robert Blake? This title lay in Blake's time (1617) with John Egerton, of no local fame or associations.

There is an interesting and hitherto unpublished account of a certain lawsuit, in 1637-8, between Humphrey Blake, the Admiral's brother apparently, and Algernon Earl of Northumberland, lord of the manor of Wick-Fitzpayne, in Stoke Courcy, and owner of portion of Over Stowey on the Quantocks. This Algernon was, it may be noted, Lord High Admiral of King Charles the First at that date. The subject of dispute was a right of common on the Quantock Hills. Humphrey Blake, as owner of Plainsfield, claimed pasture on the hills "by reason of vicinage upon the said (*vastum*) waste of Quantocke." Blake is the defendant, and it is shown that he is "lawfully seised in his demesne of fee or fee-tail of the capital messuage, barton, farm and manor of Planesfield bordering upon the said waste of Quantocke held of His Majesty as of his manor of Hampton Court by knight's service." Humphrey Blake and his ancestors before him from time immemorial, so the pleading runs, had always enjoyed common of pasture on Quantock Waste for all their cattle, except when any part of the hill was tilled or sown with rye or corn. Such, we may presume, had been the privilege of the Williams family before the Blakes inherited Plainsfield. The depositions of wit-

THE ANCIENT BOROUGH OF BRIDGWATER

nesses taken at Glastonbury, 19th December, 1637, before William Coward, are interesting as throwing a sidelight upon the Quantocks. One of the witnesses had known Humphrey Blake personally for six years, and had always heard that "the common called Quantock and reputed to be parcel of the manor of Wick-Fitzpayne contained about 1200 acres." The matter ended by Humphrey Blake having 120 acres of land set out for him from the common of Quantock on Plainsfield Hill (July, 1639), and the wood survives to this day.

The Quantock traditions, therefore, were strong in the Blake family, and there could have been no property more prized by these merchants of Bridgwater than this. The very transference of the manor is symbolical of the change going on in England. Originally it had formed part of the great Stowey Barony, held up to the reign of Henry VII by the Audley family, and the barony marched with the still greater Stoke Courcy Barony, both of them claiming part of the great Quantock Common or Waste. Nether Stowey Barony claimed 1000 acres with pasturage for 1000 sheep, and the Stoke Courcy Barony 1200 acres with pasturage for 1200 sheep. Presently both these feudal rights get split up, and the barony of Nether Stowey, becoming forfeited to the Crown by the attainder of the last Lord Audley, was divided up amongst many claimants. The old order went and the men of trade and commerce stepped in and took the place of the old feudal nobility. Humphrey Blake holds his title "of the King, as of his manor of Hampton Court," in this lawsuit. The Act for making the manor of Hampton Court an honour, with divers lands and manors attached, dates back to 1540 (31 Henry VIII c. 5). However this may be, the Herald's Visitation of Somerset (1623) amply testifies to the position of the Blake family as landed gentry, *generosi* and *armigeri*.

## ADMIRAL BLAKE

In Commonwealth and indeed in Stuart times Church patronage indicated a peculiar local influence, scarcely intelligible at the present time. There were root divergences of religious thought, and the Blake family used their territorial influence to secure certain nominations. In the little parish church of Aisholt, close to Plainsfield Court, Blake traditions lasted long. The advowson was originally inherited from the Williams family; then, just before the Civil War it fell into the hands of the King. But in 1660 Humphrey Blake the Admiral's brother held it, then Nathaniel Blake, both described as *generosi;* then Elizabeth Blake, *vidua.* As late as 1790 a rector, Nathaniel Blake Brice, seems to point to a kind of continuity of family patronage derivable from the days when the Blakes held the contiguous Quantock manors of Tuxwell and Plainsfield.

Blake influences in Church appointments can be traced also at this time in the ecclesiastical annals of Over Stowey, where a Caractacus Butler, evidently a Blake nominee and associated very closely with the family as joint patron of Aisholt living, was appointed in 1671.

At Enmore the Church patronage appears also to have passed for the time into the hands of two men of Puritan traditions, Hugh Saffin or Saffyn, of a family known at Bicknoller and Lydeard St. Lawrence on the west side of the Quantocks, and "Nathaniel Blake clericus." About this time that notorious wastrel of the Restoration, John Wilmot, Earl of Rochester, was owner of Enmore, and under the circumstances, the nomination of a Puritan rector might have been for the benefit of the parishioners. The earl died at the early age of thirty-three, chiefly owing to his extravagant excesses, his father confessor towards the end of his career being the celebrated Bishop Burnet, who has left on record some curious stories of this poor Restoration wastrel.

In Over Stowey Church there is still an inscription to Humphrey Blake of Over Stowey, clothier, buried March 20th, 1619: also to Ann his wife who died December 11th, 1645. On the south wall there is a monument to John Blake, junior, of Court House (Plainsfield), who died May 2nd, 1723, aged 32. In Nether Stowey churchyard there are inscriptions to Roger Blake who died July 15th, 1785, aged 66: to Jane wife of Roger Blake and daughter of Lancelot St. Albyn of Alfoxton who died March 29th, 1751: also of Robert Blake of Churchill in this county, son of Roger and Jane Blake, who died March 2nd, 1830, aged 86 years: also to Frances his wife who died October 31st, 1848, aged 88: and to Frances St. Albyn their daughter who died January 9th, 1864, aged 75.

Knowle (or Knoll) Hill was not so closely associated with the history of the Blake family as Tuxwell or Plainsfield manor. It had formed part of the old Nether Stowey Barony in feudal days, like Plainsfield, and had been purchased by Blake's father. The income of the estate was calculated to be in those days about £200 a year, and it was here that Robert Blake first lived when, after his Oxford career, he took up the management of the family affairs. He seems to have been very fond of this spot, as his biographer says that he took much pleasure in the walks round his lands at or near Knoll, "in which walks he was very contemplative; and I have heard his brother say, who was wont to take these walks himself, that he learned to do so by his practice with him."

The view westward from Knoll Hill takes in the wide plains around Bridgwater, from which it is two or three miles distant, with the tidal Parret meandering across a dyked and empoldered region. In those days the road that runs in a straight line from Bridgwater to Downend, just at the foot of the Poldens, did not exist. At Downend itself, once a separate manor and called in old documents the " Burgh de capite montis," was an ancient landing place, Downend Pylle being reckoned within the boundaries *by water* of the borough of Bridgwater. Here the River Parret itself used to run up close to the hill and form a distinct loop, a geographical feature still to be recognized in old maps. The Admiral, therefore, at Knoll Hill would be in very quick and close touch with the River Parret itself and would get the earliest information from ships and traders. His partiality for the Polden ridge as apart from the Quantocks would thus be easily understood, and Downend Pylle was an active place in Blake's days as it had been in far more ancient times. The house the Admiral lived in was said to have been inhabited by a family named Balch for sixty years, and it did not remain long in the possession of the Blakes, but was repurchased from the Admiral's brother or his assignees about 1682 by Robert Balch, member for Bridgwater. Historically the whole region lying between the Poldens and Taunton was full of traditions of King Alfred and his campaign of 878 against the Danes, culminating in the famous battle of Æthandune or Edington, said to be Edington on the Poldens. Downend and Chisley Mount, the little castle or fort overlooking the Parret still, is associated with the great king's doings and is probably the castle at which the Danes surrendered previously to the signing of the "Peace of Wedmore."[1]

In Blake's case the smaller or more local patriotism by no means obscured the larger patriotism. Proud

[1] *Athenæum,* August 18th, 1906.

enough of being a "Somerset man, born and bred,"
he was prouder still of being an Englishman and
extremely jealous of the glory of his nation. This
was a hard thing to do in Commonwealth times, and
it was owing to Blake that the navy was really more
English than merely Parliamentarian. Naval officers fell
under the influence of Admiral Rich, Lord Warwick,
yet were never seething with the passions of the mob,
"keeping the ring" as the discreet but not violent servants of the Parliament. If a Parliamentarian seaport town was threatened by Prince Rupert and Prince
Maurice, up sailed a ship or two of the Commonwealth
and the intruders had notice to go or be classed, as
they really were, as privateers. Supposing a European
king sympathized with King Charles and the Royalist
exiles wished to come, there lay the "silver streak"
between them, patrolled by Commonwealth ships easy
for all to see and claiming the honours of the flag. It
was best to leave these ocean patrols alone, dipping flag
or topsail as they went. Admiral Blake told his seamen
"that it was his and their business to act faithfully in
their respective stations and to do their duty to their
country, whatever irregularities there might be in the
councils at home ; and he would often say amongst his
officers that State affairs were not their province, but that
they were bound to keep foreigners from fooling us."
A wise and historic saying ! He was also heard
frequently to say "that he would as freely venture his
life to save the King, as ever he did to serve the Parliament."

The many-sided life of Admiral Blake can be illustrated in five different periods. There was the period of
his education as a scholar, the period of his commercial
life as a man of business engaged in the heavy task of
righting the family affairs. Then there was the political

period when he took up politics and represented the borough of Bridgwater; next his fighting life as a colonel in Popham's Regiment, a magnificent levy of 1500 men who have never been excelled in deeds and training.

Finally, there was his career as a naval officer and a "General-at-sea." The late Professor Burrows, Chichele Professor of History at Oxford, himself a naval officer by training to begin with, has pronounced a strong encomium on Blake. He stands alone amongst naval and military heroes in the peculiarity of his training for noble deeds. Certainly no other seaman began his career as a naval officer as late as the age of fifty and then crowded into a space of seven years a series of brilliant victories which even Nelson did not surpass in a lifetime.

With these public acts in detail we are not here concerned to treat. They are written broadly in England's annals and furnish a most illustrious page. Clarendon's estimate of him was that he was "of a melancholic and sullen nature, and spent his time most with good fellows who liked his moroseness." As a character sketch we cannot accept this as true, for although Robert Blake was of a serious temperament, as indeed he had cause to be, he was by no means lacking in a genial and pleasant West-Country bonhomie which made him the idol of his sailors. He was open and chivalrous enough in fight and was of invincible courage. What cavalier of the day could have surpassed him in courtesy and in the rules of chivalrous bearing than when he met with a French man-o'-war, a ship of forty guns, in the Straits of Gibraltar? Commanding the captain to come on board his ship Blake asked him whether he was willing to deliver up his sword. The Frenchman boldly answered "No," and then the English Admiral bade

him return to his ship and fight it out as long as he
was able. A strange tournament, we exclaim, as we
call it up! Fought out there upon the heaving space of
blue waters with no other witness but the clouds of
heaven. The duel ended with the victory of the
English crew after a stern engagement of two hours,
and then, with torn rigging and splintered decks, the
Frenchman yielded, kissing his sword impulsively as
he handed it to the victorious Admiral. The celebrated duel between Captain Broke of the *Shannon* and
Captain Lawrence of the *Chesapeak* off Boston harbour
has often been quoted, but this naval duel of Admiral
Blake is more noticeable, as Englishmen were then fighting for the honour of the flag and were struggling to
lay the first foundations of national strength by sea.

The fact is there were so many great exploits done
by Blake, both by sea and land, that we hardly know
which to select as most typical or as most honourable. What more gallant than the defence of Lyme?
or of Taunton? Blake was the very mainspring of that
tough resistance against odds of an overwhelming
kind, proving how a "Puritan," as he was scoffingly
called, could fight even against such a skilled captain
of the age as Prince Rupert. As long as English
history is read the contrast between Blake's Somerset
men and Goring's rascally and debauched troopers
will remain and point the moral of quiet and sober
courage. When Blake became General-at-sea he was
equally at home, as a Blake naturally would be, and
chased Prince Rupert's fleet from the Irish Seas to the
Mediterranean. He subdued the Scilly Islands, which
had been made a centre of Royalist resistance, he
humbled the pride of Spain, reduced Portugal to
reason, broke the naval power of Holland, (the most
difficult task of all), suppressed the rovers of Barbary,

who had been the curse of the seas for centuries, and twice triumphed over Spain. Perhaps the capture of the Spanish Plate-fleet off Cadiz is of the greatest interest to Bridgwater people, because a ship called the *Bridgwater* was engaged. Blake and Montagu had long been investing the Spanish port when the Plate-fleet was expected, challenging the Spaniards who could not be prevailed to leave the shelter of their forts and castles. Blake and his crew suffered much from want of fresh water and provisions and from the wearisome monotony of keeping up a blockade during the winter months. Fortunately, the opportunity for striking a blow came when Blake was close to Wyers Bay in Portuguese territory and the glad news came that the Spanish merchantmen were sighted at last. Hoisting all sail, Stayner, Blake's right-hand captain, swooped down upon the Spaniards like a falcon on its prey, and the action was fought amidst the horrors of the growing night. Stayner had three ships with him, the *Speaker,* the *Bridgwater,* and the *Plymouth,* and with them, first of all, he engaged eight Spanish men-o'-war and the galleons within four leagues of Cadiz Bay. The Spanish admiral, Don Marco del Porto, with 600,000 pieces of eight on board, ran his ship ashore, thinking the rocks more hospitable than the shot and shell of the English. Two ships, one commanded by Don Francisco de Esquevil, in which were 1,200,000 pieces of eight, and another commanded by Don Rodriguez Calderon, were fired, one designedly and by the Spanish crew themselves, the other by accident. In one of them the Marquis of Badajos, Viceroy of Mexico, with his wife and eldest daughter, betrothed to the Duke of Medina, perished in the flames. His other daughter and his two sons, Don Francisco de Lopez, and Don Joseph de Sunega, and nearly 100 others, were saved by Blake's seamen. The *Rear Admiral* with 2,000,000 pieces of eight on board was taken and secured. So also was another ship richly laden with hides and cochineal. A man-o'-war and an advice-boat got into Gibraltar and the other two ships ran ashore and bulged. Six of these eight were destroyed or made prizes. Admiral Blake ordered Montagu home with the Plate-ships, and coming to Portsmouth, the silver was taken out and carried by land in many waggons to London and so through the city to the Tower, where it was coined. The prisoners, among whom was the young Marquis of Badajos, were brought up with the plate and entertained in the Tower. "The sight occasioned great discourse and joy, and Oliver, whose glory was radiant before, received a new increase of it by this achievement." Edmund Waller, the poet of the Commonwealth, thought fit to celebrate Cadiz in verse, and although his muse does not strike the critic as rising altogether to the occasion, still there are a few lines which were passable, as they indicated the fact of England's naval supremacy. For instance :—

Others may use the ocean as their road,
Only the English make it their abode ;
Whose ready sails with every wind can fly
And make a cov'nant with the inconstant sky.
Our oaks secure as if they there took root,
We tread on billows with a steady foot.

Apropos of the treasures, the poet sang not so discreetly about Cromwell :—

Let the rich ore forthwith be melted down
And the State fixed, by making him a Crown ;
With Ermine clad and Purple, let him hold
A Royal sceptre made of Spanish gold.

Whether the Protector would have accepted a crown made of the captured wealth of Spanish galleons is more than doubtful. The Admiral's humble biographer, speaking the gossip of his family, thought these lines would have been very disagreeable to Blake as a simple State servant. In his own private opinion Blake understood that there was no Government in the country but the Commonwealth, and this was what the English fleet was fighting to maintain. However, it seems tolerably certain that the great Admiral did not live to criticize the effusions of the poet of the day, much though he might have sympathized with the poet on patriotic grounds.

The Cadiz capture recalled the old days of the *Madre di Dios* again, after an interval of fifty years, and old salts round Bridgwater and the Severn ports must have furbished up again their yarns of Sir Robert Crosse. Blake himself, born in 1598, might just have linked the interval with memories of what he had seen and heard, and remembered how the little villages of Spaxton and Over Stowey had been thrilled with tales of "derring do."

For, if we think of it, Blake's lifetime, although he lived only sixty years, covered a marvellous and epoch-making time. He knew the England of Shakespeare and of Sir Walter Raleigh; the England of Queen Elizabeth, of King James, and of Charles the First. Born ten years after the defeat of the Armada, he lived to see Spain—proud Spain—humbled to the dust for her crimes in the Old World and the New. And of many great events he might have said, "Quorum pars magna fui!"

It is necessary to think of Admiral Blake not only as a man of action, but a man of thought deeply influenced by religion. It has been objected to him by some that he was tinged with Puritan principles of a somewhat dour and destructive tendency, and this prejudice was surely in Clarendon's mind when he passed his judgment of this great Englishman. It may be well, however, to offer a few remarks on some aspects of "Puritanism" such as it was in King Charles's day and as it was professed by the Blake family and others. Clearly Blake's Puritanism was not fashioned, to begin with, on the stern and hard Calvinistic model. His father Humphrey had left in his will small sums of money to Wells Cathedral, to Bridgwater Church, and to Paulet Church, thus endowing Episcopacy. The Admiral's brother, Humphrey, was churchwarden of St. Mary's Church, and the Admiral himself was duly baptized as a member of the Church of England.

Episcopacy, therefore, was clearly acknowledged by two generations of Blakes at least, and we are told that when Humphrey Blake was driven by persecution to emigrate to Carolina, his son Joseph, becoming one of the lord-proprietors of the colony and an important personage, was the first governor who established a settled income and a handsome allowance for a Church of England minister. This was a very generous act, as Joseph Blake had small occasion to love Episcopacy in its extreme Caroline developments.

There was evidently a distinction in Blake's time between the Church of England as it had been left by the Elizabethan settlement and what it was about 1630–50. It seemed to be undergoing some real and radical change. In the will of a certain Somerset lady, Bridget Mahatt, dated 1655, within a year or so of Blake's death, there is this significant protestation: "I die a true Christian in that religion which was established in the Church of England in Queen Elizabeth's time." That is to say, Bridget Mahatt distinguished between two phases of the same Church, clear enough to her mind, and she desired to die in the Protestant faith of Elizabethan rather than of Caroline times.[1] In 1660 Hugh Peard of West Harptre, by his will dated September 13th, bequeathed to the parish Bishop Hall's works in folio with a shelf to place it on and a chain to fasten it with. Bishop Hall had been an old pupil at Emmanuel College, Cambridge, and was suspected of what his enemies in the Caroline days called Puritanism. But Hall had his own rightful position in the Church of England, and might easily have retorted to his Caroline critics that he represented the Church of England as left, doctrinally and otherwise, by the great struggle culminating in Elizabethan days. At any rate Mr. Peard of Harptre thought that in 1660 his works should find a place in every church library alongside of Jewel's famous *Apology* and the *Paraphrase of Erasmus,* and other works which really standardized the great doctrines of the Church of England as far as they could be standardized, by vigorous and incisive language, such as we find thundered forth in the Church homilies themselves. The style and diction of these Church homilies are old fashioned, but, doctrinally, they are plain enough on fundamental teaching.

Bishop Hall suffered much for his leanings to Puritanism, and to use his own words, "The billows went so high that I was three several times upon my knee to His Majesty (Charles I) to answer these great criminations. . . . I plainly told the Lord Archbishop of Canterbury (Laud) that rather than be obnoxious to the slanderous tongues of misinformers I would cast up my rochet." However, in December, 1642, he was committed to the Tower, his estates and rents being sequestered as a notorious delinquent, although he was

[1] *Somerset Wills,* Brown Series.

actually Bishop of Norwich at the time.  He wrote an account of his privation, under the title of "Hard Measure" (*Biographical Dictionary*).

Bridget Mahatt was the wife of Philip Mahatt, vicar of East Brent, and he is said to have been a cousin of Bishop Lake, the Bishop of Bath and Wells before the days of William Laud.[1]  The distinction alluded to in Bridget Mahatt's will gathers still more force from this connection.  Bishop Lake was, we are told, a Puritan bishop, if controversialists of the age would have allowed the reasonable sense of this appellation.  He stood for the Elizabethan interpretation, Bishop Laud for the Caroline.  Bishop Lake was an intimate friend of such a distinguished clergyman as the Rev. John White, a Fellow of New College, Oxford, and rector of Dorchester for forty years, known as the "Puritan Divine" and the father of the Massachusetts colony.  He was a man of great godliness, profound scholarship and wonderful ability, and his name is still honoured on both sides of the Atlantic. John White was plundered at Dorchester by Prince Rupert's Horse, and came to London to be made rector of Lambeth and one of the Westminster Assembly of Divines.  These little incidents throw light upon the state of the Church of England in Blake's time.  It was not hard to guess which side he would take.  By a strange and unfortunate chance Laud harried and worried the Somerset Puritans sadly, and almost drove them to extremities.  His successor, Bishop Pierce, suspended one of Blake's favourite ministers in Bridgwater, and enjoined Humphrey Blake, his brother, to do penance as a favourer of the delinquent.  Were these petty persecutions necessary?  Were they wise? Robert Blake, a learned scholar himself, with Oxford

[1] Brown's *Wills.*

traditions, was fully able to point out the proper position, doctrinally or otherwise, of the Church of England as it was in the days of Queen Elizabeth. There have been and, probably, will always continue to be two parties in the English Episcopal Church, and certain distinct lines of cleavage were apparent enough in 1630–50. We are not concerned to defend one position at the expense of another, for the controversy would lead us far afield, but simply to explain Robert Blake's attitude, common not only to him but to many others. At this date the terms "Anglican" or "Anglo-Catholic," as applied to the Church, were unknown. The attempts to divide England into Presbyterian "classes," although formulated, fell still-born. There was never any real enthusiasm at that time for Presbyterianism, nor any burning zeal to upset the old parochial church system if it could be purified. There were, of course, great leaders of thought and opinion, and the Admiral would have preferred George Abbot to William Laud as his Metropolitan, Arthur Lake to William Pierce as his Diocesan, whilst his general attitude on doctrinal points would have been more in agreement with the writings and opinions of Bishop Jewel, the West-Country divine, and Joseph Hall, Bishop of Norwich. These men were, of course, the theological prototypes of Bishop Burnet and of Archbishop Tillotson who came after them.

Next to Blake's religion must be considered that burning flame of patriotism which illumined his whole soul as an Englishman and fired his blood as a seaman. Nothing aroused his wrath more than the idea of ship-money, which was levied, not for the sake, as he saw, of national protection, or "to keep out foreigners and prevent their fooling Englishmen," but to let them in by shoals and bring England under their influence.

Blake and William Strode were at one with Hampden here. Close to Bridgwater and living at Brymore in Cannington was John Pym, the stalwart friend of constitutional government. Here is a passage from a letter of Walter Strickland to John Pym dated November 19th, 1642: "I am more and more confirmed that there are designs upon Harwich, Yarmouth, Hull and Portsmouth, and that it is intended to have considerable forces at sea to beat the Parliament's ships, if it be possible."[1] Why should Strode, Blake, Pym, and the rest be forced to subscribe money to build ships with which would at once be turned against their own liberties? They were not men of this stamp and naturally objected to forging their own fetters.

Further, there was the King's marriage with Henrietta Maria of France, a marriage cordially detested by Englishmen as a rule. This had been preceded by the attempt to secure a Spanish match in 1623 when Prince Charles, accompanied by Buckingham, had paid a visit to "His Most Catholic Majesty." This continental flirtation and these dynastic intrigues brought nothing but trouble to England, and the French marriage was the unluckiest event in the unlucky life of the weak and uxorious Charles I. The Queen might influence the King, and behind the Queen stalked the shadow of a father confessor, possibly a Jesuit. Englishmen like Blake cared little for political Jesuits and their ways. The Queen herself in 1642 was on the side of England's bitterest antagonists by sea—a point that touched Blake and the rest of the English seamen to the quick—and from the Hague in January, 1642, the Queen, who had gone thither ostensibly on a visit to her daughter Mary, the wife of the Stadtholder, William of Orange, began to organize naval forays

[1] *Bouverie Papers*, Hist. MSS. Commission.

against England. The Hague had been the asylum of two very evil counsellors of King Charles, viz. Chief Secretary Windebank and Lord Keeper Finch. In addition to sea rivalry and fishing disputes, the fact of the Hague being used as a base against Parliamentary England by the Queen sharpened the animosity of the Commonwealth leaders. Here is an extract from a letter written to John Pym by Walter Strickland from the Hague (November 19th, 1642):—

"The Queen is not satisfied with the small number of ships (from Holland against England). Some think that others will meet her on the way and make her able to do something against our fleet or to get some place in England, Harwich, Yarmouth, Hull or Portsmouth." All these machinations of the Queen would be well known to Robert Blake through John Pym.

As one result of these intrigues, which lost none of their venomous meaning because hatched in a professedly Protestant state as Holland, English trade suffered everywhere. The massacre of Englishmen by the Dutch at Amboyna in 1623, and the expulsion of England from the Spice Islands, grated on the feelings of Blake and the Commonwealth leaders. There was no security for English trade anywhere, not even in the home waters. The complaint of the Earl of Warwick is notorious in which he stated that Irish pirates, whose field of unlawful adventure covered the seas from Ushant to the ports of the Severn Sea, were making captures of English merchantmen. Intolerable ignominy! How could even a Cavalier or Loyalist say that the arm of their Prince protected them in their lawful occupations? "It grieves me much," wrote Lord Warwick, "that I cannot help them or send any of our ships to take these rogues. All our ships are out of victuals and none of them go well enough to catch them, except the *Providence* and the *Expedition*, which might be fitted out for the service." The Royal Navy could not catch a pirate !

The following extracts from the State Papers supplement this evidence :—

June, 1629. A French man-of-war lies between the Holms and Bridgwater and took a "Trow" [i.e. a small coasting smack] which was coming to Bristol with lead. The Englishmen told them of the Peace, and the Frenchmen answered they knew not nor did they care.

Dec., 1631. Petition of Robert Pawlet, John Norris, Comptrollers of Customs at Bridgwater and Minehead, to, Lords of Admiralty about the English and Irish coasts being infested with Biscayners, etc.

May, 1634. Petition of Robert Pawlet, sometime Customer of Bridgwater and Minehead, to the Lords of the Admiralty for relief concerning losses for more than three years by piracy of certain Dutch of Rotterdam.

In August, 1629, an order was issued that in consequence of the decay of the town of Bridgwater, that town shall hereafter pay for itself and for the tithing of Heygrove no more than one-eighth part of the sum assessed upon the hundred of North Petherton towards furnishing the provision of His Majesty's household.

It was time, indeed, for men like Robert Blake to gird on their armour and man their own ships. "What! a Frenchman off the Holms !" we can fancy Blake exclaiming, and at the same time twirling his moustaches, a habit of his when spurred by righteous wrath. Englishmen saw two kinds of fetters being forged for them : first, the political fetters of their own misguided King (the most galling of all to Englishmen), listening to such men as Chief Justice Finch, who actually endeavoured to revive the Forest Laws and exact the Forest Fines. In the words of Lord Falkland, who impeached him, "he gave our goods to the King, our lands to the deer, and our liberties to the Sheriffs." Even Lord Clarendon pointed out the unwisdom of such measures. Behind the King's ministers and backing them up were the King's foreign auxiliaries. In a letter (October 16th, 1634) from Francis Windebank (who died in the Roman Catholic faith) we learn that the King of Spain had promised twenty ships to coerce King Charles's subjects! Shades of Sir Francis Drake, Captain Crosse, and Walsingham, we exclaim! This was carrying Court intrigue too far!

The other fetters threatened were spiritual fetters. Englishmen whose fathers had gone through the perilous times of Queen Elizabeth knew too well what these meant. The Blakes and Strodes and all Severn merchants, whose occupations had led them continually to Bilbao and San Sebastian, had a first-hand acquaintance with the country ruled over by "His Most Catholic Majesty." They required no further lessons. The sailors of Bridgwater who brought the first news of the coming of the Armada, as already noted, were the sailors of Humphrey Blake. In other parts of England the Spanish, and indeed the continental, danger might be half known or, perhaps, misunderstood. Not so in Severn waters, a first line of quick intelligence, whither the beacon signals of alarm were likely to come more swiftly than even to London.

Blake's attitude towards the Roman Catholic faith, a very militant and aggressive faith in his day and in the days of his father and grandfather, is best shown in the following episode. "The Admiral being at Malaga, some of his seamen going ashore met the Host (the consecrated element) carried about, and not only paid no respect to it but laughed at those who did. Whereupon, one of the Spanish priests put the people upon resenting this indignity, and they fell upon the English and beat them severely. When they returned to the ship they complained of this usage to the Admiral, upon which he immediately sent a trumpeter to the Viceroy to demand the priest who was the chief instrument in that ill usage. The Viceroy answered that he had no authority over the priests and so could not dispose of them. Upon this Admiral Blake sent word that he would not inquire who had the power to send the priest to him, but if he were not sent within three hours he would burn their town. The Spaniards hearing this, obliged the Viceroy to send the priest to the Admiral, and he justified himself upon the petulant behaviour of the sailors. Blake answered that if he had sent a complaint to him he would have punished his men severely, since he would not suffer them to affront the established religion of any place. But he took it ill that he should set the Spaniards on to do it, for he would have all the world to know that an Englishman was only to be punished by an Englishman. So he treated the priest civilly and sent him back, contenting himself with the thought that he had him in his power. Cromwell was highly delighted with this and read the letter himself in Council, saying that he hoped he should make the name of an Englishman as great as that of a Roman."

The justice which Admiral Blake would have measured out to the Spaniards was not the kind in vogue throughout Spain. Their officials were accustomed to treat all "heretics" with severity, and there is an entry in "Letters and Papers Foreign and Domestic" (Henry VIII) from which we learn that two British subjects, Bridgwater men, were sentenced to public penance in the Church of St. Sebastian and to pay 600 ducats within three days, and, further, to stay within the town for two years on penalty of 10,000 ducats, "all because, six years previously, they had said that they did not believe in the Pope and in the prayers to saints." At the same time a boy of Bridgwater was fined twenty ducats for words spoken in England. On one occasion Admiral Blake fluttered the dovecots at Rome when, in 1654, he appeared off Leghorn. "The city of Rome and all the Pope's territories were alarmed at the name and approach of Blake. Several of the principal citizens retired with their effects to the mountains, though Sir Richard Tambot, as the Italians call him, assured Cardinal Berberini, the Cardinal patron of England, that Cromwell had given no orders to insult the patrimony of St. Peter. Yet the terror of the people was such, that public processions were made and the Host exposed forty hours to avert the wrath of heaven should Blake attack the dominions of the Church. New works were raised around the Chapel of Loretto to defend it. Upon his arrival in sight of Leghorn he despatched his secretary to demand of the Great Duke £60,000 for the damages sustained by the English in his duchy, where Prince Rupert had taken so many ships belonging to the English .... The Great Duke offered to pay part of the sum and desired him to consult the Pope about the payment of the rest. Blake replied that the Pope had nothing to do with it and that he expected the whole sum from him. Upon this the Duke paid down 35,000 Spanish and 25,000 Italian pistoles. The Duke pretended that some of the ships had been sold to the subjects of the Pope and therefore his Holiness ought to pay part of the damage, which Alexander VII did, and paid him 20,000 pistoles, the only " Peter's pence " that was ever brought from Rome and put into the treasury of England."

Whatever his opinions on the more burning Church questions of the day, it would be impossible to ignore the strong vein of personal religion that ran through Admiral Blake's life and character. He lived in contentious times, but in a homely practical way the Admiral tried to do his duty as a simple straightforward Englishman without cant or fuss. His biographer writes: "I was told by a countryman of his and mine, Mr. Thomas Bear of Bridgwater, when he was afterwards mayor of that town, that though he was with him two or three years and officiated and lay in Blake's cabin, he never heard an oath sworn aboard that ship or indeed aboard the whole fleet. It has been said that General Blake prayed himself aboard his ship with such of his men as could be admitted to that duty with him, and the last thing he did, after he had given his commands and word to his men, in order to retire to his bed, was to pray with the above-mentioned Mr. Bear. When that was over he was wont to say, 'Thomas, bring me the pretty cup of sack,' which he did with a crust of bread. He would then sit down and give Thomas liberty to do the same and inquire what news he had heard of his Bridgwater men that day, and talk of the people and affairs of that place."

Here came in that old spirit of West-Country sympathy and camaraderie which carried these West-Country crews together towards the attainment of their laudable ends, whether it was to seek for the North-East or North-West Passage or, still better, to fight the enemies of their country. No wonder that "his tenderness and generosity to the seamen so endeared him to them that when he died they lamented his loss as a common father." Whenever a Day of Thanksgiving or of Humiliation was ordered by Parliament it may be noted that Admiral Blake always kept them and had them observed. Penance with him, as with many other Puritans, was a real religious duty and it was a public and congregational matter.

The circumstances of the death of Admiral Blake were glorious and at the same time deeply pathetic. Blake had heard that the Spanish Plate-fleet was on its homeward voyage in 1657 and that it would probably put in at Santa Cruz in the island of Teneriffe, a strongly fortified station in the Canaries. Leaving the blockade of Cadiz he sailed at once for Santa Cruz. There he found the Spanish galleons already anchored and protected not only by sixteen men-o'-war, but by a well-fortified bay and by a castle. There were also seven forts each mounted with heavy artillery, all united by a line of communication and manned with musketeers. Enough to terrify and appal a less stout heart than that of Robert Blake ! But already in answer to the Dey of Tunis, who braggingly cried, " Here are our castles of Guletta and Porto Ferino, do your worst, we fear you not !" Blake had replied by shot and shell and had struck terror into the hearts of the sea rovers of the age. No castle or fort could withstand his onset. It was the Spaniard's turn now, and the Admiral Don Diego Diagues was to learn a stern lesson. In Santa Cruz harbour was a Dutch skipper who, knowing something about Blake and his seamen, craved leave to quit the harbour as a neutral. " Get you gone if you will and let Blake come if he dares !" was the answer of the piqued and enraged Spaniard who thought himself secure. And Admiral Blake did come, and where, in 1797, the great Nelson failed, won a brilliant and most unparalleled success. Again Captain Stayner, who the year before had commanded the *Speaker*, *Bridgwater*, and *Plymouth* frigates, swooped upon the galleons, boldly standing in for the harbour.

What he and Blake did then is ranked amongst the greatest of British naval achievements, and when the English ships, almost miraculously it is said, returned from the swoop into the bay favoured by the wind that sprung up, they had captured the galleons and annihilated the Spanish fleet.

This victory was the climax of Blake's naval successes and at the same time marked the end of his career. Slowly the fleet returned to England covered with much glory, but at the same time carrying a dying Admiral. With a frame weakened with wounds and sickness but with a spirit struggling bravely to the last, his one passionate desire being to see again the shores of old England, Robert Blake was borne from the Canaries to Plymouth. Lovely was that island of Teneriffe, beautiful its orange groves, rivalling those of Seville, magnificent its towering peak lifted 12,000 feet to the subtropical skies, splendid the numerous and countless forms of nature by sea and land, but, far from the scene of his triumph, lay Blake's island home for which he yearned. Shall I live to see the ridges of the Poldens? or the long low line of the Quantocks? or the grey muddy reaches of old Father Parret meandering up the green moorlands? or the old bridge of Bridgwater and the Cornhill and the old familiar West-Country faces I know so well? They will greet me, and nothing better than such a home-coming as this! Then I will, perchance, rest awhile, if my country's needs permit it! Alas! the hopes of the dying sailor were not destined to be fulfilled nor his "passionate" desire to be granted him. The fleet sighted Plymouth, and as the ships came up by the Eddystone the sailors might have seen the green slopes of Mount Edgcumbe, the Hamoaze, Drake's Island, the Hoe, the houses of the old town of Plymouth rising like a city they loved from the sea, and behind the Devon highlands and the moorland. But not the Severn Sea or the combes and hills of Somerset! And so Robert Blake's spirit passed away on the element he knew so well, the heaving, changing, restless sea. We may conclude with a stanza or so of that well-known poem by Henry Newbolt on the death of the Admiral (August 7, 1657).

Low on the field of his fame, past hope lay the Admiral triumphant,
    And fain to rest him after all his pain :
Yet, for the love that he bore his own land ever unforgotten
    He prayed to see the western hills again.

Fainter than stars in a sky long grey with the coming of the daybreak,
    Or sounds of night that fade when night is done,
So in the death-dawn faded the splendour and loud renown of warfare,
    And life of all its longings kept but one.

Oh ! to be there for an hour when the shade draws in beside the hedgerows,
    And falling apples wake the drowsy noon :
Oh ! for the hour when the elms grow sombre and human in the twilight,
    And gardens dream beneath the rising moon.

Only to look once more on the lands of the memories of childhood,
    Forgetting weary winds and barren foam :
Only to bid farewell to the combe and the orchard and the moorland,
    And sleep at last among the fields of home !

    .    .    .    .    .    .

Dreams ! only dreams of the dead ! For the great heart faltered on the threshold,
    And darkness took the land this soul desired !

The heart of Admiral Blake was taken from his body and buried in St. Andrew's, the mother church of Plymouth, where a sermon was preached over it by the learned Obadiah Hughes. The body was embalmed and taken to Greenwich, whence it was conveyed by water on September 4th, 1657, to London, with all due solemnity, in a barge of State covered with black velvet and adorned with escutcheons. In addition to his brother Humphrey and his immediate relations, the cortège consisted of the members of the Privy Council, the Lords of the Admiralty, the Commissioners of the Navy, the Lord Mayor and Aldermen of London, the Field Officers of the Army, and several other persons of honour and quality rowed in boats draped in mourning and marshalled by heralds-at-arms. Blake's body was buried finally in a vault made on purpose in Henry the Seventh's Chapel, but to the eternal disgrace of English rulers at the Restoration it was taken from there and transferred to the churchyard outside. Such revenges are paltry and mean. But what else could you expect from Charles II and his profligate Court?

It is strange that no public memorial was ever erected to Robert Blake in Bridgwater till the year 1898, when, owing to the untiring zeal and enthusiasm of Dr. Winterbotham, a prominent leader in that town, a sum of money was raised to erect a statue to his honour. In 1897 Professor Montagu Burrows, Chichele Professor of Modern History in the University of Oxford and Captain R.N., prepared the way by reading an appreciative notice before the members of the Somerset Archæological Society. The statue, the work of Frederick Pomeroy, with two bas-reliefs giving stirring scenes in the hero's life, was subscribed for and completed, and now stands for all to see in the Cornhill. The features and attitude of the Admiral were copied from a painting in the possession of the Rev. Raymond Pelly, of Great Malvern, a direct descendant of the Admiral's niece, Sally Hitchin

Blake. Stranger, we would say, if you pass this way
and love honour, piety, and simplicity, and that noble
patriotism that works for England solely and keeps her
foes, whether inside the gate or out of it, "from fooling
her," take off your hat to Robert Blake's statue as it
stands in the Cornhill, Bridgwater.

### THE WILL OF ROBERT BLAKE

The last will and testament of me, Robert Blake, written
with my own hand as followeth : First, I bequeath my soul
unto the hands of my most merciful Redeemer, the Lord
Jesus Christ, by Him to be presented to His heavenly Father,
pure and spotless, through the washing of His Blood which
He shed for the remission of my sins, and, after a short
separation from the body to be again united with the same
by the power of His Eternal Spirit, and so to be ever with
the Lord.

Item, unto the town of Bridgwater I give £100 to be
distributed amongst the poor thereof at the discretion of
Humphrey Blake, my brother, and of the Mayor for the
time being.

Item, unto the town of Taunton I give £100 to be distributed among the poor of both parishes at the discretion
of Samuel Perry, once my Lieutenant-Colonel, and Mr.
George Newton, Minister of the Gospel there, and of the
Mayor for the time being.

Item, I give unto Humphrey Blake, my brother, the
manor of Crandon-cum-Puriton, with all the rights thereto
appertaining, to him and to his heirs for ever.

Item, I give unto my brother, Dr. Wm. Blake, £300.

Item, unto my brother George Blake I give £300, also
to my brother Nicholas I give £300.

Item, unto my brother Benjamin Blake I give my dwelling-house, situate in St. Mary's Street, Bridgwater, with the
garden and appurtenances, as also my other house, thereto
adjoining, purchased of the widow Coxe ; likewise I give
unto him all the claims I have in eleven acres of meadow or
pasture (more or less) lying in the village of Hamp, in the
Parish of Bridgwater, lately in the possession of the widow
Vincombe, deceased.

Item, unto my sister Bridget Bowdich, the wife of Henry Bowdich, of Chard Stock, I give £100, and to her children, of the body of Henry Bowdich aforesaid, I give the sum of £900, to be disposed among them according to the discretion of Humphrey, William, George, Nicholas and Benjamin Blake, aforesaid, my brothers, or any three of them.

Item, unto my brother Smythes, goldsmith, in Cheapside, I give the sum of £100.

Item, unto my nephew, Robert Blake, son to Samuel Blake, my brother, deceased, I give the gold chain, bestowed on mè by the late Parliament of England, also all the claim I have in an annuity of £20, payable out of the farm at Pawlett.

Item, unto my nephew, Samuel Blake, younger son to Samuel, my brother, deceased, I give £200.

Item, unto Sarah Quarrell, daughter of my late niece, Sarah Quarrell, by her husband, Peter Quarrell, now dwelling in Taunton, I give the sum of £200 to be disposed of for the benefit of the said Sarah Quarrell, according to the discretion of Humphrey, Nicholas and Benjamin Blake, my brothers aforesaid.

Item, unto my nephew John Blake, son unto my brother Nicholas, I give £100.

Item, unto my cousin John Avery, of Pawlett, once a soldier with me in Taunton Castle, I give £50.

Item, unto Thomas Blake, son of my cousin Tom Blake, once commander of the *Tresto* frigate, deceased, now aboard of the *Centurion* frigate in the service, I give £50.

Item, all my plate, linen, bedding, with all my provisions, aboard the ship *Naseby*, I give unto my nephews Robt. and Samuel Blake, aforesaid, and unto my nephew, John Blake, aforesaid, to be divided by them by even and equal portions.

Item, unto the negro called Domingo, my servant, I give £50, to be disposed of by my aforesaid nephèw, Capt. Robt. Blake and Capt. Thomas Adams, for his better education in the knowledge and fear of God.

Item, unto my servants James Knowles and Nicholas Bartlett, I give to each of them £10.

Item, unto the widow Owen, the relict of Mr. Owen, minister, I give £10.

Item, unto Eleanor Potter, widow, I give £10.

All the rest of my goods and chattels I do give and bequeath unto George, Nicholas, and Benjamin Blake, my brothers aforesaid, and also to Alexander Blake, my brother, to be equally divided amongst them, whom I do appoint and ordain to be the executors of this my last Will and Testament.                                   ROB. BLAKE.

Signed and sealed aboard the *Naseby*, March 13th, 1655, in St. Helens Road in the presence of Roger Cuttons, J. Hynde, John Bourne, Antho. Earming.

NOTE.—The Admiral's charitable bequest to his native town of Bridgwater was at first carried out in the way it was intended, but Charles II succeeding to the Crown, and the Corporation Test having put the borough of Bridgwater in the hands of men of Restoration principles, not the least notice was taken of Admiral Blake's name in the distribution of his legacy which, from the field his money purchased, was called "Jacob's Land Charity." The immortal name of the Admiral was dropped by the worshipful corporation as unworthy to be recorded! Could adulation sink deeper? Blake's local biographer, "bred in the family," adds, "I did not know the charity, though I lived in and frequented the place near fifty years. I took it to be Jacob's Charity as well as Jacob's Land till, even in the present reign [George I?], George Balch, Esq., son of Robert Balch, Esq., who was one of the trustees for the bequest, observed to the two other trustees, Mr. Jeanes and Mr. Pitman, honest men of Bridgwater, 'It was a shame to forget General Blake in the distribution of his legacy, which should go no more by the name of Jacob's Land but of Admiral Blake's Charity.'" By which name it has been known ever since. St. John's Church, Eastover, occupies a part of this land, and the school and some houses cover the remainder. In accordance with the suggestion of Hepworth Dixon, the biographer of Robert Blake, this site has been called Blake Place, perpetuating the name of the gift of the Admiral.

o

# CHAPTER XV

## THE SIEGE OF BRIDGWATER

FEW men ever combined so many private virtues with public transgressions as King Charles I. He was a good husband and father, a man of intense kindliness, a loyal and devout Churchman, and a prince possessed of many high ideals. Yet he embroiled himself fatally with the nation and with the Parliament, and in his attempts to extricate himself from the difficulties which in many instances were those of his own creation, he erred most grievously in his judgments, in perception, and in act. It was his dealings with the nation, and the protest of a powerful section of the nation against his policy, which led to the siege of Bridgwater in 1645.

Charles inherited a legacy of ideas from his father which contained in themselves the seed of national discord. James I was a man of small natural capacity, but he compensated for this by fostering to every extent that lay in his power the notion that kings could do no wrong. In his time the theory was evolved that all power lay inherent in the sovereign; that though he might choose to delegate certain of these powers to Parliament, or to some other agent, he could recall these concessions at will, and re-invest them in his own sacred person. His son Charles I, a far abler man, thus entered upon his reign handicapped by an inherited tradition which could only imply, in those times, disaster sure and swift. For

before the seventeenth century had run half its span,
political ideas of a most directly opposing nature were
current, and were daily gathering strength. The Parliament, and the strongest men within it, were determined that the sovereign, whoever he might be,
should rule in conformity, and only in conformity,
with their wishes. Monetary supplies, without which
the king could not govern, were to be granted only at
their bidding. The king might have his full share
of power, but not independently of them. They were
to be reckoned with, to be consulted, and to some
extent they thought that they should even be cajoled.
Here, then, were two theories of government which
were as directly in opposition as the poles ; both sides
held to their position ; both assumed the *non possumus*
attitude ; each was inflexible.

Charles found difficulties with his first Parliament ;
they held the purse-strings too tight. So he dissolved
it, and convoked another, which proved to be yet more
intractable. This assembly also was dissolved, and he
began to raise taxes on his own authority. But so
great was the discontent that the King was obliged to
call together his third Parliament, which he found,
to his great dismay, to be less tractable and less easy to
manage than either of its predecessors. It was evident
that some compromise must be arrived at, and indeed
such an one was soon called into being. The Petition
of Right, which bound the King to abstain from raising
money without the Parliament's consent, and which
forbade the imprisonment of any subject without the
law having first been appealed to, was drawn up, and
was ratified by Charles. If he had adhered to this
undertaking all might have gone well. But he did
not. All the old troubles broke out again. At length
the third Parliament was dismissed, and in an evil

hour the King resolved to rule without one. For eleven years, from 1629 to 1640, Parliament never met. The unpopular ship money was raised; the nation waited, sullen and disgusted, yet not willing lightly to plunge into civil war. Then, in a moment of supreme folly, Charles attempted to force the Anglican Liturgy upon the Scots, and the pent-up feelings of the nation at last gave way. In November, 1640, the famous Long Parliament had to be summoned, which sat for thirteen years, until Cromwell, who like Charles tried to rule England as a despot, without check or hindrance, contemptuously turned it out by force in 1653. Within two years of the assembling of this Parliament the Civil War began, when the King raised his standard at Nottingham on August 22nd, 1642.

But other forces beside these were also at work. The Puritan position in matters of religion had been deepening for years, notably in Bridgwater and in Taunton. Mr. Devenish at St. Mary's had diligently taught these doctrines, and his influence was great. It was about this time that some eight thousand clergymen were turned out of their benefices, and their places filled by such men as would obey the Parliamentary Committee of Religion. Thus the livings of the Church of England for a time were filled by those who disbelieved her doctrines and sneered at her ceremonial, yet were glad to accept her posts of honour. George Wotton, the rightful vicar, was ejected in 1644 or 1645, and evidence seems to point to his not having been in Bridgwater at the time of the siege. Probably John Norman, the intruded minister who conformed to the religious standard of the Covenant, was then in possession. Thus from the religious point of view Bridgwater, when the siege came, in all probability had within its walls more who sympathized with the

Parliamentary position than who owned loyalty to the King. In theory it was a Royalist town, since Colonel Wyndham commanded the castle; in practice it was a divided community. Four hundred years before, when the Briweres ruled in Bridgwater, the policy of the lords of the castle was the policy of the borough, but times had changed since then. All England was in a ferment; so too was Bridgwater. There were many who hated the puerile and vacillating policy of the King; there were many who hated the abominable tyranny of the Committee of Religion.[1] There was no man in the town who was strong enough to take the lead. Colonel Wyndham was a brave soldier, but he was no leader of men. Devenish had passed away; Wotton was either ejected or just about to be ejected from St. Mary's; Norman was not yet fully installed. The town possessed every element of weakness; it was at the mercy of any really strong man who was prepared, in 1645, to take the side either of Royalist or Parliament.

The strong man soon appeared. Oliver Cromwell, then forty-six years of age, had steadily forced his way

[1] "The Puritans in the day of their power had undoubtedly given cruel provocation. They ought to have learned, if from nothing else, yet from their own discontent, from their own struggles, from their own victory, from the fall of that proud hierarchy by which they had been so heavily oppressed, that in England, and in the seventeenth century, it was not in the power of the civil magistrate to drill the minds of men into conformity with his own system of theology. They proved, however, as intolerant and as meddling as ever Laud had been They interdicted under heavy penalties the use of the Book of Common Prayer, not only in churches, but even in private houses It was a crime in a child to read by the bedside of a sick parent one of those beautiful collects which had soothed the grief of forty generations of Christians. Severe punishments were denounced against such as should presume to blame the Calvinistic mode of worship. Clergymen of respectable character were not only ejected from their benefices by thousands, but were frequently exposed to the outrages of a fanatical rabble. Churches and sepulchres, fine works of art and curious remains of antiquity, were brutally defaced."—Macaulay's *History of England,* chap II

upwards. He had sat in Parliament; he had trained
soldiers. As a captain of Parliamentary horse he
fought at Edgehill. At a military engagement near
Gainsborough he had distinguished himself. Only the
year before, in 1644, he joined Fairfax's troops before
York, and the terrific charge of his cavalry at Marston
Moor decided the issue of the day. Now, as against
the Presbyterian and Moderate party, he was the leader
of the Independents, or thoroughgoing faction. He
thought fit, after the second battle of Newbury, to
impeach Manchester's conduct, and by the decision of
the Self-denying Ordinance, while the Presbyterian
and aristocratic generals were set aside, Cromwell was
retained in command. Under Fairfax, his junior by
some thirteen years, he led the new model army to a
splendid victory at Naseby, and then first decisively
turned the fortunes of the war from the Royalist to the
Parliamentarian side. Henceforth he was the representative of the army in its contest with the Presbyterian Parliament, who wished to disband it. Cromwell
promptly marched to London and bluntly coerced the
members, for by this time he had found out that it was
by a military despotism that England was for a time to
be ruled. So, while Fairfax was Captain-General of
the Parliamentary forces, and nominal head of the
army, Cromwell was in reality the directing genius and
force, though in actual rank only Lieutenant-General.
He early recognized the need of strenuous discipline
amongst his troops, and he gained it. There was no
drunkenness, no licence, no pilfering amongst his
Ironsides. He looked out for men who had convictions, who felt that they were fighting for a worthy
cause, who fought for conscience sake. His rule was
the rule of an iron hand, yet only so to put down
breaches of discipline. It must be frankly said that he

made his troops respected as well as feared; honoured as well as dreaded. He gave them a moral stimulus which was terrible in its power; he restrained them with a curb which was inexorable in its rule. This was the man, and these were the men, who came into Somerset in July, 1645.

On July 10th General Fairfax, with Cromwell, severely defeated the forces of Lord Goring, the Royalist General, at Langport, capturing some horse, prisoners, ordnance, and colours, and pursuing the Royalists to within two miles of the East Gate of Bridgwater. The following extract is taken from an account of the Bridgwater siege, compiled by Joshua Sprigge, M.A., in his *Anglia Rediviva*,[1] published in 1647. It may perhaps more faithfully show what happened—being written at the time—than the most elaborate later research can reveal. It was obviously written from the Parliamentarian point of view.

The next day, (July 10th) the whole Army, horse and foot, with the Train, were drawn up in Westonmoor, otherwise called Pensy pound, two miles from Bridgewater. The Country-men thereabouts, that had been vexed with the Cavaliers, hearing of the defeat given unto them, and fearing to taste of their former cruelties, rose in great numbers, and with their colours, clubs and arms, appeared upon Knol-hill; which being made known to the General,[2] he with the Lieutenant-Gen.[3] and other Officers marched up to them, who seemingly received him with joy, and in token thereof gave a volley of shot: whence after some conference with them, and their Leader, who made a Neutral Speech, the General returned, and the Army that night went

---

[1] *Anglia Rediviva*, England's recovery: being the history of the motions, Actions, and successes of the Army under the immediate conduct of His Excellency Sir Thos. Fairfax, Kt., Captain-General of all the Parliament's forces in England. Compiled for the Publique good by Joshua Sprigge, M.A. London: printed by R. W. for John Partridge, and are to be sold at the Parot in Paul's Church-yard, and the Cock in Ludgate Street, 1647.

[2] Fairfax.                    [3] Cromwell.

to quarter, the head-quarter that night being appointed at Chedsay, within two miles of Bridgewater.

Friday, July 11. Colonel Welden's Brigade was commanded on the North side of the Town towards Devonshire, and the rest of the Army on this side towards Chedsay; the guards being set, the General with the Lieutenant-Gen., went to view the Town, which they found to be very strong, standing in a valley, yet glorying in the equality of its level with the ground about it, there being not a clod that could afford any advantage against that place; The Fortifications very regular and strong, the Ditch[1] about it very deep, and about thirty foot wide, which for a great part about the town, was every Tyde filled up to the brim with water, the compasse of ground within the line and works not great, very well manned, having in it about 1800 Souldiers to defend it; within the town was a castle of indifferent strength, (there was planted on the severall Batteries about 40 peece of Ordnance;) well stored with ammunition and victuals, being a magazine for all the petty garrisons thereabouts.

Saturday, July 12. The Army continued in quarters, and new places for guards were appointed.

Lord's day, July 13. The Army rested at Chedsay; and Colonel Okey having, from that day the battel was at Langport, besieged Burrough-garrison with his Dragoons, had the same surrendred unto him upon quarter, wherein were 140 prisoners, the Officers being promised fair usage.

Monday, July 14. A Councel of war was called, great debate whether to storm the town,[2] or not: Some inclination to it, but no positive resolution; Notwithstanding preparations were made in order to a storm, the Souldiers cheerfully made their faggots, and were drawn in readines for a storm, but upon further consideration were for that time drawn back to their quarters; and more time being taken, there were 8 long Bridges, betwixt 30 and 40 foot length, devised to be made by Lieutenant-general Hamond, the

---

[1] On the west side of the town a ditch ran from the North Gate, past the Castle, to the Parret; also in an opposite direction from the North Gate along the entire length of the Mount, joining a ditch in North Street which ran southwards to Moat Lane (near Albert Street). The south side of the town was similarly protected. On the Eastover side there were also ditches, but the course of these is now difficult to trace accurately.      [2] i.e. Bridgwater.

# THE SIEGE

Lieutenant-general of the Ordnance (a Gentleman of approved fidelity, and of a most dexterous and ripe invention for all such things) which were approved of by the Commanders and Officers, and accordingly ordered to be made, and were of very great use to the Souldiers in the storm.

This day, the General going over the river to view the posts on the other side, was graciously delivered from a great danger he was near unto by a sudden surprisal of the Tide called the Eager, where he very narrowly escaped drowning.

Wednesday July 16 a Counsel of War was again called, and several propositions were made for the framing of our Army, and reduction of the town, both being of great consequence, and vehemently desired by us. To rise with our whole Army and leave the town unattempted, was conceived to be very prejudiciall to our future progresse; To sit down before it (being a place of that strength, and we not sure to carry it) leaving the Enemy[1] at Liberty to rally his broken forces, seemed very hazardous.

The *blocking* of it up by Forts on both sides with a part of our Army was propounded, but the difficulty of laying a Bridge over the River through the violence of the current, (which yet was necessary for the maintaining a communication between our quarters on both sides) hindred that designe.

It was propounded to attempt it by *approaches;* But it was considered, that if we should have gone that way, it would have proved very tedious; and if during our stay about it any great glut of rain should have fallen, it would have laid us wet in our trenches, and disabled us from effecting the business.

At last, a resolution to storm it was agreed upon, though it carried the greatest danger with it: yet the desire which the Army had to be speedily free for the further service of the Kingdom, surmounted all difficulties: the storming being thus happily resolved on, to the great and generall satisfaction of all the Army, both Officers and Souldiers; Lots were drawn for every one to take their posts, some to storm, some to be reserves, others to alarm, but the time of falling on not yet determined.

Friday July 18. It was resolved at a Counsel of War, that the time of the storm should be on Monday morning towards dawn-

[1] The Royalist troops.

ing of the day. The Brigade appointed to storm on that side towards Devon was commanded by Major General Massey, being the Regiments of Col Welden, Col. Inglesby, Col. Fortescue, Col. Herbert, Col. Birch, and Major General Massie's own Regiment: the Regiments designed on this side, were the Generals, Major-Generals, Col. Pickerings, Col. Montagues, Sir Hardresse Wallers, the Regiment commanded by Lieut. Col. Pride, Col. Rainsboroughs, and Col. Hamonds. The General rode round about the town this day, to see if all things were in readines for the storm, that both sides might fall on together. On the Lords day, July 20, Mr. Peters in the forenoon preached a Preparation Sermon, to encourage the Souldiers to go on : Mr. Bowles likewise did his part in the afternoon. After both Sermons, the Drums beat, the Army was drawn out into the field :[1] The Commanders of the forlorn hope who were to begin the storm, and the Souldiers, being drawn together in the field, were there also afresh exhorted to do their duties (with undaunted courage and resolution) by Mr. Peters, who did it (as one says of him) *tàm Marte, quàm Mercurio*. As soon as it grew dark, the Souldiers drew every one to their severall Posts allotted them to storm ; the signe when the storm was to begin, was, the shooting off three peeces of Ordnance on this side, which the Forces on the other side were to take notice of, and to fall on at the instant : and on Monday, July 22, about two of the clock in the morning, the storm began accordingly on this side of the town, (the Forces on the other side only alarming the Enemy, which kept them upon the Line, expecting a storm). Our Forlorn hope was manfully led on by Lieut. colonel Hewson ; and as valiantly seconded by the Generals Regiment, commanded by Lieut. colonel Jackson ; and the Major-generals, commanded by Lieut. colonel Ashfield. The Bridges prepared to passe over the Moat,[2] were quickly brought to the Ditch, and thrown in, on which the Souldiers with little losse got over the deep ditch, and with undaunted courage mounted the Enemies works (notwithstanding the

[1] In the neighbourhood of Horsey and Bower.
[2] Eastover was thoroughly well fortified. *Vide* a petition from Sir Edmund Wyndham to the King (January 31st, 1668) for sums of money expended in ammunition and soldiers' clothing, and for the repayment of £1200 which Wyndham and others had advanced for fortifying Eastover. State Papers (Domestic)

great and small shot which showred about them) beat them from their Ordnance, turn'd them upon the enemy, and let down their drawbridge; which made many of their Foot instantly cry, "Quarter, quarter." The Bridge being let down, Captain Rainolds, who commanded the forlorn hope of horse, immediately entred, and scoured the streets of that part of the Town so gained, called Eastover, with much gallantry and resolution, even up to the Draw-bridge[1] over the main Ditch, leading to the second Town: whereupon the rest of the Officers and Souldiers that were in a body, and yet annoyed us in that part of the town which we had won, threw down their arms, and had fair quarter given them: (there were about 600 taken prisoners, Officers and Souldiers). The Enemy instantly made barracadoes at the gate upon the bridge, and drew up the bridge that divided one part of the town from the other. Our forces had not been two houres in the first town, but the Enemy shot granadoes, and slugs of hot iron, and fired it on both sides, which by the next morning burnt that part[2] of the town (of goodly buildings) down to the ground, except three or four houses, Major Cowel, who had a good share in that service, standing all that while in the midst of the street, which was both sides on fire, keeping guards to prevent the Enemies fallying upon them: Captain Sampson, in that remarkable action, received a shot.

The General, hoping that the Storm might have wrought upon the Souldiers, and the Fire upon the Townsmen, so far, that they would have hearkened to a treaty; renewed his Summons, which the Governour[3] peremptorily refused, according to his allegiance (as he said) whereupon, Tuesday, July 22, it was resolved to alarm the town by our forces on this side, and to storm it by the other forces on the other side, at two of the clock the next morning; for which purpose the General was there in person to see it done, though it was held fit on after considerations, only to alarm on both sides, which much amazed the Enemy, and kept him waking that night: Also about two of the clock in the afternoon, the General sent to the Governour a Trumpet with a message to this purpose, that his denial of fair tearms had wrought in him no other thoughts, but of compassion towards those that were innocent, who otherwise might suffer

[1] The bridge over the Parret.
[2] Eastover.          [3] Colonel Wyndham.

251

through the Governour's obstinacy : Wherefore he signified his noble pleasure, that all women and children that would accept of this liberty, should come forth of the town by four of the clock in the afternoon, which being made known to them, the Governour's Lady and divers others came out They were no sooner come forth, but our Cannon plaid fiercely into the town, Granadoes were shot, and slugs of hot iron in abundance, whereby several houses in the town were fired, and the wind being high increast the flame, the townsmen within were in great distraction, every man imployed how to save his house and goods, the Enemy in a great amazement, and the Governour so far melted with the heat of the fire, as to send forth Tom Elliot in haste, to desire to know the General's tearms; The General refused to admit of any treaty at all, resolved that the Governour and they within that had destroyed so fine a town, should have no conditions, but should submit to mercy; which being signified to the Enemy, they yet would try the General with these three particulars.

First, that the Governour with all the Officers and Gentlemen that were in the Town, with their servants, horses, swords, pistols and cloak-bags, might march with a safe Convoy to Exeter.

Secondly, that all the souldiers might likewise march to Exeter leaving their armes.

Thirdly, that all Clergie-men in the town, and Townsmen may have liberty to march with us, or abide at home.

The General returns these.

1. To all their lives.

2. To the inhabitants, their liberty and freedome from plunder.

3. Neither Officers nor Souldiers to be plundred of the clothes they have upon them.

4. The Gentlemen to be disposed of as the Parliament shall appoint, and in the mean time to have civil usage.

Six Hostages to be sent, and an answer in a quarter of an hour.                              THO. FAIRFAX.

The Governour returned answer, that he found those Propositions so ill resented, both by the Gentlemen and Souldiers,[1] that he could not accept of them.  The general

---

[1] i.e. of Bridgwater.

thereupon gave order to the souldiers to stand upon their guard, and go to their duties; Tom Elliot desired nothing might be done till he returned, leaving Sir John Heale as caution, which was agreed to; and he presently returned with an answer of submission to the Generals Articles, only slipt in a motion for himself, that he might have liberty to carry the news to the King upon his Parol. May he have more such imployment till peace be setled!

Thereupon the Hostages were sent, Sir John Heale, Sir Hugh Windham, Mr. Waldron, Mr. Warr, Mr. Siddingham, Mr. Speake. And we sent some into the Town to them.

They were to deliver the Town and yield themselves prisoners the next morning by eight of the clock, and all that night they imployed themselves to quench the fire in the town. The losse of men in this storm was not many, Mr. Martin an Officer in the train had his leg shot, and afterwards cut off, whereof he died, he behaved himself valiantly.

Wednesday July 23. The town was surrendred, about 1000 Officers and Souldiers, besides Gentlemen and malignant Clergy,[1] marched out as prisoners. There were taken in the town about 44 barrels of powder, 1500 armes, 44 piece of ordnance, 400 weight of match, Enemies goods of great value, that had been carried for security into that place, and were seized by the Commissioners of the Parliament, and sould; and 5. s. a man raised upon the sale, to be bestowed as a reward upon the common souldiers for their good service in the storming of the place.

That which may seem to allay the happiness of the successe was, that the town was fired; but truly though in strictness of souldiery this might be very well justified, yet God in his providence concurred to the justice of it, and our acquittance: They refused treaty after part taken, they fired the part we had taken, and rang the bels for joy when they saw it blaze: and as we are credibly informed, they fired the town themselves[2] in many places where fireworks could do no hurt, the souldiers saying, "The Town did it to be rid of them;" the town said, the souldiers did it, when they were in little hopes to hold it. But God be thanked

[1] The "malignant" clergy were those who were not for the Parliament.

[2] Mr Sprigge is here evidently trusting to rumour only. He is anxious to make the Parliamentary case good.

THE ANCIENT BOROUGH OF BRIDGWATER

we found much more of it standing then we expected. Some things there are which made the businesse considerable. As first, that by it a line of garrisons was drawn over that isthmus of ground between the South-sea and Severne, by Bridgewater, Taunton, Lime, and Langport, it being from Bridgewater to Lime little above twenty miles, by which the Counties of Devon and Cornwall then wholly in the Enemies possession, except Plymouth, were in a manner blockt up from all entercourse with the Eastern parts, a business of no small consequence, if we had procceded no further. Likewise this being taken, our Army was at liberty for further work, which was a great mercy at that time of the year. It was a great gain with little losse: and that which addes as much to the commendation of the action, as any thing, we kept our Articles exactly, which is not only honourable in the eyes of men, but acceptable in the sight of God, and that which this war had scarce formerly attained; and it was not done without some difficulty now, in regard our souldiers had suffered so much, and Cornwal was so near.

Thursday July 24. All the day was spent in ordering the manner of sending away the prisoners, and securing Malignants goods in the town. And thus you have that gallant fight at Langport crowned with an easie recovery of that considerable strength of Bridgewater, whose natural fortification by water, they that knew, must needs conclude, God was the Bridge by which our Army got over.

Such is Mr. Sprigge's story of the storming of Bridgwater. The very quaintness of his diction, and his unrestrained partiality for the cause of the Parliament, are interesting, and significant in their way. He omits to relate the very narrow escape which Cromwell had of being shot on July 12th. He and Fairfax were viewing the town defences, and venturing too near the Castle, a shot was fired by Mrs. Wyndham, the governor's wife, which killed the man standing at Cromwell's side. Within a few days Cromwell again was in danger. He narrowly escaped being drowned in the Parret. Either of these accidents, had it ter-

minated in a different manner, would probably have
changed the history of England.

The town suffered deplorably. In Eastover scarcely
a house was left undamaged, and the fire raged fearfully.[1] Wyndham, furious at the success gained there,
poured a perfect rain of hot shot across the river at
Fairfax's men, seeking to dislodge them, or to put
Eastover in a blaze. Tactically, of course, he was
right. Better to lose Eastover than to lose all. But
there were abler men storming at the gate of the great
bridge, and directing the Parliament's forces, than were
defending the town from within. When Cromwell
turned the great guns which had been taken from the
Royalists at Naseby, and the mortar pieces, upon the
western part of the town, all was soon over. The streets

[1] Sir Thomas Fairfax wrote the following appeal on behalf of the
Bridgwater people two years after the siege :—" To the Commissioners
for the monthly assessment in the Countie of Somersett, and to the High
Constable of the hundred of North Petherton, and every of them.

"Having perused a certificate under the hands of Tho. Wroth,
Knight, Col John Pyne, and Col. Rob^t Blake, members of the Honb^le
House of Commons in this present Parliam^t, in the behalf of the Burrow
of Bridgwater, in the Countie of Somerset, importing an inequallitie of
taxes and paym^ts charged upon the same by the Hundred of North
Petherton, whereof the said burrow is a part ; and particularly in this
present monthly assessment, wherein the rest of the said hundred doth
presse the said burrow, and limits thereof, to pay a third part with the
said hundred, whereas upon good informacon it is but the eighteeth
[eighth] part of the said hundred. I therefore desire yow all that accordingly you lay no more on the said burrow and limits thereof, in the said
monthly assessm^t and other publique rates, then according to the pro-
porcion of the eighth part as aforesaid ; forbearing to trouble the said
towne anie farther in that behalf; and the rather, for that the said
towne hath susteyned exceeding great losses by fire ; almost one third
part thereof being burnt down to the ground in the late seidge thereof;
the Parliament having besides declared their desires and intencions to
redresse all grievances of this nature through the inequality of rates in
the kingdome . thus not doubting of your readie conformitie to a thing
soe just and equall, thus attested by the members aforenamed, who well
know the different state and condicon both of the said towne and
hundred.      " I remaine,

" Windsor, the second      " Your verie assured frend,
of December, 1647.            " T. FAIRFAX."

255

were fired [1] in three places, notably at the Cornhill, in High Street, and St. Mary Street. The fire spread rapidly, and threatened to consume the whole town. Wyndham was bound to surrender, or to see the place burned to the ground. He rightly yielded, though it must have been with a heavy heart. Having only the horse that carried him, he took his quarter and rode to Weston the same night.

The booty was considerable, as Mr. Sprigge has pointed out. Beside the arms and prisoners, there was all Lord Goring's and Colonel Wyndham's baggage, a great stock of provisions, and a hundred thousand pounds in money, jewels, and plate. Many people, relying upon the impregnability of the town, had lodged their belongings there for safety. A huge sale of the spoils held in the market-place provided further largess for the soldiery, who were already highly paid, and so delighted was the Parliament with the capture of Bridgwater that another £5000 was sent to Fairfax to dispose of as he would amongst his men. Many old buildings, of course, were greatly damaged. When the Ironsides succeeded in storming the Bridge Gate they drove the defenders before them into the market-place, past the High Cross, and into St. Mary's Church. It was probably at this time that the beautiful north porch was so sadly damaged, for the one blot upon Cromwell's men was that they were simply

---

[1] December 23rd, 1656. Henry Milles, mayor of Bridgwater, writes to John, Lord Desborow, General of the West and M P. : " Your ready assistance encourages me to represent our cases, we having no help towards repairing 120 dwelling houses consumed in the late war. We beg your order for some stones undisposed of, belonging to the late garrison, viz. a small sconce at the foot of the bridge, and a wall near the castle, 50 feet long and 5 or 6 high, towards the rebuilding of our alms-houses, which were utterly demolished ; many poor shall bless you for them." [An order thereon in Council was made that the mayor and aldermen may take down and carry away the said stones for repairing the almshouses, without payment.]—Cal. of State Papers.

vandals and ruffians in a church.[1] There was little likelihood of any trace of mediævalism remaining in St. Mary's under Devenish, but the Parliamentary troops so hated churches and churchmen that they were not scrupulous. It was a mercy that the building was not more seriously damaged.

Considering the probabilities of the result of the storming of Bridgwater, as from this distance of time they may be estimated, it is clear that the advantage lay on the side of the forces of Fairfax and Cromwell. They were united; they were splendidly disciplined; they were inspired by the most vigorous mind and personality of that age. These qualifications much more than outweighed the advantages of the well-manned, well-fortified, well-provisioned town. If the same fight, in the same conditions, had to be fought out again to-day, the same result would follow. War is largely an affair of the genius of the generals. It cannot be denied that Cromwell possessed a genius for war. He ruled England by the sword for fifteen years; the army which the Parliament created mastered its makers, and reduced them to impotence. Under any other leader save Cromwell this would probably have been ruin to the country, and when he died, leaving a standing army of fifty thousand men on English soil, the liberties of England were never nearer to becoming the prey of a military despotism which might have wrecked the state. The situation was critical; only the Restoration, and the disbanding of the Ironsides, saved the position until Parliament could recover its real power.

[1] "One of Cromwell's chief difficulties was to restrain his musketeers and dragoons from invading by main force the pulpits of ministers whose discourses, to use the language of that time, were not savoury; and too many of our cathedrals still bear the marks of the hatred with which those stern spirits regarded every vestige of Popery."—Macaulay's *History*, chap. I.

But other events which transpired showed that Wyndham had no real chance of success in defending the town. When Eastover was gained by Fairfax's forces, and Captain Reynolds had secured possession of that part of the town, 500 of the Royalist foot surrendered. Of these 300 promptly took the Covenant and joined Fairfax, expressing their pride at being captured by such an enemy. Thus within the walls were divided counsels, and men who had no loyalty and no stability. In a word, Bridgwater Castle was Royalist, so were its governor and garrison, and some of the inhabitants. But Taunton was for the Parliament, under the famous Blake of Bridgwater, and there were many people in Bridgwater who shared the same views. In conditions such as these, the result was a foregone conclusion. The town was doomed to fall because of its divided adherence; and it did fall.[1] It had against it the greatest military genius then living in Europe. But it did not need a Cromwell to reduce it. The real enemy was the half-heartedness of many within the town gates.

Some of the waverers, one would think, were sorry when the order came from London at the end of the year to dismantle the old Castle, once the pride of the town. Indignation at the order was openly expressed, but this was futile. It was clearly the natural thing for

[1] Letter from Sir Thos. Fairfax to Lord Fairfax, 24th July, 1645:— "Yesterday I gave an account to both Houses of our taking Bridgwater, part of it by storm, and finding their obstinacy I was forced to fire two or three houses which presently made them to render the toune." In a P.S. he adds: "The King is expected this night in Bristowe, if the news of taking Bridgwater stay him not. His greatest hopes now seemes to be in the club-men; and God's providence is much seene in the timely taking of this toune. If the King had had time to have got out his forces and these numerous club-men together, we must have left it." Dated from Neare Bridgwater. [N.B.—This letter is exceedingly valuable as showing what might have been done if Bridgwater, with a whole heart, had vigorously resisted the attack of the Parliamentary forces.]

the Parliament to wish to see the Castle slighted and dismantled, for it was in some sense a badge of the Royalists and of ancient feudal power. *Vae victis!* William Briwere's fine old building was thrown down, and it became a quarry for the builder. Had Bridgwater men been truly united in the day of their siege, had they really been inspired with the stimulus of a great conviction or by the possession of a splendid ideal, they might have won the day, and their castle would have been standing now.

# CHAPTER XVI

## THE MONMOUTH REBELLION

ON April 9th, 1649, a baby boy was born at Rotterdam who was destined to bring ruin and death to thousands in the West-Country, and to embroil Englishmen in a rebellion which, though speedily quelled, was lamentably fruitful in disastrous consequences. This child was James, the son (as was believed) of Charles II, the mother being one Lucy Walter, "a browne, beautifull, bold, but insipid creature."[1] After the Restoration the boy was brought to England[2] with Queen Henrietta and Lord Crofts, the latter of whom acted as his guardian. In 1662 the handsome lad was taken to Hampton Court with the suite. He was received with extraordinary fondness by the King, and Pepys described him "as a most pretty spark of about fifteen years old."[3] Even thus early Charles had been busy about scheming a matrimonial alliance for young James. In the previous year he had written to the Countess of Wemyss, acknowledging "the affection which you shew to me in the offer you make concerning the Countesse of Buccleugh, which I do accept most willingly, and the rather for the relation she hath to you."[4] Within a year of the writing of the letter the Countess of Wemyss and her daughter, "a lively tall young lady of her age," came to London,

[1] *Evelyn's Diary.*
[2] In 1656 he had previously been in England with Lucy Walter.
[3] *Pepys' Diary*
[4] Copied from a transcript of the original letter at Wemyss Castle.

and preparations were made for drawing up the marriage contract.

In the draft of this contract ran, by Charles's own order, the significant phrase "Filio nostro naturali et illegitimo." In November, 1662, the boy was made Duke of Monmouth, Earl of Doncaster, and Baron Tynedale. In April of the following year his marriage with the Lady Anne, daughter and sole heiress of Francis Scott, second Earl of Buccleuch, was solemnized at Whitehall, and on the same day the bridegroom was further created Duke of Buccleuch, Earl of Dalkeith, and Lord Scott.[1] He was fourteen years of age, his bride was twelve. It was a great start in life, indeed, for Lucy Walter's son.

But there was more to come. He now took precedence over all dukes not of the blood royal, and honours and distinctions multiplied upon him. He soon became Knight of the Garter, Chancellor of Cambridge University, Captain-General of the King's forces, Privy Councillor, Lord Great Chamberlain of Scotland, Governor of Kingston-upon-Hull, and Lord-Lieutenant of East Yorkshire. The King doted upon him, and they were constant companions everywhere.

From very early days there was always the possibility of trouble arising about the Duke of Monmouth. The failure of the King in regard to legitimate offspring rendered the succession to the throne a disputable matter, and it soon transpired that many about the Court held to the belief that Monmouth was Charles's lawful son. The King's brother James, Duke of York, not unnaturally conceived a violent aversion to the young Duke, which he made no effort to conceal. Charles's fatally easy nature complicated the *status quo ante*, and there can be little wonder that Monmouth,

---

[1] Calendar of State Papers, 1663.

:

surrounded by flatterers, and by others whose designs
were more far-reaching, conceived ambitious notions
as to his future. The King, however, when it came to
an issue, peremptorily settled the knotty point. "Much
as I love him," said he, "I had rather see him hanged
at Tyburn than I would confess him to be my heir."
A disgraceful intrigue which occurred just then, in
which Monmouth, the Duke of York, and the Earl of
Mulgrave were all implicated, further widened the
breach between the King's brother and the King's
son. Strife is quickly bred, and tardily allayed. The
uncle and nephew were at enmity as long as the latter
lived.

Meanwhile Monmouth gained no small reputation as
a soldier in the second Dutch War of 1672, and seven
years later his politic action—and his clemency to the
rebels—at the battle of Bothwell Bridge told immensely
in his favour.[1] He was beginning to pose, too, as the
champion of Protestantism. Lord Shaftesbury, always
eager to oppose the Catholic Duke of York, fanned
the hatred already existing between the two men.
Charles grew weary of all the strife. At length he
cut the Gordian knot by sending Monmouth to Holland
for a while, at the same time insisting that the Duke
of York should be despatched to Scotland. The
leisure-loving King wanted only to be left in peace.

However, both men were soon back again, and
Monmouth, now the admitted champion of the Protestant party, scored a magnificent success by setting
out, at Shaftesbury's instigation, upon a grand tour in
the west of England. The West-Country folk were then
great manufacturers of woollen goods, and amongst
them were many Nonconformists. Charles's attitude

[1] He received the freedom of the city of Edinburgh in a golden
casket, and banquets were given in his honour.—Allan Fea's *King
Monmouth*, p. 70.

to the Nonconformists had never been quite fair. The Acts against Dissenters were too rigid in many ways, and their meeting-houses were being suppressed. No doubt this was partly owing to the Dissenters' own hardness to churchmen in the time of the Commonwealth, yet to retaliate with hardness for hardness is always an error. It merely perpetuated the grievance. Monmouth was received in Wiltshire, Somerset, and South Devon, as a popular hero. Just over thirty years of age, handsome, with fascinating manners, well travelled, the son of a king, and withal possessing a *penchant* for Protestantism—what could be better? His progress was like a royal progress; he stole the hearts of Israel. To Longleat, to White Lackington, Barrington Court, Chard, Ford Abbey, Colyton, Otterton House, he went and was most hospitably received. At Hinton Park he touched a poor girl—one Elizabeth Parcet—for the king's evil. The girl was declared cured, and the belief in Monmouth's legitimacy was thereby vastly strengthened. On his way he was received with acclamation, "God bless King Charles and the Protestant Duke." It was this tour in the west which determined him to strike a blow for the crown when the right time should come.

Events quickly culminated. Disaffection grew, and the wretched Rye-House Plot, which but for an accident would probably have cost Charles his life, implicated many persons. Monmouth was tinged with suspicion, and no wonder, for many were only too eager to make him their tool, and he had not wit enough to perceive it. The King temporized; he seemed to be surrounded by traitors, yet knew not what or whom to believe. Ultimately, after much correspondence and plotting, interspersed with visits to Lady Henrietta Wentworth, Monmouth fled, leaving his duchess behind in England. At the last the King had been roused, and in a towering passion had bidden the Duke quit the Court immediately. The latter embarked in a fisher-boat at Greenwich, and escaped to Brussels. There Lady Henrietta joined him,[1] and there, we read, the Prince of Orange welcomed him with open arms. This was in 1684.

Poor Charles! Wronged as he had been by Monmouth, he could hardly bear to have him out of his sight. He yearned over his son, as David yearned over Absalom. But it would never do, he thought, to have him back yet. He must wait a little while. Then Monmouth should return. One hasty but secret interview, indeed, took place between them in England, yet unknown to the Court. The days passed by, and the King grew ill. It seemed to be nothing. Yet he did not rally, and Father Huddleston was hastily brought in to his bedside. Charles received extreme unction at the priest's hands, and then passed peacefully away. At two o'clock on the 6th of February, 1685, James Duke of York was proclaimed to be, *Dei Gratia*, of the United Kingdom of Great Britain and Ireland King.

When men mean to strike a blow for power, it is well to minimize delay. London and Amsterdam were thick with plotters, yet there was more talking than acting. Three months elapsed before Argyll's expedition, which was to accomplish so much for Monmouth, set out to raise forces in Scotland. It was a failure from the very beginning, and ended in Argyll's[2] capture, after a desperate resistance, and his safe detention in Edinburgh. Monmouth himself, with the

[1] Lady Henrietta Wentworth stayed in Holland with Monmouth—save for one short visit to England—until he sailed for Lyme in May, 1685. She never afterwards saw him again.
[2] Archibald Campbell, ninth Earl of Argyll.

erratic Lord Grey and Andrew Fletcher, a Scottish laird, sailed from the Texel on May 30th in the frigate *Helderenburgh*, with two other vessels, and landed at Lyme, in Dorset, eighty-three men all told. With these, and with the aid of the huge numbers of men who, he had been informed, were eagerly waiting in England to join his standard, he hoped to seize the English crown. Never was a wilder expedition planned by man. The very day after the Duke's departure from Holland the Prince of Orange sent Bentinck post-haste to London to give information to King James that his rebellious nephew had now irrevocably taken up arms.

Lyme, however, welcomed Monmouth warmly,[1] and his manifesto, which was the ill-judged handiwork of the fanatical Ferguson, was read in the market-place. It did not mince matters. "We do solemnly declare and proclaim war against James Duke of York, as a murderer and an assassin of innocent men ; a Popish usurper of the Crown ; Traitor to the Nation, and Tyrant over the People." James was accused of poisoning the late King, and of every other sort of crime. Englishmen were called upon to rise against him. Meanwhile Monmouth stayed four days in Lyme, and there lost two of his ablest supporters. One was Fletcher, who in a quarrel killed Dare of Taunton, a man of some influence there, a goldsmith, and withal devoted to Monmouth's cause. Fletcher took flight to Holland to escape the vengeance of Dare's son, and the moody Duke saw nothing but ill-omen in the disaster. Recruits, however, came in, and by the 12th of June 1000 foot and 150 horse had joined the rebellion. A little skirmish, wherein Grey's

---

[1] William Stradling's *Priory of Chilton-super-Polden, with a Miscellaneous Appendix*, 1839, p. 53.

horse hardly distinguished themselves, occurred the next day near Bridport, but this was more than compensated for at Axbridge, where Monmouth's numbers, having greatly increased, caused the Royalist forces under Albemarle to fall back in some confusion. On June 18th, the Duke having just passed through the district full of happy memories of his visit five years before, Taunton was entered, amidst the wildest acclamations and manifestations of joy.[1] The populace yelled, shouted, cheered, and waved green boughs. All promised well, save that the country gentlemen held aloof. It was the rank and file who mustered, but the rank and file could not carry all things before them, unaided. The Duke stayed at the house of Captain John Hucker, a serge manufacturer. It was then that the Taunton school girls presented to him their banners, prettily worked and bearing the initals J. R. Then, too, Monmouth, receiving the present of a sword and a Bible, declared that he came now into the field with a design to defend the truths contained in that book, and to seal it with his blood, if need be. Then he was proclaimed "our lawful and rightful Sovereign and King." All this was delightful: *"c'est magnifique, mais ce n'est pas la guerre."* A council of war was held, and it was determined to push on to Bridgwater with the army (now 7000) with all speed. Meanwhile Churchill was watching his movements, and the Earl of Feversham was on his track.

At Bridgwater (June 21st) Alexander Popham, who was mayor that year, and the corporation, "dressed in their formalities," were effusively eager to welcome the Protestant Duke. Taunton, their old rival, must not be allowed to outdo them, and they boisterously proclaimed him king before the old High Cross then

[1] Stradling's *Priory*, p. 59.

standing in the market-place. Of King James they knew but little, and that little they did not like; of Monmouth they knew less, but he was a Protestant, or at least they thought he was. Hence his popularity. Weapons were forged, pledges were given, and all seemed to bid hopefully for him in the old town. Yet, moving on in pursuance of their plan to Shepton Mallet, by Wade's advice it was thought necessary to go towards Bristol, and the army encamped at Pensford near Keynsham. But the attempt was given up. Bath would have none of them, and shot their herald. Retreating to Philip's Norton, and thence to Frome, his followers began to melt away. All this marching about seemed to lead to nothing. It was seriously considered whether the attempt had better not be abandoned. To Shepton Mallet again, to Wells, to Glastonbury; then back again once more to Bridgwater, to make the final stand. Monmouth had erred; he should have pushed forward via Gloucester to London, where aid was; or attempted Bristol; or he might have made for Exeter, a strong city with many adherents to his cause. Meanwhile Lord Feversham was at Somerton, and was preparing to march on Weston Zoyland, ready and eager to attack the rebel troops. By July 5th he had encamped his foot soldiers there (five regiments) and his five hundred horse, while five other regiments were near at hand on the moor. A force of militia was stationed at Middlezoy, and at Othery hard by. The net was being fast drawn around the Protestant Duke.

It was on Thursday the 2nd of July that Monmouth entered Bridgwater for the last time, and his forces, depleted as they were, amounted then to about 3500 men. The town was strongly in his favour, and did everything it could to succour him.[1] Taunton, it would

---

[1] Stradling, p 69

appear, had wavered, since on his way back from Glastonbury it had sent a deputation urging the Duke not to return thither. Monmouth sadly retorted that it would have been better if they had induced him not to go there when he first landed at Lyme. However, Goodenough, paymaster of the rebels, issued an injunction commanding the aid of carpenters and labourers, with pickaxes, barrows, saws, and other implements, with corn and all kinds of provisions. Roger Hoar, the merchant, was most generous in his assistance ; so were the inhabitants. Monmouth lodged in the Castle, or in what remained of it after the siege of twenty years before ; his army lay in the Castle field on the east side of the river. His cannon and ammunition were placed on the road leading out of the east end of the town. According to Colonel Wade, the forces were : Grey's Horse, 600 ; Blue regiment, 600 ; White, 400 ; Red, 800 ; Green, 600 ; Yellow, 500 ; with an independent company of 80 more. Besides these were the scythemen, and four guns. As things now were he had but two courses to adopt ; either to give battle to Feversham's troops, or to break away northwards. The latter, it transpired, he could not do. Feversham had the roads watched too well.

The Royalist army (excluding the militia, who took no part in the battle) are stated to have numbered about 700 less than Monmouth's forces. There were fourteen troops of horse and dragoons (about 700), and thirty-four companies of foot (2100) with sixteen field-pieces. Feversham's artillery, with Churchill's dragoons, lay on the left of his line of defence. His camp was well chosen, for it was protected on the north and west by a great ditch. Moreover in order to attack the Royalist forces on their right and rear it was necessary for Monmouth to make a circuit of some miles, passing north of Chedzoy, in

order to outflank them. The danger of a slip lay in
the presence of the great rhines, or ditches, and into
this very danger the rebel army fell.

On Sunday morning at noon news reached Monmouth
from Chedzoy as to the location of Feversham's troops,
whereupon a consultation was promptly held. All
notion of a dash to northwards was abandoned, and it
was agreed to make a night attack upon the Royalists
if upon further examination it should be found that
they were not entrenched. Monmouth and Lord Grey
rushed up the steps of St. Mary's tower to reconnoitre,
and by eventide further news was brought to them by
the spy Godfrey. The Royalists were *not* entrenched,
it was said ; the infantry and artillery were separated ;
moreover the men had been drinking, discipline was
relaxed, and the duty of sentries was being neglected.
Monmouth's spirits rose, for indeed there seemed to be
a chance for him. He and Grey formulated their scheme.
Grey's Horse were to make a circuit via Peasy Farm
round to the back of Weston Zoyland, which was to be
set on fire. Then he was to attack the enemy's right
flank and rear, Monmouth's infantry in the meantime
coming up and making a frontal attack on their line.
It was a bold plan, and an excellent one. "We shall
have no more to do," said he, "than to lock up the
stable doors and seize the troopers in their beds."
Godfrey was to show the way. Quickly the news was
circulated, and Ferguson preached most fervently before
setting out. His sermon was ingenious, for it implied
that the Royalists, and not his own party, were in rebellion. Yet that it had an immense effect, none can
doubt. Protestantism was then the dominant view in
Bridgwater. It was only twenty-five years since Cromwell had ruled, and the Puritan position had by no means
lapsed. Ferguson knew his men, and he knew exactly
what he ought to say.

At eleven at night the Duke set out, and Oldmixon, then a boy, noticing him pass by, saw an alteration in his look, "which," said he, "I did not like." Colonel Wade led, followed by the infantry; then came Grey's Horse; lastly the guns and baggage. Along the Bath road, to the right down Bradney Lane, past Bradney Green, by Peasy Farm, on to the North Moor, keeping Chedzoy[1] on the right, they went. It is not easy to follow the *exact* route here. For some, beyond doubt, passed down War Lane (hence the name). At any rate, Grey's Horse now took the lead, and passing along by the Black Ditch to Langmoor Rhine, crossed it, and aimed at passing to the rear of Feversham's artillery. The guide, it is said, was dismissed at Langmoor Stone, and then, in the silence of the night, a pistol-shot suddenly roused its weird echoes over the moor. The mystery as to who fired the shot will never be known; the Rev. Andrew Paschall,[2] then rector of Chedzoy, says that it was currently reported that Captain Hucker was the man. However that may be, the Royalists heard it, and spread the alarm. Lord Grey urged on his horse to attack, but he was stopped unexpectedly by a rhine (the Bussex Rhine) which they could not cross, and on the other side of which lay Dumbarton's regiment and a battalion of foot-guards. Great confusion at once arose. Feversham's forces were no doubt taken completely by surprise, but the shot, and the terrible bungle on Monmouth's part about the crossing of the rhine, spoilt all. He brought up his men as quickly as might be, and they opened a furious fire across the rhine. But little execution,

---

[1] In 1683 the total population of Chedzoy was 398. Stradling, p. 168.

[2] The Rev. Andrew Paschall, B.D., Fellow of Queen's College, Cambridge, was inducted parson of Chedzoy on November 10th, 1662. He "did toll the Bell when he took possession, and did read his Articles on the Sunday following." He was inducted by George Wotton, vicar of Bridgwater (Chedzoy Church Registers).

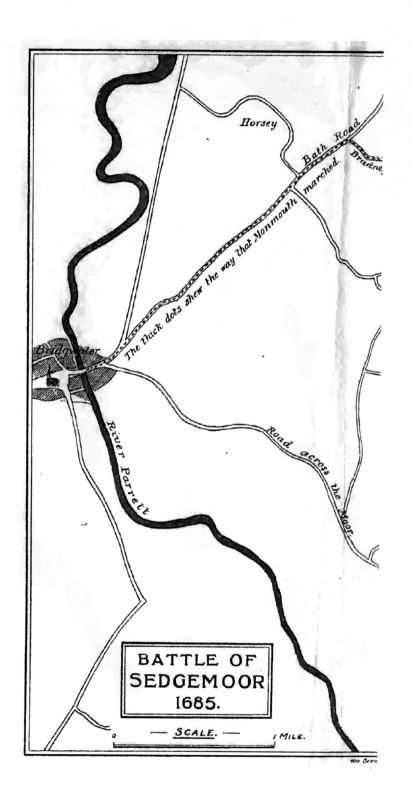

Horsey

Bath Road

Bradne

The thick dots shew the way that Monmouth marched.

Bridgwater

River Parrett

Road across the Moor

BATTLE OF
SEDGEMOOR
1685.

SCALE.

0 — — — — — 1 MILE.

Wm. Brem

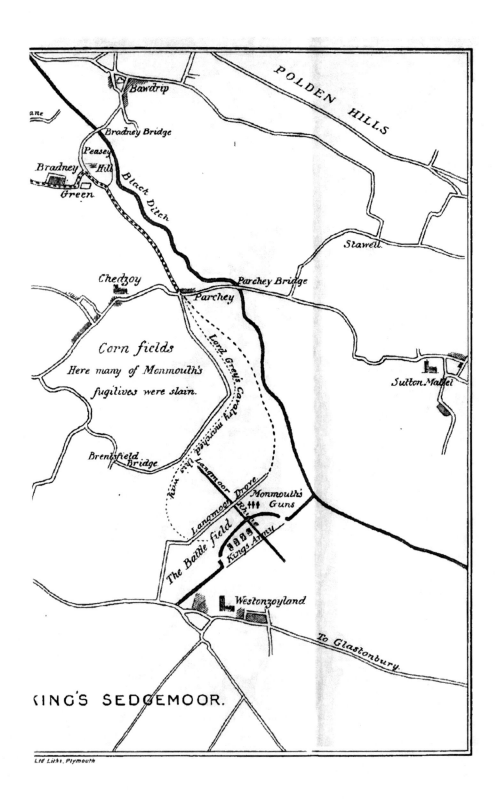

POLDEN HILLS

Bawdrip

Bradney Bridge

Peasey Hill

Bradney

Green

Black Ditch

Stawell

Chedzoy

Parchey Bridge

Parchey

*Corn fields*

*Here many of Monmouth's*

*fugitives were slain.*

Sutton Mallet

Lord Greys Cavalry mislead this way

Brentzfield Bridge

Langmoor Drove

Monmouth's Guns

The Battle field

Kings Army

Westonzoyland

To Glastonbury.

KING'S SEDGEMOOR.

however, was done, as the firing was too high.  His cannon, nevertheless, did deadly work upon Dumbarton's company and the foot-guards, until the Royalist cannon, by the aid afforded by Bishop Mews of Winchester (formerly of Bath and Wells) in sending his horses to get the guns in position, wrought terrible havoc in the ranks of Monmouth's followers.  Powder began to run short on the rebel side, yet, being attacked by Oglethorpe's troop, they held their own, compelling him to retreat.  But Lord Grey's fiasco with his horse ruined all.  The foot were unprotected, and could not resist the swarm of infantry which now rushed over the ford, and charged.  The wildest confusion ensued, culminating in panic, and a retreat.  Retreat it could hardly be called; it was a mêlée, a flight.  The poor scythe and pike men, untrained and without proper weapons, were driven into the ditches, and perished.  Utterly at the mercy of the royal troops, they were slain in heaps.  It was all over so far as fighting went, yet the victorious Royalists pursued vagrant bodies of Monmouth's men hither and thither, as they sought to escape by flight, hurrying along the Bridgwater road.  By half-past two o'clock they were carrying the wounded and dying into Weston Zoyland church, which was soon filled with men.  The battle was over.  An hour and a half's fighting had scattered the unhappy forces of the ambitious Duke, ill-trained, ill-led, and ill-guided as they had been.

But what of Monmouth? *Proh pudor!* He and Grey, disarming before the battle was over, had taken to horse and fled away by the Polden Hills, leaving their wretched followers to escape, to be killed, or to be captured as they list.  About two thousand of them, it was estimated, perished, more in their flight even than in the actual battle.  The Royalists lost still more;

2300 and upwards, it is said. Huge graves were dug: a great mound was thrown up, and to-day it is not difficult to find skeletons a little beneath the earth. The Weston Zoyland church registers tell their own story. One entry records how 500 prisoners were taken into the church, "of which there was 79 wounded, and 5 of them died of their wounds." Another entry records the expenditure, "upon the day of Thanksgiven after the ffight, 11s. 8d. for the ringers."

Most of the details of Monmouth's flight are known, yet they hardly seem worth recording. On Wednesday, the 8th of July, he was found hidden away in a ditch in the wild and remote country near Ringwood, in Dorset. Utterly exhausted from want of rest and food, he presented a broken, a dejected and miserable appearance. Five thousand pounds, he knew, were offered for him, "dead or alive." They carried the poor creature, almost in a state of collapse, to the house of the nearest magistrate, one Anthony Ettrick, of Holt Lodge. He plucked up courage enough to say, in faltering tones, that if he had but a horse he would still bid his captors defiance. Two days later he was taken from Ringwood by stages to London, which he reached on Monday, the 13th. The Earl of Aylesbury chanced to see him being led up the stairs from the river. "I wish that I had not seen him," he wrote, "for I could never get him out of my mind. I so loved him personally." Monmouth wrote the most pitiable appeal to King James. "I do assure your Majesty it is the remorse I now have in me of the wrong I have done you in several things, and now in taking up arms against you. For my taking up arms, it was never in my thought since the King died. . . . But my misfortune was such as to meet with some horrid people that made me believe things of your Majesty, and gave me so many false arguments, that I was fully led away to believe that it was a shame and a sin before God not to do it. . . . I hope, Sir, God Almighty will strike your heart with mercy and compassion for me, as He has done mine with the abhorrence of what I have done." A letter to the Queen was also despatched. "I hope, Madam, your Majesty will be convinced that the life you save shall ever be devoted to your service." Another letter was written to Hyde, Earl of Rochester, beseeching his intercession with James. He pleaded that Hyde would not "refuse interceding for me with the King, being I now, though too late, see how I have been misled."

But all was in vain. Monmouth prevaricated to the very end. If any man had ever hopelessly sinned against his sovereign, Monmouth was that man. His proclamation had loaded James with the basest calumnies, and with a charge of murder, and it had called on his subjects to rise in rebellion against him. He had assumed the kingly title; he had invaded his sovereign's realms. One chance was left; there was to be an interview with the King. It was an awful, a fearful and degrading scene. Monmouth, with arms bound, crawled in on his knees towards James, seeking to embrace his feet. He fawned upon him, imploring life with the frantic plaintiveness of a man who has lost his manliness, and who stoops to any degradation, any bitter humiliation and servility, in order to escape the due reward of his misdeeds. The two men had hated each other for twenty years; they had been rivals in amours, in the race for fame and popularity, and in the long keen struggle for power. Monmouth had staked all upon one last mad throw of the dice; he had failed miserably; now he was abjectly, finally, and completely in the clutches of the man against whom his own life had been one incessant revolt, one bitter and deadly feud. James was fifty-two years old; his nephew was thirty-six. James was now a king, Monmouth was a rebel, bound at his feet, wailing and in utter despair.

There is no telling what a great man might have done, but James was never great. He turned sullenly away from his captive, and Monmouth surmised that his doom was come. One frantic promise which he urged, that he would become a Roman Catholic if only they would spare him, was refused with the scorn which it deserved. They told him, truly, that he was seeking to save his life, but not to save his soul. This was the final falseness of the Protestant Duke. On Tuesday, July 14th, he was told that he must die.

On the day following he plucked up a little courage for the final act. As they led him out to Tower Hill his wonderful fascination over the people revived, and the crowds, as they watched him being led by, guarded by officers with loaded pistols in their hands, bewailed his fate when they saw their old favourite in such dire plight. Sounds of lamentation arose on every side. He picked up the axe and tried the edge with his thumb, giving the executioner six guineas, with the promise of six more if the work should be well done. Refusing to be bound or to have any covering for his head or face, he prayed fervently for a while, and then laid down his head, fitting it with much composure into the block. The awful scene that followed is indescribable. The executioner, utterly losing his nerve, gave a false blow, and Monmouth turned his mangled head and looked reproachfully up at the man. Again the blow failed, and again. Five strokes were given upon the wretched victim, and then the butchery ended. Six horses drew his body away in a hearse, and the head having been sewn on to the trunk, he was buried within the Chapel of St. Peter in the Tower. His burial entry is simple enough. "1685, James Duke of Monmouth, beheaded on Tower Hill ye 15th and buryed ye 16th July."

Well would it have been for the West-Country, and for Bridgwater, if the consequences[1] of Monmouth's folly and insincerity had perished with him. But they did not, as such things never do. Colonel Percy Kirke, who had only returned from Tangier the previous year, promptly set about wholesale hangings of the insurgents, and Bridgwater and its neighbourhood were filled with his victims. There has been, it cannot be doubted, some exaggeration as to this, as was inevitable, yet his brutalities were great, and he seemed to rejoice in them. Men were hanged in chains; their bodies were mangled; they were executed with many tortures; they were derided as they suffered. It was a brutal age, and civil war is worse than ordinary war. Men became devils, and forgot their manhood. The victorious party grew blatant in their triumph, for religion had played a large part in the insurrection, and the very deepest feelings of men were aroused. It was no hatred for a foreign foe, when men combine, and when the virtues of patriotism and generosity are evolved; it was the feud of neighbours at home; the bitter hatred of Protestants against Royalists, and Royalists against rebels. In this case the feelings of animosity were deepened by the knowledge that the Protestants had been fooled by following

---

[1] Stradling, quoting the authorities of his time (1839), gives the total number of persons (coming from thirty-six parishes) executed as rebels to be 239. The following eleven were Bridgwater men: Robert Fraunces, Joshua Bellamy, William Moggeridge, John Hurman, Robert Roper, Richard Harris, Nicholas Stodgell, Richard Engram, John Trott, Roger Guppy, and Isaiah Davis. Roger Hoar was reprieved. (Stradling's *Priory*, p. 130.)

a fascinating libertine, a man to whom religion was as nothing, and who was eager to renounce the faith which he had sworn at Taunton to maintain, when the pinch of trial came.

Judge Jeffreys started on his journey westwards towards the end of August.[1] In our neighbourhood the work of what is known as the Bloody Assize began practically on September 3rd at Dorchester, which provided, it is reported, seventy-four victims. At Exeter on the 14th he resumed his trials ; then came Taunton. Five hundred and twenty-six rebels awaited him, and of these 139, it is said, were condemned. He left for Bristol on Monday the 21st, where there were no prisoners to be tried for rebellion, but where he gave the corporation of the city a most drastic and prolonged castigation. Proceeding to Wells, he found some 500 waiting for trial, of whom ninety-nine, it is alleged, were executed and 283 transported. From Wells he returned to London to report himself to the King.

It does not appear that Jeffreys actually held any assize in Bridgwater, and it is probable that the Bridgwater prisoners were tried at Taunton. Kirke took six prisoners and two cartloads of wounded men there before the assizes began. Stories are rife, in scores of books, of his utter callousness, his cruelties to those whom he had to try, and his brutal conduct on the bench, and many of these stories are miserably true. But here again there has been exaggeration,[2] so that it is by no means easy to state with accuracy how many were really executed. The number was great, and it was appalling. All the West-Country ran with blood. It was a short reign of terror, which our place can

[1] H. B. Irving's *Life of Judge Jeffreys.*
[2] *Ibid.*, p. 266.

never forget. Yet it is sometimes forgotten that the chief actor in the dreadful drama was the King. Kirke and Jeffreys were two butchers who enjoyed their task, yet it was James who sent them to be butchers. "I was not half bloody enough,"[1] said Jeffreys when in the Tower, "for him who sent me thither," i.e. upon the Western Assize. The stern judge, indeed, was set a horrible task to do, and a task incompatible with the rules of justice. He was sent to condemn the rebels, and to hang as many of them as he could. The trials were a mockery; it was a foregone conclusion. He *must* cry havoc, and let loose the dogs of war. Jeffreys had no choice. At the head of things was the saturnine, maddened King, who would be obeyed. Unhappily Jeffreys was only too eager to obey; for him the awful task of hanging men was as pleasant a thing as when trout rise to fly after fly in the calm waters of a summer day. It was this dreadful ferocity, this unrelenting joy in what he did, that has made his name loathed and his memory abhorred in western counties even until to-day.

It was very long before calm reigned again in Bridgwater. Never will it be known how many poor Somerset lads lost their lives in following the wild Duke, who seemed to cast a spell over every one. Many, indeed, refused to believe that he was dead, and were certain that he would come again. The pike and scythe men did bravely indeed at Sedgemoor; would that they had had a worthier cause and a better leader! What, we may ask, were the feelings of the municipal authorities of the old borough, who had so grievously failed both in judgment and in loyalty? It might have cost them their lives, even as their action in upholding the rebel Duke cost many lives. They escaped, albeit,

[1] Woolrych's *Life of Jeffreys*.

one imagines, with trembling hearts and guilty consciences. Never did men come much nearer to laying their heads on the executioner's block, or to hanging upon a gibbet, than did Alexander Popham and the aldermen of Bridgwater, when they fostered the rebellion and proclaimed Monmouth to be king in the year of grace 1685.

### NOTES

Monmouth was granted two interviews with his Duchess previous to his execution. They were of a painful nature, and the poor lady was terribly overcome. She was superior to him in education and in everything else. By her he had four sons and three daughters. By his mistress Eleanor Needham, youngest daughter of Sir Robert Needham, Bart., he had four children. And he also left a son by Lady Henrietta Wentworth, only daughter of Lord Wentworth. She succeeded to the barony in 1667. Nine months after Monmouth's execution she died. (Fea's *King Monmouth.*)

Before his death Monmouth (in order that further trouble might be spared to the throne from any future action of his heirs) signed a declaration in the presence of the bishops, thus: "I doe declare that the late King told me that Hee was never married to my Mother." From the original document in the Bodleian Library.

The sentences upon the rebels were carried into execution with great severity. The High Sheriff's letter to the officials of Bath directs that they shall erect "a gallows in the most public place," with "halters to hang them with," also "faggots to burn the bowells of the Traytors, and a cauldron to boyle their heads and quarters," etc. etc. The executions in Bridgwater, no doubt, were carried out on similar lines. See Letter dated 16th November, 1685.

Another note directs that "you are also to provide an axe and a cleaver for the quartering the said Rebells." (Collinson's *Somerset.*)

The following extract is from the Report of the Hist. MSS. Commission, 1874, p 108. Wells Corporation Papers "The Receivers' Books, Second Volume, 1684-1755.—Under the date of September 1685 is an account of the town's expenditure for the entertainment of Jeffreys and the other four Judges at the Special Assize for the trial of the Duke of Monmouth's adherents. Among them is the item: 'Paid to Johnson 4 days and nights attendance on my Lord Jeffries his coach horses. oo—o6—oo.'"

# CHAPTER XVII

## AFTER SEDGEMOOR

FOR nearly fifty years Bridgwater had enjoyed but little rest. Soon after 1640 the troubles incidental to a civil war and to the rule of the Commonwealth set in with relentless severity. Speedily the siege followed, the terrible losses to the inhabitants, the burning of many houses, the wrecking of property, and the ruin of individual citizens. When Charles II ascended the throne of the Stuarts in 1660 there was some improvement, and the glamour and joy of the Restoration brought a gleam of sunshine to the harassed town. But this was not a permanent settlement of things so much as a sharp reaction from the Cromwellian rule, and it took Charles some time to feel secure as the sovereign of England. His reign was rather the thankful acquiescence of his people in that they once more possessed a monarchy, than the skilful and strong rule of a wise king. Charles possessed the most fascinating manners, which were hard indeed to resist. But neither his private life nor his public rule was exemplary, and the plots which arose in his reign bred a wide feeling of insecurity. In 1685, of course, this ripened, in the west, into a strong and dangerous rebellion which convulsed all Somerset, and which placed Bridgwater and Taunton under a ban. James II had little reason to think highly either of the loyalty or of the good sense of the western towns which followed Monmouth. They had placed a notorious libertine at the head of their Protestant manifesto ; they had committed their leadership of religion to a man to whom all religions were equally indifferent, and they had striven to put Lucy Walter's illegitimate son upon the throne of England. Never was a more utterly foolish, utterly hopeless effort made. But these reasons rarely appeal to the crowd or to the thoughtless. Monmouth was the people's darling; for King James no one cared. Not until the grey light of that day dawned which followed the execution of Monmouth, did his followers perceive the grievous error which they had made. They had now to sit down and count the cost.

In 1686 James came on a visit to the West-Country. On August 27th he arrived at Bridgwater from Bristol about five o'clock in the afternoon. On his way he made a point of going to look at the field of Sedgemoor, the scene of last year's fateful battle. Then he made his entrance into the town. The mayor and aldermen, who since June in the previous year had managed to develop a passion for loyalty, met the King at the East Gate, and "in their formalities" bade him welcome to the ancient and loyal borough. The people, it is said, followed His Majesty with continued acclamations.

It is difficult to resist the wish to linger upon this strange, this almost incomprehensible scene. All these men had once sworn fealty, when admitted to office, to their Sovereign. Presumably it was only upon the supposition that they were loyal servants of the King, and not perjured men, that they were allowed to retain the offices which gave them the government of the borough and its people. In June of the previous year the mayor and aldermen had broken faith, forsworn their vows, and proclaimed a rebel to be king. The same maces[1] which were now carried in pomp to do honour

[1] At least one of the Bridgwater maces had been made some years before the Restoration. There is a letter extant, dated the 16th October,

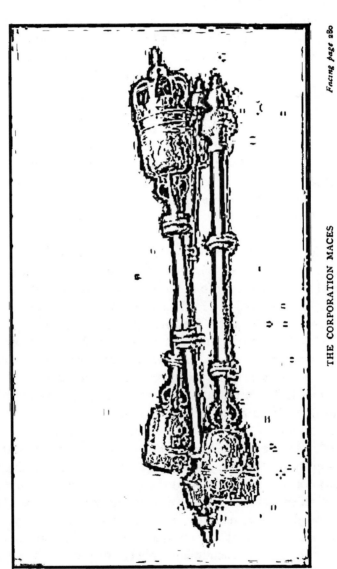

THE CORPORATION MACES

to King James had been borne in the procession which wended its way to the High Cross, where Monmouth was proclaimed king just over a year before. William Knight was the new mayor; at any rate it must have been a relief to Alexander Popham, the ex-mayor, that he did not still hold office, though he may have made one of the procession. What did these municipal officers do? Did they ignore the past episode? Did they crave pardon from the dour and cynical King? Or did they, now that Monmouth was dead and his cause for ever perished, renounce him and swear eternal fealty to this last and worst of the Stuart kings? Happily there is no answer to these questions; the shame of the position is forgotten and passed out of mind. James could sum up men well; he could value as well as most men the welcome and the loyalty, the *Punica Fides*, of these councillors. Of the glad cries of the populace there is nothing inimical to be said. They had only followed the lead of their rulers; they were not to be blamed; they had taken no oaths of loyal service. Alas! Deluded Monmouth! *Sic transit gloria mundi.* Their love for him had not lasted as long as the official gowns which the town officers wore upon their backs. The critical moment passed. James left the town. Intense, indeed, must have been the relief of the mayor and aldermen of Bridgwater when they saw him depart. Henceforth they would dally with rebellion no more. They had not, however, yet quite done with King James.

A letter arrived in the following year bearing the Royal Seal of England; signed by " William Blathwayt," and dated from the Court at Whitehall, the 4th December, 1687;

1653, addressed to Humfry Blake, asking him to use his influence with the mayor of Bridgwater on behalf of Thomas Maundy, of Fetter Lane, London, for the payment of £25. 11s. 6d. for the making of one of the maces for the borough, which weighed 56¼ ounces, at 9s. per ounce, and 5s. for the case.—Bridgwater documents.

the King's most Excellent Majesty being present in Councill : reciting that, "by the Charter granted to the Town of Bridgwater, a power was reserved to His Majesty, by his order in Council, to remove from their employments any officers in the said town ; His Majesty was pleased to order thereby that William Masey, John Rogers, William Symons, Town Clerk, Robert Baker, William Criddle, John Curry, and Robert Reeves, capital burgesses, be removed and displaced from their aforesaid offices in the said town of Bridgwater."

Here was a bolt from the blue ! For although it is a pleasant thing to be appointed to municipal office, it is distasteful to most men to be ejected therefrom. They had not long to wait for the names of their successors. By a similar letter headed James R., dated "Whitehall, 6th December 1687, in the 3rd of our reign," and signed, by His Majesty's command, by " Sunderland L$^d$," and directed "to our trusty and well beloved the Mayor and Corporation of our Borough of Bridgewater," etc., they are required forthwith to elect and admit "our trusty and well beloved John Gilbert, Sen$^r$, Robert Balch, Roger Hoar, Thomas Turnor, Samuell Pitman, and John William Briknell, to be capital burgesses and Town Clerke in the room of the persons removed by former order, without administering any oath, except the usuall oath for the execution of their respective places." Roger Hoar had been sentenced to death in 1685 for active aid given to Monmouth's cause, and his reprieve was gained with no little difficulty. However, he paid a fine of £1000, and Sunderland's letter proves that he was amply pardoned. James loved money, and would forgive almost anything in order to get it. Hoar lived to be mayor of the town in 1692, as also did John Gilbert and Robert Balch, later on. Of the ejected townsmen, Masey had been mayor in 1683, and Criddle afterwards held that office in 1716, when all the storm had blown over.

AFTER SEDGEMOOR

It was not long to wait until 1688, but in the meantime both Churchmen and Nonconformists suffered severely. Under a plea of affected tolerance James harassed all who were not Roman Catholics. Encouraged at first, the Nonconformists were treated with great injustice and severity, and their meetings were frequently broken up by fanatical opponents. But long before this there was trouble, even when Cromwell was at the height of his power. In Bridgwater the mayor and aldermen had applied for the confirmation of Mr. John Norman's appointment to be minister of St. Mary's in 1646, and he was accordingly installed. There seems to have been discord even from the first. A rather remarkable letter from the Council of State[1] at Whitehall, dated July 1st, 1651, addressed to the mayor and recorder of Bridgwater, states that "We have received the petition signed by yourselves and other inhabitants concerning the malignity and disobedience of John Norman, preacher there, tending to the danger of that place, and the articles annexed. You are to call him before you and tender the Engagement, and if he refuses to subscribe you are then to give him notice to leave the town within 10 days and not to come within 10 miles of it without special licence of Parliament or Council of State, and if he will not conform thereto you are to commit him to prison until he has entered into a recognizance in £500, with two sureties of £250 each, to obey the aforesaid order. If he takes the Engagement, you are then to prosecute the said articles before the Committee for Plundered Ministers, to whose cognizance offences of that nature most properly belong; and the articles being there proved, you need not doubt but that the Committee will

---

[1] By this time Cromwell had expelled the Rump Parliament, and had formed a Council of State, of which he was the head. There was now no Parliament. The country was under military rule.

do the Commonwealth speedy justice against him."[1] This is an excellent instance of the warring of the religious sects in Cromwell's days. For by this time the Presbyterians were losing their power, and the Independents were rising to dominance. The latter, much to the disgust of the Presbyterians, demanded that these should take the *Engagement* (*ut supra*), declaring that they would be faithful to the Commonwealth as it was then established. Norman, presumably, signed the Engagement, against which he seems at first to have protested, for on June 24th, 1656, a minute of the day's proceedings records the passing of "an Order, on the petition of the inhabitants of the town and corporation of Bridgwater, that the trustees for Maintenance of Ministers be advised to settle a fitting augmentation on the minister there, the former restraint notwithstanding."[2] This was approved on June 27th. In 1649 the King, despite the protestations of the Presbyterians, had been put to death. Their power was now gone. Cromwell tolerated the various sects as far as he could, although he would not tolerate the Church of England. But the Committee sitting in London was relentless. First Norman is put in power, and all promises well. Then he is threatened with imprisonment (under the Commonwealth, be it noted) unless he will sign the Engagement. He has to sign ; his protests are all in vain. Thus he retains his place. In 1660 the chaos ceases, the restoration is effected, and Norman gives place to the real vicar, Wotton. The unfortunate servant of the Commonwealth appears to have suffered all round. He has been described as "a minister of more than usual talent and firmness."[3] At first the Commonwealth put him into St. Mary's. Next, when

[1] State Papers, Domestic Series, I. 96, p. 263.
[2] *Ibid.*  [3] Jerom Murch's History, 1835.

the Independents grew all-powerful, it threatened him
with all sorts of terrors, imprisonment, and with expulsion. Next, when he had yielded to their demands,
it passed over his offence. Norman's treatment under
the Commonweaith is typical of the religious chaos,
persecution, and strife which prevailed then. In
Taunton it was even worse. There were too many
who, like certain of the ministers there, "strongly
condemned the error of toleration, which allowed every
man to worship God as he pleased."[1] Unhappily these
Commonwealth tyrannies led on to the harshness—
which was just as lamentable—which was meted out to
Dissenters under Charles the Second.

George Wotton's career in Bridgwater was certainly
an eventful one. In Devenish's time he signed his
name in the church registers as curate of the parish;
in 1644 or 1645[2] his name appears as vicar. After his
expulsion and exile he returned to power in 1660, and
worked on as vicar for nine years. He was buried on
December 22nd, 1669, and he seems to have done his
duty well, and to have left behind him a reputation for
sterling work and worth. At any rate, some kindly
hand, in making the entry of his burial, has written
the words: *Georgius Wotton, parochiæ hujus Pastor
vigilantissimus.* No man need crave a better record
than this.

The reigns of William and Mary, Queen Anne, and
George I brought quieter times to Bridgwater, but
it took many years for people to settle down after
the stirring days they had seen. It seemed to be
really a relief to some when the claims of the
unfortunate son—or alleged son—of James II to
the English crown gave the Jacobites an excuse for
embracing the cause of young James, otherwise known

[1] Hunt's *Dio. Hist., Bath and Wells,* p. 214.
[2] The pages of the register book have been mutilated about this date.

as the Old Pretender. Thus in 1718 a warrant was issued under the hand of Edward Raymond, the mayor, addressed to the borough constables, to warn John Gilbert, John Allen, and John Oldmixon, to appear before him at his house by eight of the clock in the forenoon of that day, to give an account of the names of the persons (which it was stated they knew) who went up and down the streets of the town on the Friday night or Saturday morning previous, in a riotous and seditious manner, disturbing the inhabitants, crying out, "Ormonde for ever!"—"He is come!" This suggests a revival of the old Monmouth days. In 1717, too, Richard Miller, John Mounshire, and William Morse declared on oath that on the 28th and 29th of May, being the anniversaries of His Majesty's birthday, and the return of King Charles II, upon the request of Ferdinando Anderdon, mayor, they played upon musick at the Swan Inn in Bridgwater, where Mr. Anderdon and others were assembled, to make public rejoycings suitable to so great occasions, and that to the best of their remembrance they did not play the tune "The King shall enjoy his own again"; and that Mr. Coles, then lately elected a capital burgess, did not desire them to play it, or offer them 5s. to do so. It is clear that the "Swan," which was one of the most famous hostelries of the West-Country, had many such jovial and exciting gatherings. On January 8th, 1718 (George I's reign), William Prior, anxious to prove his loyalty, declared on affidavit that

He did blot the name of Queen Anne out of his Prayer Book, which he usually made use of in the church, and wrote the name of his then Majesty King George in the Litany and other prayers therein; and that he always made his responses on his knees; that he did not (as falsely accused) drink the health of "the king on the other side of the water," or endeavour to make a bonfire on the Pretender's birthday.

The Pretender evidently had some friends in Bridgwater. In the same year Katherine Welles solemnly
asserted that her late husband, John Welles, "went
into Wales to escape being taken up for drinking the
Pretender's health by the name of King James III,
and for speaking seditious words: and that he kept
himself quiet there until the passing of the Act of
Pardon and Indemnity." Four burgesses of the
borough in the same year signed an affidavit attest-
ing their loyal feelings. Two of them, they averred,

sit in a pew [in St. Mary's Church] between Joel Gardner
and James Bowles; and that Joel Gardner usually makes his
responses to the services of the Church in time of divine
service loud enough to be heard by any one near him (if not
asleep), and especially on his knees, when the King and
royal family are prayed for; and that the said James
Bowles doth usually sleep or lye in a sleeping posture upon
his seat in time of service; and therefore 'tis no wonder if he
does not hear the responses made by others to the prayers
of the Church, at the reading of which he seldom or never
kneels.

James Bowles was apparently not *persona grata* with
the authorities. His orthodoxy, they felt, was not un-
impeachable. Rigidity for Conformity, and a strong
dislike of Dissent, became very prevalent at this time.
The well-known Roger Hoar was accused of dis-
loyalty. In October, 1718, he stated by affidavit that
he constantly knelt at the prayers of the Church
according to the directions of the Common Prayer
Book, "except when he was troubled with the gout;
and that, being then lately churchwarden, the sexton
brought him a box, for collecting brief money, and
delivered it to him while kneeling on his knees."
Hoar's defence was called for by an information
which had been laid in July of the same year by
Henry Player, the sexton, and Richard Coles, parish
clerk, of the parish and parish church of Bridgwater,

who say that George Balch, John Trott, and twelve others
(therein named) are all Dissenters from the Church of England, and, save occasionally, never come to the divine services
of the Church. Also, that Roger Hoare, Joseph Farewell,
Joseph Grandway, John Roberts, Robert Methwen, James
Bowles, and John Oldmixon [the historian] had applyed themselves to, and frequented the Presbyterian and Anabaptist
Conventicles; till of late they are thence withdrawn, and
come to the service of the Church of England; and that
Robert Methwen was generally looked on and much taken
notice of as a troublesome man, and a great disturber of
the peace and quiet of the town. That they never saw the
said Hoare, Farewell, Grandway, Roberts, Methwen, or
Mr. John Gilbert kneel at the reading of the prayers of the
Church.

They also depose as to the manner in which the mayor
was wont to celebrate great occasions, etc., such as
Coronation Day, royal birthdays, etc., by ringing of
bells, bonfires, going to church in state, and meeting
in the evening at a public-house to drink the health
of the sovereign.

Thirty years had now passed by since William of
Orange came to England, and Sedgemoor was getting
an old story. But the passions which Sedgemoor had
raised were hard to allay. Thus it would appear that
the aforesaid Richard Coles, the parish clerk, and
others, report with a certain self-complacency how, by
the order of Robert Steare, the then mayor, "they
prevented an attack by the country folk on the Meet-
ing-house at Bridgwater; keeping a night watch, and
being provided with bills and other weapons." These
disturbances, however, slowly passed away. By the
time that the eighteenth century had run half its course
England had sunk into a quiet somnolence of prosperous passivity, and Bridgwater shared in the general
calm.

# CHAPTER XVIII

## INHERITANCES FROM PAST DAYS

IT lies beyond the scope of this work to enter upon the story of Bridgwater during the eighteenth and nineteenth centuries. Broadly, one may speak of the days preceding the reign of William and Mary as being, in a sense, ancient. And the new spirit which came in with the Prince of Orange was the precursor—if not the medium—of what is summed up in the word modern. Yet to-day there exist in the town some links with ancient times; some reminiscences of old-world life and thought. They can only be here touched upon sparingly, and in a manner which is confessedly inadequate and slight.

The ordinary visitor to the town may be apt to complain that he can see but few traces of its antiquity. This is to some extent true. Yet if he will exercise a little diligence and some patience, he will find himself surrounded by many memories of the past. The old parish church has changed but little in outward appearance since the latter part of the fourteenth century. It stands to-day even as then, in the midst of the houses which grew up around it. The narrow passage leading to it from the High Street (until lately known as *Danger's Ope*) has always been there. Within the church the main lines of the building are unchanged from mediæval days. The western arch, the aumbry and piscina in the chancel, and the hook from which the . old rood once swung, are as they were five hundred

years ago. The Elizabethan chalice which is still used
at the service of Holy Communion has been used by
worshippers who were living before the old order of
worship passed away, and when the chantries, the
many altars, and the full mediæval services were in
daily evidence. The parish registers go back to 1558;
they are full of signatures and of entries which are
venerable in every way. There one can see the signatures of Wills, Devenish, and George Wotton; there
occur the pathetic entries at the time of the Civil War,
recording the burial of many a soldier whose name
was unknown. The three and a half centuries of duration of the registers are a real link with past days.

It is the same with the streets. Their course and
direction have changed but little for ages past. Eastover, in the old days, began where now the main road
branches off to join the Bath Road, at the Queen's
Head Inn. There stood the East Gate, so furiously
stormed in the time of the siege, and upon which, a
century earlier, a quarter of poor Abbot Whiting's body
was impaled. Near to the "Queen's Head" was the
Hospital or Priory of St. John, which finds its modern
representative in the Eastover Church of St. John the
Baptist. Fore Street is exactly as of yore; the bridge
is on the very spot where Briwere's great bridge was
built; the Cornhill, though changed in appearance, is
identical in outline with old times. St. Mary's Street
has many old houses in it still; Mary Court, the old
vicarage, the beautiful house now occupied by Mr.
Willis, and the Priory. It is as narrow as it was in
the fourteenth century, and its boundaries have not
changed half an inch. Friarn Street is but little
changed from the thirteenth century, save where the
old buildings were taken down just above Friarn Lawn,
leaving now a rather distressful gap. It is terribly

narrow up at the Penel-Orlieu end, and so the friars must have found it to be in 1250. North Street is partly new and partly old; but Moat Lane shows where the old moat ran. West Street is very old. Originally it stood outside the West Gate; now, alas! the old gate has gone. High Street has lost its group of houses known as the Island, stretching from the "Bristol Arms" to Mansion House Lane, but the old drain which served the butchers' stalls can still be seen, close to the Old Oak Inn. North Gate and South Gate are no more; each was close to a stream which in some way served as a protection to the town. Clare Street is full of queer old premises; so is Old Oak Lane. Some of the houses hereabouts are of immense age. Dampiet Street, King Street (a continuation of which was formerly known as Frog Lane, near to which was a bridge), and Blake Street form a most ancient quarter of the old town, in which was situate the town mill. Binford House probably preserves the name of a former ford over the river.

The Castle is no more, save one tiny remnant at the top of Chandos Street. But the splendid Norman Water Gate, close to Messrs. Major's offices on the West Quay, is in excellent condition. Through it, probably, many a boat-load of stores passed from the river into the Castle in William Briwere's day. Castle Street is fairly modern, but its cellars beneath the houses were once parts of the underground storage of the Castle itself. The Castle keep was in King Square. Old Saint Bridget's Church, I think, was a little northward of the Mount. Holy Trinity Church, close by where the South Gate once stood, commemorates the favourite Trinity chantry in St. Mary's, and nearly opposite to it formerly stood the Chapel of St. Saviour, built by a merchant, one William Pole. Dr.

Morgan's School, which now embraces the former
St. James's School, is a true relic of the past. Its
foundation is of late date, yet it is curiously linked
with mediæval times by its having absorbed some
small endowments which originally were attached to the
chantries in St. Mary's Church. One wishes that all
the chantry endowments had been devoted to so good
a purpose.

The municipal offices, and their appendages, are of
great age. The charters are a mine of wealth in
themselves. Indeed, a book might well be written on
the development of town government in England, as
instanced by the charters and documents of Bridgwater. It is a study in itself, and is of surpassing
interest. John Kendall was the first mayor, in 1469.
The maces date from 1660, and they are of great beauty.
No serious trouble has shaken the borough to its
foundations, as happened in 1685, when Monmouth
came within its gates, and the story of the progress of
the government of Bridgwater is much on a par with
that of many other ancient English towns. But it was
and is a port as well as a borough, and the importance
of the great river and sea trade was never neglected or
forgotten in the olden time. Bridgwater became what
she is by the aid of the River Parret and the Severn
Sea, and all her history is bound up in these great
waterways. The trade on the river to-day is the truest
link of all with the days when Bridgwater traded with
the ports of Ireland, Flanders, France, and Spain, and
when her ships and mariners took their share in the
daring expeditions of Elizabethan times.

There is one building in the town which represents
in a most interesting manner the expansion of thought
which was an outcome of the religious upheaval in
England in the sixteenth century, known as the Refor-

mation. Expansion of thought usually ends in diver-
gence of the lines of thought. It was so here. The
teaching and influence of John Norman, and all the
tendency of the like-minded people who followed him—
with many others also—resulted in the building, in
1688, of the old Dampiet Street Chapel. It was established, in the first instance, on Presbyterian lines.
Norman can hardly have ministered there himself, for
the exclusive laws of that period forbade him, and the
Five-Mile Act would be a barrier. Nevertheless in
1688 there was a building put up, and a minister, the
Rev. John Moore, officiated therein in that, the first
year of the reign of William of Orange and Mary.
It was an auspicious year in which to commence ; it
was the inaugurative year of something like freedom
of worship and freedom in religious methods. Mr.
Moore was succeeded by his son John Moore, junr.,
M.A. (1717-47), and it seems probable that he adopted
Arian views. "This was probably the theology of his
successors Matthew Towgood (1747-55) and Thomas
Watson (1755-93)." Mr. Howel (1793-1803) exercised
his ministry at the time when the Western Unitarian
Society was active, and no doubt causing a good deal
of division in the older congregations. "His senti-
ments were decidedly Unitarian, and he did not hesitate
to avow them."[1] Dampiet Street Chapel has since
then been the centre of Unitarian teaching in the
town.

The chapel has an old-world air about it, and it is
clear that it can hardly have been much altered
since first it was built, in Jacobean times. There
is a calm within it, and in the quiet street where
it is situated, which seems to speak of the days

[1] I am indebted to Dr. J. E. Odgers, formerly minister of Dampiet
Street Chapel, for many of these notes and items of information

when many men sought to escape from the hurly-burly
of strife, and to settle down in the green pastures
of a quiet nook where they might worship after their
own desire, all undisturbed.   It is a result partly of
the Commonwealth period, partly of Monmouth's
blustering days, partly again of James the Second's
wretched rule, and, yet once more, of the emancipation
which came in with William the Third.   The chapel is
a historic landmark in the town, showing at what time
religious convictions—having then grown fiercely diver-
gent—consolidated into a new society, possessing a
visible habitation of its own.   No student of history
can pass by it without gathering his lesson from the
story which more than two centuries of its existence
and duration have to teach.

One suburb of Bridgwater is still, and will ever be,
replete with memories of old.   This is the field of
Sedgemoor.   There can hardly be found a more inspir-
ing walk than to go out from Bridgwater along the
Weston Zoyland road, and, just before reaching the
village, turn to the left down past the quiet houses and
orchards, until the open moor appears.   There, bounded
by the little road on one side, and by a long drove,
is the battlefield.   The course of the old Bussex Rhine,
filled up long ago, can still be traced, and one can
stand on the very spot where the Royalists poured
their deadly fire into the ranks of Monmouth's deluded
followers, and broke their brave attack.   The spot
is absolutely peaceful; only the browsing cattle are
there.   Chedzoy tower, in the near distance, has its
tale to tell too; so also have the Langmoor drove, the
Black Ditch, Parchey Bridge, Peasy Farm, Bradney
Green, and Bradney Lane.   All these are, in a sense,
hallowed places.   They are the abiding relics of the
last great revolt of English folk against an English

sovereign—a revolt headed by an adventurer who was without principle or moral stability, and who cozened the Somerset people into the belief that he was the champion of the Protestant cause. All the area within the boundary made by the five church towers—Bridgwater, Weston Zoyland, Sutton Mallet, Chedzoy, Bawdrip—is overflowing with incident and with history. At night time the silence is almost oppressive. By day the lazy calm of the fields seems to try to efface from memory the brief yet bloody and fateful fight which awakened the echoes of the great moor in 1685. These still pasture-lands are, and will ever be, eloquent of the melancholy truth that the paths of glory lead but to the grave.

Such are some of our inheritances from the past doings of old Bridgwater times. The chain is a long one, and some of its links are weakening. Yet, such as they are, they appeal to the imagination and to the moral instinct. They suggest that the forces and passions and influences which move mankind are even now as they were of yore, and that these do not change with the rolling years.

## NOTES

During the course of writing the foregoing chapters, a considerable number of questions have been received referring to incidents, places, and things connected with Bridgwater. It would be difficult, in attempting to deal with even a few of these, to weave the answers to them into a continuous narrative. It is, therefore, thought better to refer to them *singulariter*, and with necessary brevity.

*The oldest existing gravestone in St. Mary's churchyard.*— The alterations in the positions of many old gravestones have been very numerous in past days, and they have resulted in the loss, breakage, and defacement of some most interesting inscriptions. One of the churchyard paths is paved with old headstones, many of them being cut in two, and damaged in other ways. Other such stones abound within the church walls. The oldest known gravestone is situated at the west side of the tower, and bears the following inscription : HERE LYETH THE BODY OF AGNES GROVE WHO DEPARTED THE FIEF OF FEBERARI 1635.

*Oldmixon's grave.*—It has been frequently stated that the body of John Oldmixon the historian lies in Bridgwater churchyard. This appears to be an error. There is an Oldmixon vault containing "ye body of Elinor Oldmixon daughter of John Bawdon who departed this life ye 3 of Aug. 1689," also "ye body of Hannah ye daughter of John and Elinor Oldmixon who departed this life ye 13 of November 1689." John Bawdon was buried here in 1643, and Elinor, his wife, in 1645. But it is practically certain that the historian is buried elsewhere.

*Bradney Chapel, near Chedzoy.*—On November 5th, 1330, a licence was granted for the alienation in mortmain by Simon de Bradeny of certain property, for a chaplain to celebrate divine service daily, on Sunday, Monday, Tuesday, Thursday, and Saturday at the altar of St. Mary in the church of St. Michael the Archangel, Bawdrip; and on Wednesday and Friday in the chapel of All Saints, Bradeny, for the souls of the said Simon, Beatrice his wife, and others. Bradney Chapel is marked on the map of Sedgemoor, which dates from the time of Antony Paschall, rector of Chedzoy, 1686. It is now utterly destroyed. Its former position was adjacent to the present Bradney Lane.

*The Holy Well of Wembdon.*—Wembdon Church is dedicated to St. George, but the famous well, which is now in a garden rather more than half-way up Wembdon Hill, on the left side as one goes out from Bridgwater, was called St. John's Well, because the prior and brethren of St. John's Priory, Bridgwater, were the possessors of the advowson. In mediæval times this well was resorted to by many pilgrims and others by reason of the supposed healing power of it waters. As lately as 1903 people were still asking for bottles of the water, chiefly for diseases and weakness of the eyes.

*Chilton Trinity Church bells.*—These are four in number. The inscriptions upon them are exceedingly difficult to read No. 3 bell has "*Sancte Peter et Paule orate pro nobis.*" No. 2 bell dates from 1635. No. 4 bell is inscribed, "You that heare me, Marke my call, Awake from sin." Its date is 1656, thus showing that during even the troubled days of the Commonwealth the church's work was not laid aside. In the inscription on No. 1 bell the words *nomen Domini* occur, but the remainder of the sentence cannot be identified.

*The Bread Charity.*—Gilbert Bloyse, who died in 1717, left moneys for the weekly distribution of loaves of bread "in ye Parish Church of Bridgwater, equally amongst twelve pooré people of ye said Burrough and Parish." The loaves, now thirty in number, are still given away, every Sunday afternoon at four o'clock, to selected poor and needy people who assemble to receive them in the north porch.

*Market crosses.*—Bridgwater had two; one, the High Cross, by the existing Corn Market, and the other—frequently referred to as the Pig Cross—near the old West Gate. The name Pig Cross had nothing to do with pigs. Its origin was *Horsey Pigeus*, or *Pignes*, or *Pegenes*, ultimately abbreviated to Peg or Pig. Horsey boundaries ran up to those of Bridgwater. The Pig Cross was still standing in 1800.

*Penel-Orlieu.*—Numerous inquiries have been made as to the origin of this curious name, which now is allocated to the part of the town east of where the old West Gate stood, as far as the west end of High Street, and round by the Cattle Market. In early days there was a Bridgwater family named Pynel. In their honour, presumably, a street was named, called variously Pynel, Pynell, Pynelle, or Penelle Street. The name may, of course, be a corruption of the famous family name Paganel or Paynel. Pynel Street extended from about the West Gate to a spot somewhere near the west end of the present Market House Inn. Over the entrance to the inn is inscribed the date 1563. Extending eastwards, and veering round in a northerly direction towards the North Gate, was another street called variously Orlof Street, Orlones Street, Olav Street, Orloue Street, Orlewe Street, or Orlowe Street. These streets eventually became one, and their junction produced the combination Pynel-Orlewe, which finds its modern representative in Penel-Orlieu.

*Mr. John Chubb.*—This gentleman came of an old family that had long been settled in Bridgwater. His drawings and paintings (which the writer has had the great pleasure of seeing) are works of real genius, and they hit off the life and manners of the eighteenth century in Bridgwater in a remarkable way. His sketches of scenery, and of places in the town which have now ceased to exist, are of surpassing interest. I am indebted to Mr. John B. Chubb, the present head of the family, for his great kindness in permitting me to see his ancestor's sketches.

*Bridgewater in the United States.*—Our old town, like many old English boroughs, has its daughter in the vigorous New World in America. Transatlantic Bridgewater is in the State of Massachusetts. What was once the original town is now divided into Bridgewater, East Bridgewater, West Bridgewater, and the city of Brockton. Thus in a measure are reproduced our own Eastover and the West Borough. Brockton, which was the north parish, it is said, contains more of the descendants of the early settlers from England than the other divisions. I am indebted to the courtesy of Mr. Edward A. Hewett, the town clerk of Bridgewater, for this information. The Selectmen are Mr. William Bassett, Mr. Harrison D. Packard, and Mr. Edwin D. Josselyn. Mr. Edmund L. Linnett is the town treasurer. Their municipal seal contains the castle and bridge of our own town arms, and is inscribed "incorporated 1656."

*The Bell Foundry.*—In Dr. Raven's excellent book *The Bells of England*, he refers to a group of towns of which Bridgwater is one, which possessed bell foundries, but of which he does not give any particulars. A friend of Mr. A. O. Pain, of Dampiet House, Bridgwater, who was recently travelling in Wales, found a bell in a church near Tenby, bearing the founder's name: "T. Pike, Bridgwater." The foundry was in St. Mary's Street, opposite the church. Enmore Church has two bells, the third and the tenor, cast by George Davis of Bridgwater, in 1796. In the same church also is a bell, No. 5, which was cast in 1825 by J. Kingston of Bridgwater. A bell at Middlezoy was cast by Davis, and one at Stockland Bristol, by Kingston, in 1827. (Stockland formerly had four bells by Kingston, but three of them have since been recast.) Chedzoy Church tower also has a Bridgwater bell. Another bell founder who traded at Bridgwater was one J. Bailey.

*A thirteenth-century bell.*—Documentary evidence exists showing that late in the thirteenth century a bell was cast in the town. Collections made in the parish, with gifts from others, came to £8 18s. 10d. As Dr. Raven says, "leaden vessels, trivets, pots, brass, and a bason with laver, augmented by a shilling for a ring sold, brought the amount to £10 16s. 1d."[1] The warden of the goods of the Holy Cross advanced twenty shillings. Having collected £14. 3s. 2d. (a very large sum of money, bearing in mind the change in value since then) the authorities purchased 896 lb. of copper, 40 lb. of brass, and 320 lb. of tin. Many parishioners, unable to subscribe in money, gave of their household gear to add to the metal-heap for the new bell. Thus 180 lb. was received in gifts of pots, platters, basons, lavers, and kettles; and 425 lb. from one old bell. The items are thus: an old bell, 425 lb.; metal given, 180 lb.; tin bought, 320 lb.; brass bought, 40 lb.; copper bought, 896 lb; total, 1861 lb. weight. Casting the bell absorbed 1781 lb.; 80 lb. remained over. For repairing the mould and founding the bell the " master " received in part payment of his wages, 40 shillings. This is very strong evidence of vigorous church life in the town before 1300 A.D.

*Bells now in St. Mary's tower.*—Many questions have been made as to these, and for details I am indebted to Mr. A. E. Coles, who is an expert in such matters. The first or treble bell, weighing over 6 cwt., was cast by T. Bailey in 1745. The second, weighing a few pounds more, is of the same date and by the same maker. The third was made in the year 1650, and weighs 8 cwt. 1 qr. The fourth, weighing 10 cwt. 3 qrs. 7 lb., dates from 1615. The fifth bell bears the inscription SANCTAE MARIAE ANNO 1634; it was recast in 1899, and weighs over 11 cwt. Bell No. 6 is marked A. R. (Abram Rudhall) 1721, weighing 12 cwt. 1 qr. On it is written FROM LIGHTNING AND TEMPEST GOOD LORD DELIVER US. The next or seventh bell is similarly by A. R., in 1721, and weighs 16 cwt. Last comes the eighth or tenor bell, weighing 25 cwt. 1 qr. 11 lb. It was recast in 1868, and was probably originally made in 1721 by the Rudhall firm. Its inscription is a favourite one for the early eighteenth century, especially by the Rudhalls.

> I CALL THE LIVING, MOURN THE DEAD;
> I TELL HOW DAYS AND YEARS ARE FLED.
> FOR JOY, FOR GRIEF; FOR PRAYER AND PRAISE;
> MY TUNEFUL VOICE TO HEAVEN I RAISE.

Thus the oldest existing bell (No. 4) dates from 1615, nearly

---

[1] *The Bells of England*, p. 63.

three centuries ago. The newest, No. 1 and No. 2, were made in 1745 (excepting the two which have been recast, No. 5 and No. 8). The peal is an excellent one in every way.

*The Swan Inn.*—This famous hostelry was one of the most noted inns of the West Country. It was on the Cornhill, covering the space around and occupying the site of the business premises of Messrs. Thompson Brothers. It is officially mentioned in 1672 and 1682, and it was probably in existence from early in the seventeenth century up to near 1800.

*The Balch family.*—This is a very ancient Somerset family, well represented in Bridgwater by numerous inscriptions on gravestones. John Balch emigrated (probably from Bridgwater) to Maryland in 1658. In 1327 four taxpayers named Balch appear upon a Somerset tax list, e.g. Wilhelmus Balch of Purye, in the hundred of North Petherton. Robert Balch was mayor in 1689 and 1696; George Balch in 1699 and 1709; Robert Balch in 1777. George Balch was returned member of Parliament for the borough in 1700, 1701, 1702, 1705, and 1708; Robert Balch in 1753 and 1754. The John Balch who sailed from the town in 1658 is represented in the direct line of descent to-day by Mr. Thomas Willing Balch of Philadelphia.

*Bridgwater church spire in the storm of* 1813.—On Wednesday, November 17th, 1813, a great thunderstorm occurred, damaging the church and spire. Mr. R. Anstice, on the same evening, wrote an account of the event to Dr. Wollen, the vicar of the town. He says : "About half-past seven in the morning a very violent storm of hail took place, accompanied by a very heavy squall of wind from the N.W., it having blown a strong gale from that quarter during the night. The weather afterwards became dry and moderate at intervals, with occasional storms of rain and hail. At about half-past twelve o'clock some distant noise of thunder was heard, and during the next quarter of an hour the thunder increased, and some flashes of lightning were seen. About this time the weather became extremely dark, and a heavy shower of rain began to fall. I was sitting in the Custom House looking out of the window, and saw on the shute of the house opposite a dash of fire, appearing of nearly a solid consistence, and, breaking on the shute, seemed to spread itself from that point, but particularly in the direction of the shute. A very strong and explosive clap of thunder almost immediately followed. It occurred to me that the spire of the church (from its being of greater elevation than any other surrounding body, and being composed of materials of different conducting powers, ill arranged to convey the lightning harmlessly to the ground) was in danger of having suffered. I went out to examine it, and found the effect had been as I apprehended." A lengthy description, in very full detail, follows the letter, giving an account of the injuries which the church had suffered. They were serious, and made it necessary to have extensive repairs done, which were duly carried into effect in the following year.

*The Kingsmill monument.*—The Kingsmill family have a fine seventeenth-century monument in the chancel. The inscription is as follows: *Hic jacet corpus Francisci Kingsmill de Ballibeg in comitatu Corke intra regnum Hiberniae Militis reique militaris scientia praecellentis qui obiit 25 die Julii anno Domini 1620. Per fidem sancti effecti sunt Validi in bello. Heb. xi. 34.*

*Hic jacet corpus Henrici Kingsmill armigeri filii dicti Francisci patris. Qui obiit 22 die Aprilis 1621 Hic etiam jacet corpus Francisci Kingsmill generosi . . . qui obiit 16 die Augusti anno Domini 1640.*

Sir Francis Kingsmill was born in 1570 He served as an officer in the royal army in the Irish wars at the close of Queen Elizabeth's reign, and was buried in Bridgwater. His eldest son Henry, born at Ballibeg, died at the age of fourteen. Francis, the third son, also died in the town, in 1640, aged twenty-eight. Sir Francis' granddaughter Elizabeth became the wife of Samuel Pepys, who was the author of the famous diary. The monument was probably erected by the second son, Colonel William Kingsmill of Ballibeg, who suffered heavily in the royal cause. In 1620 Sir Francis Kingsmill presented a handsome chalice of beaten silver to the church, which is still in constant use. It bears the inscription: *Calix ecclesiae Bridgwateriensis. Ex dono Francisci Kingsmill, generosi.*

# INDEX

# INDEX

Dampiet Street Chapel, 292, 293, 294
Daubeny, Lord, 55
Davy, John, 65, 126
Dodington, 7, 33
Domesday reference to Bridgwater, 1
Douai, Walter de, 1, 4, 15, 26, 28, 29, 103, 104
Downend, 15, 217
Druidism, 37 *et seq.*
Dulverton, 22
Dunster, 28

East Quantockshead, 140
Edgar Atheling, 26
Edington, 18
Edmeston, Daniel de, 35
Edmund de St. Maur, 39
Edward the Confessor, 18, 21, 26
*Emanuel*, Voyage of the, 175–87
Engilby, Thomas, 99
Exe, River, 22
Exeter, 21–22
Exmoor, 19

Fairfax, Lord, 58, 246 *et seq.*
Falaise, William de, 43
Flat Holm, 22
Fraternities, Church, 65
Friars Minor, *vide* chap. III, p. 76; *vide* chap VI
Friars, Regulations of, 78, 79, 80
Friars, Influence of, 81, 82, 83
Frobisher, 177, 178, 179, 180, 182, 184
Frompton, Nicholas, 100–101, 128
Funerals, Mediæval, 64, 65

George Inn, 124
Glastonbury, 13, 27, 38, 150, 195
Goathurst, 140
Gothelney, 23
Grammar schools, 152, 156
Grey, Lord, 109, 265 *et seq.*
Grygg, Richard, Will of, 75
Guilds, 113, 139, 140, 147, 155
Guthrum, 19
Gwent, Lower, 39

Hadley, James, Will of, 72, 73, 74
Hakeluyt, Sir Leonard, 66
Hakeluyt, Lady, 66
Ham Hill, 12
Hamelyn, Adam, Will of, 68
Harold, King, 22, 23, 25
Henry VII, King, 56
Hill, John, 70
Hill, Thomasine, Will of, 70
High Altar, 113
Holy Trinity, Altar of, 112
Holy Trinity, Chantry of, 141

Holy Cross, Altar of, 113, 124
Horsey Chapel, 153, 154
Hospital of St. John, 94
Hospital, rules of, 95, 96
Huntspill, 12

Idstock, 148, 149, 150, 151
Ilchester, 8
Inscriptions in Parish Church, 114, 115
Interdict, Papal, 88 '

James, Duke of York, 261, 262, 264
James II, 265, 273, 274, 277, 280, 281, 282, 283
Jeffreys, Judge, 276, 277, 278
Johannes Hostiarius, 34
John, King, 25, 45, 46, 47, 48, 49, 52, 88, 89

Kilve, 33, 140
Kingsmill family, 301
Kinwith Castle, 3
Kirke, Colonel, 275
Knights of St. John of Jerusalem, 97, 101
Knowle, 23

Labourers' Insurrection, 89
Lamps, 113, 140
Langport, 8, 11, 14, 15, 17
Langport Bridge, 8, 17
Lights, 113, 140

Marmoutier, Abbey of, 20, 25, 105, 106
Masses, 65, 77
Matilda, Queen, 27
Mayor of Bridgwater, 5, 69, 92, 115
Mediæval church services, Hours of, 131
Mendip, 19
Merchants' Guild of Bridgwater, 129, 144, 145
Merlesuain, 1, 26
Michaelchurch, 34
Mohun, William de, 28
Monmouth, Duke of, 109, 260–278
Montacute, 8, 19, 24, 32
Montfort, Simon de, 49
Mortimer family, 50 *et seq.*
Mulchelney, Abbots of, 121
Murillo, 118

Neroche, 19, 54
Nether Stowey, 214, 216
Newfoundland, 14
New South Wales, 14
Norman, John, 171, 174, 244, 245, 283, 293

# INDEX

North Petherton, 19, 29, 46, 47, 49, 50, 54
North Newton, 47, 127
Nova Scotia, 13

Obits, 77, 139
Oldmixon, John, 296
Oratories, 140
Over Stowey, 23, 212

Paganel, Fulk, 103, 106
Paganel family, 26, 103, 105, 106
Parewastel, Isólda, 112, 142, 143
Parret, River, 8, 9, 11, 17, 19, 22, 23, 27, 30, 125
Pembroke, Earl of, 48, 49
Penel-Orlieu, Origin of name, 297
Peter de Bruges, 35, 41
Picture in parish church, 116, 117, 118
Policy of William I; 44
Pons Walteri, 2, 4
Porlock, 22-23
Poulett family, 116, 117
Preaching, Mediæval, 134
Purgatory, Doctrine of, 63
Puritan influences, 167, 168, 169, 170, 171, 172
Pym, John, 208, 228, 229

Reformation changes, 157-74
Rood, Altar of the, 113
Rood loft, 113
Rowley, Albert, Will of, 77

Screens, Church, 114, 115
Selwood, 19, 28
Siege of Bridgwater, 242-59
Somerton, 14, 19
South Petherton Bridge, 17
Spanish Armada, 117
Spaxton, 210, 212
Sprigge, Joshua, History of, 247
St Erasmus, Altar of, 113
St George, Altar of, 113
St. George, Chantry of, 141
St. Gregory, Altar of, 113
St. James, Altar of, 113

St Katherine, Altar of, 113
St Mary, Altar of, 112, 123
St. Mary, Chantry of, 141
St. Sebastian, Image of, 114
Stigand, Archbishop, 21
Stoke Courcy (or Stogursey), 2, 23, 25, 43, 47
Strete, Thomas (vide chap. XI), 137
Stringston, 23
Summer, John, 87
Swan Inn, 300

Tasmania, 14
Taunton, 14
Taunton, Archdeacon of, 47, 48
Tiverton, 22
Tone, River, 9, 17
Trade and Traffic, chap. XVII
Trental, 77, 139
Trinoda necessitas, 3
Trivet, Sir John, 6, 7
Trivet's Bridge, 6, 7

Vicars of Parish Church, 85, 118, 120, 124, 125, 126, 127, 128, 136, 137, 244
Vigils of the dead, 65

Walshe, Richard, 101, 102
Walter, Lucy, 260 et seq.
Wembdon, 26
Wembdon, Holy Well of, 296
Wemedone, William de, 35-36
Westonzoyland, vide chap XVI
Wheler, John, Will of, 71, 128
Whiting, Abbot, 159, 165
William of Orange, 265, 285, 289, 293
William the Conqueror, 18, 21, 23 et seq., 34, 43
Williton, 19
Wills of Bridgwater folk, 61 et seq
Wotton, George, 171, 172, 173, 285, 290

Yeo, River, 8, 9
Yeovil, 8

304

# LIST OF SUBSCRIBERS

Agapemone, The, Spaxton, near Bridg-
water.
Allen, Mr. F. H., Northfield, Bridg-
water.
Alway, Mr. S. B., Pedwell, near Bridg-
water.
American Library and Literary Agency,
Trafalgar Square, London, W.C.
Anderson, Miss, Elmwood, Bridgwater.
Andrew, Mrs., Fore Street, Bridgwater.
Anstice, Rev. J. B., Burnham.
Ashford, Mr. E., Wembdon Road,
Bridgwater.
Ashill, Mr. S. G., Northgate, Bridg-
water.
Ashton, Mr. R., St. Mary Street, Bridg-
water.
Ashton, Mr. R., Bridgwater.
Ashton, Mr. R., jun., St. Mary Street,
Bridgwater.
Ashton, Miss S., Taunton Road, Bridg-
water.
Atchley, Rev. H. G. S., Portishead.
Axford, Mr. W. H., London.

Bagg, Miss, Blake Street, Bridgwater.
Baker, Mr. W. Proctor, Sandhill Park,
Taunton.
Baker, Mr. Ernest E., The Glebe
House, Weston-super-Mare.
Baker, Mr. A. G., Puriton, Bridgwater.
Baker, Mr. H., Haygrove, Bridgwater.
Baker, Mr. W. J., Penel-Orlieu, Bridg-
water.
Baker, Mr. W. T., Wembdon, Bridg-
water.
Baker, Rev. S. Ogilvy, Red Lodge,
Clevedon.
Balch, Mr. T. Willing, 1412 Spruce
Street, Philadelphia, U.S.A.
Balch, Mrs. T. Willing, 1412 Spruce
Street, Philadelphia, U.S.A.
Barnett, Miss, Northfield, Bridgwater.
Barnett, Mr. G. A., Wembdon Road,
Bridgwater.
Barnicott and Pearce, Messrs., Athen-
æum Press, Taunton.

Barton, Mr. T. J., King Square, Bridg-
water.
Bates, Rev. E. H., Puckington Rectory,
Ilminster.
Bath and Wells, Right Rev. the
Bishop of.
Batten, Col. Cary, Abbots Leigh, near
Bristol.
Belcher, Mr. Walter, Cornhill, Bridg-
water.
Bell, Rev. W., Charlynch Rectory,
Bridgwater.
Bennett, Mrs. C. H., College House,
Hammersmith.
Berry, Mr. S., Taunton Road, Bridg-
water.
Betty, Mr. C., West Street, Bridgwater.
Biddick, Mr. T., Northfield, Bridg-
water.
Bishop, Miss, King Square, Bridgwater.
Bishop, Mr. F. W., Westfield, Bridg-
water.
Blackburn, Mr. H., High Street, Bridg-
water.
Blake, Mr. E. J., Old House, Crew-
kerne.
Bolderstone, Mrs., Woolavington Vicar-
age, near Bridgwater.
Bond, Mr. G. W., Taunton Road,
Bridgwater.
Boodle, Mr. R. W., Pershore Road,
Birmingham.
Bouchier, Mr. W., Eastover, Bridgwater.
Bouverie, Mr. H. H. P., Brymore,
Bridgwater.
Bovett, Mr. E. W., George Street,
Bridgwater.
Bowering, Mr. A., Penel-Orlieu, Bridg-
water.
Boyland, Mr. T. E., St. Mary Street,
Bridgwater.
Boys, Mr. W. H., King Square, Bridg-
water.
Bradbeer, Mr. H., Cranleigh Gardens,
Bridgwater.
Bradfield, Mr. W., Eastover, Bridg-
water.

Braikenridge, Mr. W. Jerdone, Claremont, Clevedon.

Braithwaite, Mr. J B , Blencathara, Burnham.

Braithwaite, Mr. John B , The Highlands, New Barnet.

Bramble, Lieut.-Col. J. A , Seafield, Weston-super-Mare

Brewer, Mr. C., North Petherton, near Bridgwater.

Brice, Rev E. H., Coleford Vicarage, near Gloucester.

Brice, Miss E. M , Goathurst Rectory, Bridgwater.

Brice, Mr. F., Friarn Street, Bridgwater.

Broadmead, Mr. W. B., Enmore Castle, Bridgwater.

Broderip, Mr. E., Cossington Manor, near Bridgwater.

Brooks, Mr. J., Chedzoy, Bridgwater.

Brown, Mr. E , Hamp Green, Bridgwater.

Brown, Mr. W. H., Sutton Mallett, near Bridgwater

Brown, Miss, King Square, Bridgwater.

Brown, Mr., Dampiet Street, Bridgwater.

Brown, Mr Frank, High Street, Bridgwater.

Brueton, Mr Huntworth, Bristol.

Bryant, Mr. E., Eastover, Bridgwater.

Bryant, Mr. H. G., Redgate, Bridgwater.

Bryer, Mr C , jun., Friarn Street, Bridgwater.

Buffett, Mr. R. W., Cornhill, Bridgwater

Bull, Rev. T. W., Paulton Vicarage, near Bristol.

Burge, Mr., Bridgwater.

Burrington, Mr. G. G , Westfield House, Bridgwater

Burrows, Mr. C , Neath.

Carter, Mr. S., Gosforth, Newcastle-on-Tyne.

Carver, Miss, Chilton Polden, Bridgwater.

Carver, Mr. H., Burnham.

Catlow, Rev. W., Dr. Morgan's School, Bridgwater.

Cawley, Mr H. P , Victoria Road, Bridgwater.

Chant, Mr. R., Evelyn House, Finsbury Pavement, London, E.C

Chant, Mr. C. T , Lyndale Avenue, Bridgwater.

Chard, Mrs , Shovell House, North Petherton, Bridgwater.

Chester-Master, Mr. C , Friarn Lawn, Bridgwater

Chinn, Mr. S , Bristol Road, Bristol

Chisholm-Batten, Lieut.-Col., Thornfalcon, near Taunton.

Chubb, Mr John B , Caroline Place, Mecklenburgh Square, London, W C.

Church, Rev. Canon, North Liberty, Wells

Churchill, Mr. E H., Wembdon, Bridgwater.

Clark, Mr. William S., Street.

Clench, Mrs., Wembdon, Bridgwater

Clerke, Mr. C. J., Broomfield Hall, Bridgwater.

Coate, Mr W. H., Salmon Parade, Bridgwater.

Coates, Mr. R , 38 Monmouth Street, Bridgwater.

Coles, Miss, Bridgwater.

Coles, Mr. J., Bridgwater.

Coles, Mr A. J , King Square, Bridgwater.

Coles, Mr. J., jun., 6 Keyford Terrace, Frome.

Collins, Rev. J A. W., Newton St. Cyres Vicarage, near Exeter.

Colsey, Mr. J. J , Fore Street, Bridgwater.

Comley, Mr J. W., Avalon, Wembdon Road, Bridgwater.

Cook, Mr J., Weston-super-Mare.

Cook, Mr E., West Street, Bridgwater

Cook, Mr. R., Detling

Coombs, Mr J., Castle St., Bridgwater

Cooper, Mr. W. E., Church Street, Bridgwater.

Cooper, Rev. Sydney, Christ Church Vicarage, Frome.

Cooper, Mr P. N., Mount Radford, Bridgwater.

Cooze, Mr. J , Bridgwater.

Cornish, Mr. J. H., sen , Northfield, Bridgwater.

Cottam, Mr A , Haygrove, Bridgwater.

Cottam, Mr A. B., Haygrove, Bridgwater.

Counsell, Mr. M. L., Wembdon Road, Bridgwater.

Cox, Mr , Bridgwater.

Cox, Mr W. H., High Street, Bridgwater.

Crawford, Mr. W., Northfield, Bridgwater

Cresser, Mr. G , Bridgwater.

Croker, Mr. F., Hereford.

Croker, Mr H., Eastover, Bridgwater

Croker, Mr. J, Halswell Avenue, Bridgwater.

Croker, Mr. W. T., Friarn Street, Bridgwater.

Culliford, Mr J, High Street, Bridgwater.

Cummins, Mr. W., Cranleigh House, Bridgwater.

Curry, Mr. H, High St., Bridgwater

Curtis, Mr. E. Constable, North Petherton, Bridgwater.

Daniel, Mr. H. T., Park House, Over Stowey, near Bridgwater.

Daniel, Rev. H., Manor House, Stockland, Bridgwater.

Davey, Mr. J., Albert St., Bridgwater.

Davis, Mr. Geo. E., Eastover, Bridgwater.

Davis, Mr J. M., High Street, Bridgwater.

Day, Mr. H. C. A., Oriel Lodge, Walton Park, Clevedon.

Deacon, Mr. W., High Street, Bridgwater

Denman, Mr. D. G., Haygrove, Bridgwater

Dilks, Mr. T B., Eastover, Bridgwater.

Docksey, Mr. F., Taunton Road, Bridgwater

Dosson, Mr. J. N., Longthorns, Charlynch, Bridgwater

Duckett, Mr. W, Hawker's Farm, Bridgwater.

Duder, Mr. J, Tregedna, Taunton.

Edwards and Sons, Messrs, West Street, Bridgwater.

Eveleigh, Mr T., Wembdon, Bridgwater.

Everard, Captain, Hill House, Otterhampton, near Bridgwater

Evis, Mr. R, Bristol Road, Bridgwater.

Fackrell, Mr. W., North Street, Bridgwater.

Farthing, Mr. H., 32 Camden Road, Bridgwater.

Fisher, Miss A T, Fore Street, Bridgwater.

Foley, Mr. R. Y, The Lions, Bridgwater.

Foster, Mr. F. C., Broxholme, Bridgwater.

Foster, Mr J E., Castle St., Bridgwater.

Foster-Barham, Colonel, Wembdon, Bridgwater.

Foster-Barham, Mrs. A. G., Marycourt, Bridgwater.

Fox, Mr. Francis F, Yate House, Yate.

Frost, Mr., Wembdon, Bridgwater.

Fry, Mr. Francis J, Cricket St. Thomas, Chard.

Fursland, Mr. J. E., Bristol Road, Bridgwater

Fursland, Mr J, Taunton Road, Bridgwater.

Galloway, Mr. R., Spaxton, Bridgwater.

Geen, Mr. A., Cranleigh Gardens, Bridgwater.

Gilbert, Mr. J E., St John Street, Bridgwater.

Glanville, Mr. E. J, St. Alban's Place, Haymarket, London, S W.

Gleed, Mr., Bridgwater.

Gleed, Mr W. J, Bridgwater

Gooding, Miss M. W., Clay Hill House, Cannington.

Gooding, Mr W. Forbes, Durleigh Elms, Bridgwater.

Gooding, Mr. J. Brande, Clay Hill House, Cannington, Bridgwater.

Goodland, Mr Thomas, Bridge Street, Taunton.

Goodland, Mr., Victoria Terrace, Bridgwater.

Gould, Mr. F. H., Bridgwater.

Gould, Mr J H, Wembdon, Bridgwater.

Grant, Rev. Prebendary, St. Benignus Vicarage, Glastonbury.

Green, Mrs. A. L., London

Greenham Mrs, Trieste, Austria

Gregory, Mr., High Street, Bridgwater

Griffin, Mr. W. H., jun., Bath Road, Bridgwater.

Grubb, Mr John, The Down, Winscombe

Gurney, Rev H F. S, Stoke St. Gregory, near Taunton.

Hall, Mr A., Westfield, Bridgwater.

Hallett, Mr. T., Northgate, Bridgwater.

Hamblin, Mr. E, Taunton Road, Bridgwater.

Hamlin, Mr J., Fore Street, Bridgwater.

Hancock, Rev Preb., The Priory, Dunster

Harding, Mr. H., Northgate, Bridgwater.

Harland, Rev. R, Nether Stowey Vicarage, Bridgwater

Harris, Mr. J., Westfield, Bridgwater.

Harris, Mr. C. J., Eastover, Bridgwater.

# LIST OF SUBSCRIBERS.

Harris, Mr. W. G., East Quay House, Bridgwater

Harris, Mr. W. Boundy, Wembdon, Bridgwater.

Hartcup, Mrs. F. M , Eastwood, Old Calton, near Norwich.

Hawkes, Mr. H , Bridgwater

Hawkins, Mr. C. F , North Petherton, Bridgwater.

Hawkins, Mr., Bristol Rd , Bridgwater

Hayes, Miss F M , Camden Road, Bridgwater.

Hayter, Mr. L. H., Castle Street, Bridgwater.

Hazell, Mr. W J ,High St , Bridgwater

Helps, Mr. E W., Westfield, Bridg-.water

Hembry, Mr. F. W , Langford, Sidcup, Kent

Henniker, Mr J. G., Catcott, Bridg-water.

Herninian, Mr. M., North Street, Bridg-water

Hill, Mr. E J., St. John Street, Bridg-water.

Hill, Mr E W , Wembdon, Bridgwater.

Hill, Mr. Frank, Clare St., Bridgwater.

Hobhouse, Rt.'Hon. Henry, Hadspen House, Castle Cary

Hodge, Miss B M , King Square, Bridgwater.

Hogg, Mr. E. M., King Square, Bridg-water.

Holmes, Rev. Chancellor, Wells

Hook, Mr S W., North Petherton, Bridgwater.

Hooper, Mr. E. H., jun., High Street, Bridgwater.

Hooper, Mr. E. H., Greenfield, Bridg-water.

Hosegood, Mr. A., Rochdale.

Hoskins, Mr. E. J., 76 Jermyn Street, London, S.W

Hoskyns, Mr. H W. P., North Perrott Manor, Crewkerne.

Huggins, Mr. S., Dampiet St., Bridg-water.

Humphry, Mr. H. I., Monmouth St , Bridgwater.

Hunt, Mrs., 41 Gloucester Street, London, S.W

Hunt, Mr T. O., West St., Bridgwater.

Hunt, Mr. W. A., Eastover, Bridgwater.

Hunt, Mr. J. C., Northfield, Bridgwater.

Hurman, Mr. J. L., Northfield, Bridg-water.

Impey, the Misses, Street.

Irish, Mrs., St. Leonard's Rd., Exeter.

Jarman, Mr. G. W., Bradney, near Bridgwater

Jarman, Mr S , Wrexham, Bridgwater

Jevons, Miss, Marycourt, Bridgwater.

Jobson, Mr. J., Castle St , Bridgwater.

Jones, Mr. A J , Bridgwater.

Jones, Mr. S , Westfield, Bridgwater.

Keirl, Mr. Samuel, Monmouth Street, Bridgwater.

Kemeys-Tynte, Mr C., Halswell House, near Bridgwater

Kemeys-Tynte, Mr. St. David, Royal Crescent, Bath.

Ker, Mr H M. B., Bridgwater.

Kidner, Mr F., Church St., Bridgwater.

Kidner, Mr. W., Church Street, Bridg-water.

Kitch, Mr. J H., Taunton Road, Bridgwater.

Kitch, Mr. W. H , St. Saviour's Avenue, Bridgwater.

Kitch, Mr. Howard M., St. Saviour's Avenue, Bridgwater

Kitching, Miss, The Hospital, Bridg-water.

Landor, Miss, The Grange, Cannington, Bridgwater

Lansdown, Mr. G E., Over Stowey, Bridgwater.

Lee, Mr. J. A., Haygrove, Bridgwater.

Lees, Mr W. A , Bridgwater.

Leng, Mr. W. L , Weston-super-Mare.

Lethbridge, Sir Wroth P C , Hyde Park Street, London.

Letherby, Mr. R. J., Alexandra Road, Bridgwater.

Lewis, Mr. E. W., Victoria Terrace, Bridgwater.

Livingstone, Mr J., Wembdon Road, Bridgwater

Long, Col. W., Newton House, Clevedon

Lovibond, Mr G , Eastcroft, Bridgwater.

Lovibond, Miss C. M., Eastcroft, Bridg-water

Lovibond, Mr. G. Francis, Wembdon, Bridgwater.

Lovibond, Mrs. Henry, Dartholme, St. John's Road, Clifton

Lovibond, Mrs , Exe House, Exeter.

Lucas, Mr. E. M , Blake Place, Bridg-water.

Luttrell, Mr G. F., Dunster Castle.

Macfie, Mr. R., Hamp House, Bridg-water.

Maidment, Mr. W., Bristol Road, Bridgwater.

Major, Mr. C., Wembdon, Bridgwater.
Major, Mr. H. J., Northfield, Bridgwater.
Malet, Rev. C D E, Stoke Courcy Vicarage, Bridgwater
Manchip, Mr. T. W., Northfield, Bridgwater.
Markham, Mr T. W., High Street, Bridgwater.
Marriage, Mr. Wilson, Colchester
Marshall, Miss K. Lovell, The Priory, Bridgwater.
Masding, Mr. W. H., Haygrove, Bridgwater
McAulay, Mr. G Scott, High Street, Bridgwater.
McShane, Mr. J., Monmouth Street, Bridgwater
Meade, Mr. Francis, The Hill, Langport.
Meaker, Mr. W. T., West Street, Bridgwater
Meaker, Mr. J, King Square, Bridgwater
Medland, Mr. J., Wellington Road, Bridgwater.
Medley, Rev J. B., Tyntesfield, near Bristol.
Meffey, Mr. E., Duke Street, London.
Montgomery, Mr H. G, M.P., Thornfalcon, near Taunton
Morland, Mr. John, Wyrral, Glastonbury.
Mullins, Mr. T. Ruscombe, Limber, Brocklesby, Lincolnshire.
Murch, Mr W., St Mary Street, Bridgwater.

Newton, Mr. G., Northgate, Bridgwater.
Nichols, Mr. A., Monmouth House, Bridgwater.
Nicholls, Mr S, Friarn St, Bridgwater.
Nield, Mr. W., Bath Street, Bristol
Norman, Mr. G., Brock Street, Bath.
Nurton, Mr. R., Wem, Shropshire

Odgers, Rev. Dr., Manchester College, Oxford.
Olivey, Mr. Hugh P., Mylor, Penryn.

Page, Mr. E. Godfrey, Gray's Inn, London, W.C.
Page, Mr. E. T., Fore Street, Bridgwater.
Page, Mr. Maurice E., Fore Street, Bridgwater.
Pain, Mr., Chilton Trinity, near Bridgwater

Pain, Mr. A. G, Dampiet House, Bridgwater.
Palmer, Mr. J. J., Wembdon Road, Bridgwater.
Palmer, Mr W. II., North Petherton, Bridgwater.
Palmer, Mr. W., Wembdon, Bridgwater.
Parker, Mr. Walter, St. Saviour's, Bridgwater
Parker, Mr. H. W, 11 Queen Victoria Street, London, E.C.
Parsons, Mr. H. J, Oaklands, Shalford, Surrey
Parr, Mr F, Park Road, Bridgwater.
Peace, Mr. A., Penleâ, Bridgwater.
Pearse, Mr. E., Northgate, Bridgwater.
Peirce, Mr H, Church St., Bridgwater.
Perceval, Cecil H. Sp., Longwitton Hall, Morpeth
Perrett, Mr. S., Westfield, Bridgwater.
Perry, Mrs, Clifton, Bristol.
Phelips, Rev Preb., The Vicarage, Yeovil.
Phelps, Mr. R. H., West Quay, Bridgwater.
Phelps, Mr, High St, Bridgwater.
Phillips, Mr. W. Herbert, Park Road, Bridgwater.
Pitman, Mrs. S., St. John Street, Bridgwater
Podger, Mr C., Victoria Road, Bridgwater
Pole, Mr. W. J., Taunton Road, Bridgwater.
Pollard, Mr. H. W. (Mayor of Bridgwater), St John's House, Bridgwater.
Pope, Mr. H. S, Castle Bailey, Bridgwater.
Porter, Mr. F, High St., Bridgwater.
Portman, Hon Mrs, Ashfield, near Bridgwater.
Potter, Mr. T. P., Wellington Road, Bridgwater.
Powell, Mr. R, Bideford.
Powell, Mr Septimus, The Hermitage, Weston-super-Mare.
Price, Mr. J. G., The Avenue, Taunton.
Price, Mr. W., Wellington Rd, Bridgwater.
Prideaux, Mr. W., de Courcy, Frederick Place, Weymouth.

Ramsay, Mr F., Bramblecroft, Bridgwater.
Randle, Mr. G, The Docks, Bridgwater.
Raworth, Mr. A. E., Monmouth St., Bridgwater.

# LIST OF SUBSCRIBERS

Read, Mr. W., Railway Hotel, Bridgwater.

Reed, Mr. T. M., Burnham.

Rees, Rev. S., Otterhampton Rectory,
near Bridgwater.

Richards, Mr. J, St. Mary Street,
Bridgwater.

Roberts, Mr. Guy, Wembdon Road,
Bridgwater

Robertson, 'Mr J. S, The Willows,
Bridgwater.

Roe, Mr. W. L, Eastover, Bridgwater.

Rogers, Mr. C, St Mary Street, Bridgwater

Rose, Mr. F W, Wembdon, Bridgwater.

Ross, Rev. D. Melville, Langport
Vicarage.

Routh, Mr R. H. F., Malvern House,
Bridgwater.

Rowe, Mrs G., Northfield, Bridgwater.

Rudman, Mr. H. J, West St., Bridgwater.

Russell, Mrs., West Wickham, Kent

Salmon, Mr. H., Northfield, Bridgwater.

Salter, Mr. J, Bridgwater.

Sanders, Mr F., Eastover, Bridgwater

Sanders, Mr R A., Barrwick House,
near Yeovil

Sayer, Mr. J. Phillips, High Street,
Malden, Essex.

Scott, Mr W. M, Friarn House, Bridgwater

Sellick, Mr. Sebastian J., Hazelmere,
Weston-super-Mare.

Seward, Mr. G. U, High Street, Bridgwater.

Sharman, Mr. S., Westfield, Bridgwater.

Sharp, Mr. Cecil J., Adelaide Road,
London, N W.

Sheere, Mr F. J, Cattle Market,
Bridgwater.

Shepherd, Mr. B. C., Knowle Hall,
near Bridgwater

Shepherd, Mr J, St Saviour's Avenue,
Bridgwater

Shephard, Mr. W, High St., Bridgwater.

Shore, Commander Hon. Henry N.,
Mount Elton, Clevedon.

Shrimpton, Mr. F., Northfield, Bridgwater.

Skinner, Mr. A. J. P., Colyton,
Devon.

Slade, Mr. Wyndham, Montys Court,
Norton Fitzwarren, Taunton.

Slocombe, Mr. J., Riverside, Bridgwater.

Smith, Mr. W. H., High St, Bridgwater

Smith, Mr. S., Bristol Rd, Bridgwater.

Smith-Spark, Mr. C. G., Wembdon,
Bridgwater.

Solway, Arthur J, 5 Jewin Street,
London, E.C

Somerset Archæological and Natural
History Society.

Somerville, Mr. Arthur F, Dinder
House, near Wells.

Sorby, Rev J. A, Enmore Rectory,
near Bridgwater.

Spencer, Mr. F., Oakhill, Bridgwater.

Spiller, Miss K, Sunnybank, Bridgwater

Spratt, Mr. F., St. John Street, Bridgwater.

Squibbs, Mr. A., Taunton Rd., Bridgwater.

Squibbs, Mr H J., King Square,
Bridgwater

Squire, Mr. F. J., Lyndale Avenue,
Bridgwater.

Stanley, Mr. E. J, Quantock Lodge,
near Bridgwater.

Staples, Mr. J., The Docks, Bridgwater.

Steed, Mr. H. N., Wembdon, Bridgwater

Stewart, Mr. C. Balfour, Huntspill,
Bridgwater.

Stiling, Mr. W, Northfield, Bridgwater.

Stoate, Mr W., Ashleigh, Burnham.

Stockham, Mr W, jun, Alexandra
Road, Bridgwater.

Stokes, Miss, St. John's Schools, Bridgwater

Street, Rev J, The Vicarage, Ilminster.

Sturge, Mrs. W., Clifton, Bristol

Sully, Mr. J. G., Holywell, Wembdon,
Bridgwater.

Sully, Mr R. O., Crowpill House,
Bridgwater

Sully, Mr. Thomas N., Avalon House,
Weston-super-Mare.

Symons, Mr C. J, Taunton Road,
Bridgwater.

Symons, Mr. F, Saltlands, Bridgwater.

Tapscott, Mr. F., Weston-super-Mare.

Taunton, Venerable Archdeacon of.

Taylor, Mr., Cornhill, Bridgwater

Taylor, Mr C, High St, Bridgwater

Teek, Mr. H. C., Cheddar.

Thompson, Miss, Sidcot.

Thompson, Mr. H. Stuart, London.

Thompson, Mr. H Woolcott, Cardiff.

Thompson, Mr Wilberforce, Ivy House,
Bridgwater.

Thompson, Mr. W. C., Church Street,
Bridgwater.

Thompson, Mr. W., Brent Lodge, Bridgwater.

Thyer, Mr. H., Polden St , Bridgwater.

Tite, Mr. Charles, Stoneleigh, Taunton

Todd, Rev. J. Uttin, Alcombe, Taunton.

Tomkins, Rev. W. S., Canynge Sq., Clifton

Tomlin, Mr. T., Taunton Rd , Bridgwater.

Townson, Rev F , Cossington Rectory, Bridgwater.

Tratt, Mr. G. R., Sackville House, Bridgwater

Trayler, Mr. J. N , Wembdon, Bridgwater

Trelease, Mr. C., Taunton Rd., Bridgwater.

Trevilian, Mr E B Cely, Midelney Place, Curry Rivel, Langport.

Trevor, Lieut.-Col H. P., Chatfields, Alexandra Road, Farnborough.

Trevor, Rev G , Burrowbridge Vicarage, Bridgwater.

Trevor, Mr E., Halesleigh, Wembdon, Bridgwater.

Trippe, Mr., High Street, Bridgwater.

Tucker, Mr. R., St Mary Street, Bridgwater.

Tudor, Rev C M., Over Stowey Vicarage, Bridgwater.

Underdown, Mrs R., Gordon Road, Clifton

Upham, Mr. T., Eastover, Bridgwater.

Van Trump, Mr. H. J., Taunton.

Vaughan, Rev. Preb , Wraxall Rectory, near Bristol

Vicary, Mrs., St Matthew's, Bridgwater.

Waddell, Rev. T. B , Northfield, Bridgwater.

Waddon, Mr. C. C., Eastover, Bridgwater.

Waddon, Miss R., Northfield House, Bridgwater.

Wadman, Rev. Canon, St. Joseph's Presbytery, Bridgwater

Wake, Mr., Camden House, Bridgwater.

Wake, Mr. C. F., Yatton.

Walsh, Mr. T. L., Sherwood, Bridgwater

Walters, Miss M., Castle Park, Exmouth.

Ware, Mr. T. S, Trewartha Park, Weston-super-Mare.

Warren, Rev. F. K., Exton Rectory, Dulverton

Warren, Rev. W. M. K., St. Mary Street, Bridgwater

Webber, Mr. W., Friarn Street, Bridgwater.

Weaver, Rev. F. W., Milton Vicarage, Evercreech.

West, Mr F , Blake Place, Bridgwater

Westcott, Mr. H. J , Camden Road, Bridgwater

Wells, Very Rev the Dean of

West, Mrs., King Square, Bridgwater.

Whitby and Sons, Messrs , Cornhill, Bridgwater.

Whitham, Miss. E. M., St. Margaret's, Bridgwater.

Wilkins, Mrs. A. R., Glenthorne House, Bridgwater.

Wilkinson, Mr. T., Wembdon, Bridgwater.

Williams, Mr. T. W., Greystones, South Road, Weston-super-Mare

Williams, Mr. H. E , St. John Street, Bridgwater.

Williams, Mr. Penrose, Castle Street, Bridgwater.

Willis, Mr. T. H , St. Mary Street, Bridgwater

Wills, Mr. F., Northfield, Bridgwater.

Wills, Mr. V. J , Taunton Road, Bridgwater.

Winslade, Mr W. J , Fore Street, Bridgwater.

Winterbotham, Mr. W. L., Wembdon, Bridgwater.

Withers, Miss, St. Margaret's, Bridgwater

Withycombe, Mr. Wm., St. John Street, Bridgwater.

Wood, Mr E , Wembdon, Bridgwater.

Worley, Mr. J., Eastover, Bridgwater.

Yard, Miss Lilian, Sewardston Road, Victoria Park, London, N E.

Young Men's Christian Association, Bridgwater.

PLYMOUTH
WILLIAM BRENDON AND SON, LTD.
PRINTERS

CPSIA information can be obtained at www.ICGtesting.com
Printed in the USA
LVOW121927270512

283474LV00011B/188/P